lips
unsealed

BELINDA CARLISLE

A MEMOIR

lips
unsealed

THREE RIVERS PRESS
NEW YORK

All rights reserved.
Published in the United States by Three Rivers Press, an imprint of the
Crown Publishing Group, a division of Random House, Inc., New York.
www.crownpublishing.com

Three Rivers Press and the Tugboat design are registered trademarks
of Random House, Inc.

Originally published in hardcover in the United States by Crown Publishers,
an imprint of the Crown Publishing Group, a division of Random House, Inc.,
New York, in 2010.

Library of Congress Cataloging-in-Publication Data
Carlisle, Belinda.
    Lips unsealed: a memoir / Belinda Carlisle. — 1st ed.
        p.   cm.
    1. Carlisle, Belinda.   2. Rock musicians—United States—Biography.   I. Title.
    ML420.C25557A3 2010
    782.421666092–dc22
    [B]   2009053737

ISBN 978-0-307-46350-0
eISBN 978-0-307-46351-7

Book design by Elina Nudelman
Cover design by Kyle Kolker
Cover photography: (front) Jill Furmanovsky/Jill Furmanovsky.com; (back) © Jenny
Lens/Cache Agency

First Paperback Edition

TO MY BELOVED PIERRE

HEAVEN IS A PLACE ON EARTH

FOR MUCH OF my life, I felt like my fate was determined before I stepped into a recording studio, sang a song, or even thought about the Go-Go's—long before I joined Hollywood's punk scene in the mid-1970s.

When I was twelve years old, I was a mixed-up, restless little girl living in Thousand Oaks, a working-class area in Los Angeles's West San Fernando Valley. My stepdad had a drinking problem, my mom was on the verge of a nervous breakdown, and I was teased as being fat and stupid. I was neither, but at that age, the facts didn't matter. I hated my life and wanted something better.

I came home one day from a friend's house holding a book that seemed like it might help me change my life. I hid it under my sweatshirt and went straight to my bedroom. I felt a tingle of excitement as I slipped it out and looked at the cover: *The Satanic Bible* by Anton LaVey. I read bits and pieces, and although I understood very little of the author's rant against Christianity, I focused on terms like "exorcism," "evil," and "black magic," thinking I could find out how to cast spells and take control of my life.

This wasn't the first book I'd read on the subject, but it got me in the mood to finally try to cast a spell. I slid a box out from under my bed and removed the contents I had assembled earlier: brewed tea leaves, oak twigs, string, and a candle. I arranged them in front of me as I'd seen in a different book. I chanted some words and called on the invisible powers of the universe to give my life the excitement I felt it lacked and everything else I wanted.

What did I want?

I asked myself that question for most of my life. As a kid, I wanted out of my house, a place of much torment and trouble. The punk scene became my refuge, my safe haven, the forgiving, understanding world where I could be anything I wanted—in my case, a rock star. After I became a rock star, I still didn't know what I wanted. Finally, many years later, I began to realize I had been asking the wrong question.

It was actually one night in 2005 when I finally came clean with myself, when I asked what it was I *needed*, not what I wanted. I had gone to London for business, but spent three straight days locked in my hotel room, doing cocaine. I went on the biggest binge of my life, which is saying something considering I had used, boozed, and abused for thirty years. When I looked at my eyes in the mirror, I didn't see anyone looking back at me. The lights were out. I was gone.

It scared me—yet I didn't stop until I had an extraordinarily frightening out-of-body experience where I saw myself overdosing and being found dead in the hotel room. I saw the whole thing happen, and I knew that if I kept doing coke, I was going to die.

At that moment I shut my eyes, and when I opened them again I made the decision I had put off for much too long. I opened myself up to life. I appreciated the good, faced the bad, and began to find the things I needed.

Now, four and a half years later, the bad days are behind me but not forgotten. They made me who I am today—a far better, healthier, smarter, more open and loving person than I ever thought was possible. I'm someone who lived her dream against the odds of any of it happening, and yet I never doubted it.

Who knows, maybe it was the spells I cast back when I was a little girl. Whatever it was, it's been a pretty remarkable ride. I'm writing this book at age fifty, a milestone that seems like the right time to look back, hopefully with some perspective, insight, and wisdom at my career, marriage, sobriety, and efforts to connect with a higher power.

I don't know that people make complete albums anymore. But when I was growing up, and early in my career with the Go-Go's, artists tried to put together a collection of songs that made sense as a whole. You

listened to a record cut by cut, hoping every song was great but generally discovering that some songs were better than others, some *were* great,
and some were so bad they should have been left in the studio. At the
end, there was some sort of aha moment when you "got" the work in
its entirety.

If it was any good, it stayed with you, made you think, and in the
best of all worlds it offered inspiration and hope. I feel that way about
my life thus far. It may not be everyone's cup of tea, but most of the cuts
have been pretty good, and some even great. They worked for me—a
little girl who thought she cast a spell that created the rest of her life,
and then turned into a woman who realized the real magic had been
there the whole time.

I THINK IT'S ME

AT EIGHTEEN, I worked at the Hilton Hotels Corporation, photo-copying papers for eight hours a day. When I wasn't doing that, I was ordering toilet paper for hundreds of hotels. I was bored out of my mind. Making matters worse, I had the world's most hideous boss. He looked for reasons to call me into his office and chew me out. Most people would've quit, but I didn't care. Besides needing the money, I knew I wasn't going to be there long. I was going to be a rock star.

I was absolutely certain of it.

I had always been like that: someone who dreamed big and believed those dreams could come true if I kept at them.

I probably inherited that from my mom. Raised in Hollywood, Joanne Thompson was the eldest of two children of Roy, a plant manager at the General Motors facility in Van Nuys, and Ruth, a homemaker whose head-turning beauty and dramatic flair had inspired her as a younger woman to pursue movie stardom. When those dreams didn't pan out, she turned into an obsessive fan who read all the gossip magazines and took her daughter to movie premieres where they ogled the stars walking the red carpet.

Like my grandmother, my mother was drop-dead gorgeous. Photos of her as a senior at Hollywood High show a redhead with a great figure and big, lively eyes. She was a knockout. I think she could have had a shot at a career in front of the camera if she'd had ambition in that direction. By her own admission, though, she was too naïve and short-sighted. She didn't have a plan.

"I didn't think about what I wanted to do," my mother once told me when I asked how she had envisioned her life going after high school, adding that she saw herself as Debbie Reynolds and "thought everything would be, or should be, happy, happy, happy."

"Then I got married," she continued, "and I found reality."

Actually, she found Harold Carlisle, a James Dean look-alike whom she met while still a high school student. He was her dose of reality. He worked at a gas station near the school. Though he was twenty years older than her, she fell in love with him.

"I was so stupid," she told me. "He was a bum."

They married right after she graduated and on August 17, 1958, less than nine months after she accepted her diploma, she gave birth to a baby girl, whom she named Belinda. *C'est moi!* I arrived in the world via special delivery, otherwise known as a C-section. According to my mom, I was too large for her to push out naturally. Apparently size was an issue for me from day one.

Two years later, my mom gave birth to a boy, Butch; and two years after him, she had my sister Hope.

Even now she doesn't talk much about those early years. From the little she has revealed, she was in over her head as both a wife and a new mother. She's described it as a time when she learned "the tricks of the trade." Translation: Barely out of her teens, she was juggling three small children in a cramped Hollywood apartment, making do without much money, and trying to figure out life with a much older man.

According to her, my father wasn't happy about having children. I can sort of understand his position as he was an older man who impregnated a high school girl, married her, and then found himself in a situation he may not have envisioned for himself. Why did two more children follow if he was against having a family? Good question. To this day, my mom is reluctant to speak about those early years. She has too many wounds that are still tender and raw.

When I was five and a half, we moved to Thousand Oaks, a fifty-mile drive northwest over the hills from our Hollywood apartment. It got us out of the city and into a fairly rural area with dairy farms and post–Korean War housing developments. Our neighborhood was the low end of working-class and we were among the poorest of the poor, though at my age I didn't know rich from poor.

We moved into a small, pink and brown 1950s tract home at the end of a cul-de-sac. The street was lined with trees; I thought it was beautiful. The backyard was a hardscrabble mix of grass and dirt with a cheap metal swing set lodged in the middle that was like an island of fun. The problem was getting to it. My dad had an extremely territorial pet rooster that roamed the yard with an ogrelike temper and threatened us kids whenever we went back there.

My dad had a similar temperament. He didn't threaten us, but he left no doubt that he ruled the roost. Even on good days, there was always an undercurrent of tension. I know my parents could barely afford the house, but that was only one of their problems. My mom didn't trust my dad, or his explosive temper. Sadly, I felt the same way after I was literally caught in the middle of one of their more physical arguments, with one of them pulling my legs and the other my arms until it seemed I might split into two pieces.

Our move into the Valley coincided with my dad working at the GM plant in Van Nuys, though he didn't last there long before he started a carpet-cleaning business. I don't know whether he left or was laid off. I remember my mom hand-painting a logo on the side of his van. It was like the christening of an ocean liner because after that he spent most of the time on the road.

As part of the change, my mom sought comfort and companionship with the handsome carpenter who lived across the street, Walt Kurczeski. It turned out Walt had his own demons, but I didn't know about them then. At that point, he was my mother's special friend. Many years later, when I asked how their friendship had started, she said, "He was there when I needed him—with marriage or without."

All I knew was Walt was at our house whenever my dad wasn't there, which was more often than not. I didn't question the arrangement until one afternoon when I was waiting in front of my house to ride bikes with Eddie, a little Mexican boy who was one of my best friends. He walked up to me looking uncomfortable and announced that he couldn't ride bikes with me that day or any other day. When I asked why, he said his parents didn't want him to play with me anymore.

I didn't understand. We played together almost every day.

"Why?" I asked.

"Because my mom says your mother is bad."

My mother was bad? I didn't understand what he meant or why he said such a hurtful thing, and his words left me bleeding from a hundred little wounds. I held back tears as I raced home. I ran into the garage, sat on my bike, and cried while trying to figure out why my friend's mother would've said such a mean thing about my mom.

It didn't make sense. My mom was a sweet, shy, young woman. She wasn't bad, and she didn't have the capability of being mean. She fought with my father when he called from the road, but she sounded defensive and usually hung up feeling scared.

After a few minutes, I went inside and looked for my mom. She was in the kitchen, preparing dinner. I stared at her through tear-filled eyes. She asked if I had been crying. I lied and pretended nothing was wrong. I felt like I would hurt her if I told her that someone thought she was bad, and my instinct was to protect her.

She was twenty-five years old. Her hair was in a ponytail and she was wearing a cute dress that she had made herself, as she had most of her clothes, as well as my school outfits. None of that was bad. She liked to watch movies. She also sang around the house, played piano, and clapped when I danced for her. None of that was bad either.

At worst, she was troubled. But bad?

I could think of only one possibility for Eddie's words—Walt. He was at our house for dinner and often still there in the morning. He was more of a companion to my mom than my father was. I grew used to him being around without really thinking about why he was there. Of course, in retrospect I know why. My mom and dad had split. I don't know if they had officially separated or divorced, but they weren't together anymore.

My mom never mentioned it. Walt's presence was assumed. He continued to show up after we moved to Simi Valley, and then to a rental in Reseda, and yet again to an even smaller home in Burbank that was so close to the freeway that I went to sleep and woke up to the sound of cars speeding past. Even after the final move to Burbank, my mother, sister, and I continued to shuttle back and forth between my grandparents' home in Saugus and those of various friends of my mother.

Just as we were never given an explanation of Walt's presence, my brother, sister, and I were never told why we were constantly moved around. To this day, if I shut my eyes and think back to that time, I can feel the sense I had of being unsettled and uncertain and of wondering why we couldn't stay at home. It was confusing and chaotic. Maybe this moving around was why, years later, I took to the road so easily—it reminded me of this time in my life.

It wasn't until I was an adult that I asked my mother for an explanation and she finally gave me one. She told me that her split from my father was volatile, and she felt the need to hide us while she tried to work things out with him. I didn't understand why she wanted to hide us from my father, but there were a lot of things going on between them that were beyond my comprehension.

At seven years old, I simply wanted to know where my dad was and why he wasn't coming home. I also wanted to know why he didn't want to be with us anymore. When he did call, why didn't he want to speak to me? And why did my mom always hang up in tears?

For a while I got into the habit of perching next to the living room window after dinner and staring into the darkness, looking for my dad. I thought that if I looked long and hard enough, I might wish him back and see his truck turn onto the street and pull into the driveway. As I sat there, I used to play his favorite 78s on our stereo, albums by Donald O'Connor and Burl Ives, as if they might help lure him up the driveway and through the door.

They didn't.

My mom let me go through that ritual without explaining that my dad wasn't coming back home. One day I finally threw a fit and insisted on knowing why he didn't want to be with us anymore. She said, "One day I can tell you. One day you'll understand. But not now."

Soon after that, Walt moved in with us permanently. The arrangement was never explained, even after my dad showed up one day with a girl-friend with red hair like my mom's. He parked outside for a while—I don't know why, maybe just to unnerve us—then brought her inside, where she stood uncomfortably to the side as he got into a fight with my mom in the living room.

I stood in the hall and eavesdropped from behind the door, which was open a crack, just enough so that I could glimpse them as they moved back and forth across the room. I didn't want them to see me—or my brother and sister, who were behind me.

Looking back, I guess it was the final straw between them, because after a while my dad screamed, "Good luck without me," and then stormed out of the front door.

A short while later, my mom picked me up at a friend's house and told me that she and Walt had gotten married in Las Vegas. She said we were to refer to him as Dad. Other changes happened more gradually but were no less profound and hard to understand. First there was an unmistakable bulge in my mom's tummy, and then some months later she gave birth to my sister Mary, the first of four children (the others are Josh, Joe, and Sarah, who was born when I was twenty) she had with Walt.

Given how fearful she was of my dad, I can see why my mom was drawn to Walt. He was about five-eleven, well built, very strong, and kind of rugged looking from all the time he spent working outdoors. He walked with the swagger of a badass, which he was. I know two versions of Walt. There's the man who got sober after I left home and turned into one of the most remarkable, loving men I have ever met. Then there's the Walt with whom I grew up.

That Walt was impossibly bad when he drank, and he drank a lot. The booze lit up the demons in him, and he turned them against us. He went out drinking most nights after work. As he squandered money on himself that could have helped the entire family, we ate oatmeal and Bac-O-Bit sandwiches for dinner while trying to ignore the empty place my mom had set for him at the table.

We worried about whether he was going to make it home, and if so, what kind of shape he was going to be in. We only let ourselves think of

two choices, bad or worse, though all of us knew there was another possibility, a drunk-driving accident. But that was too terrible to consider.

After doing the dishes, my mom paced the living room, chain-smoking
cigarettes and listening for the sound of his truck. The TV was always on
in the background, but somehow she could hear his motor from half a
mile away. I waited in bed, listening for the same sound. Every so often
I tiptoed out of bed and spied on my mom through the hallway door.

I had to bite my tongue because more than anything, what I wanted
to ask was "Do you think Dad is coming home soon?"

By this time I referred to Walt as Dad—and still do to this day. But
I resisted saying anything and always made it back into bed before my
mom sensed my presence. I continued to wait. Sometimes it was hours,
and other times I lost track of how long I waited in bed. Then when I
did finally hear him, I braced myself for the inevitable fight he had with
my mother.

She was ready, too—not because she liked to fight or had conten-
tious fiber in her body, because she didn't. But he came in angry and
short-tempered and put her through such worry every night that she
needed to yell back at him or she'd go crazy. Their voices ripped through
the nervous silence that had settled over the house, and no matter how
tightly I squeezed my pillow over my head, it wasn't enough to block
out their back-and-forth.

My dad's tirades never carried into our room, thank goodness. If he
did open the door, it was only to poke his head in and make sure all of
us were asleep. My eyes were squeezed tight.

In the morning, I climbed out of bed and looked for my mom in the
kitchen, pretending that none of the yelling the night before had happened. She pretended the same thing. My way of communicating that
I knew what had happened was trying to help her as much as possible.
I spent all day attempting to get that message across to her. I fed the
babies, changed diapers, and helped in the ways I could.

My dad wasn't drunk *every* night, but it was often enough that it left
me with the impression that it was more often than not. Nor did he and
my mom scream at each other every night, but they did it enough of
the time so that I expected it to happen. Each day was a walk through a

minefield. Even when there was calm, I didn't trust it, and as much as I hated it when they fought, at least it relieved the stress of anticipation.

With his quick temper, my dad lacked certain basic parenting skills, such as patience. He was of the old-fashioned school that believed in spanking children, and not only that, he seemed to think children should be spanked regularly. My mom looked the other way as we screamed. I don't know if she condoned such punishment, but once, after I complained, she said that she had read that a popular TV talk-show host also spanked his kids, as if to say that made it okay.

Butch and I made light of the beatings we received by comparing the red marks on our skin or the number of lashes. It was our way of surviving. But beneath the jokes and the half smiles were lots of pain and tears. Butch came into my room one night with red, puffy eyes and a crooked smile on his face. He sniffled.

"Twenty-seven," he said.

"I don't believe it," I said.

"Yeah. He hit me twenty-seven times—a new record!"

Deep down I resented my mom for putting us in a situation where we were subjected to Walt's volatility and violence. I don't know what I expected her to do, but I didn't think the way he treated us was right, and I wondered why she didn't say anything to him. Maybe she did in private. I just wished she had done more.

There were good times too. We would pile in the camper of my dad's truck, all of us kids crammed together, and we would go on weekend camping trips to Santa Barbara and San Diego. We enjoyed both the beach and the forests. There were so many of us and we were so poor that between the lack of space and the scrimping, we were either fighting or laughing hysterically. I remember more laughter than anything else.

It was always a relief to be away from home and setting up a tent in the outdoors. My dad was usually sober, and I loved having space of my own, something that was in short supply in our small, crowded home. It was liberating to run around. It felt good to exhale, and I swear to this day I have tasted few things as delicious as the bologna sandwiches my mom made on Wonder bread smeared with French's mustard.

My mom was a good sport and she knew those trips brought out the best in my dad. He was able to loosen up and relax. It was as if he left all of his demons at home. My mom was a very religious woman, and I wonder if, as she went to sleep on those nights when we were under the stars, she felt like God was answering her prayers.

Her faith was extremely important to her. It got her through the worst of times. Every Sunday, she sat through sermons and found hope and strength in the promise of God's love. It was a beautiful thing for her, something I didn't appreciate at the time.

To me, church was a big bother. Every Sunday morning, my mom dressed all of us kids in matching outfits that she had sewn, and she marched us like a mother duck with her ducklings into the little church around the corner from our house. I felt like I was on parade. Everyone went except my dad. My mom always had a reason why he couldn't go, as well as a reason why we had to.

When I think about it now, I am pretty sure my mom didn't want my dad there. She was happy that he stayed home. She wanted those Sundays to herself, to be able to sit quietly with her children and feel the presence of God, hoping that He would steer all of us to salvation.

I found it all a turn-off, starting when my mother had me baptized when I was eight. I didn't want to do it, and I was doubly and triply repulsed after I was baptized Belinda Kurczeski. That was Walt's last name, not mine. What was wrong with my name, Belinda Carlisle?

Despite this, I attended Sunday school until I was in my teens and hated every minute of it. I always wished I were someplace else. I can still picture myself going home and taking off my Sunday school clothes as if I was shedding a skin. I also tried to forget everything I had heard. I didn't buy those stories. I didn't care about what was going to happen to me after I was dead.

I wanted to be saved *now*.

two

C O O L   J E R K

ON THE PLAYGROUND at Burbank's Bret Harte Elementary School, I looked like any other kid my age scampering around. But in fifth grade, I had one of those moments that changes some girls for a lifetime—I discovered style. My aunt gave me a box of hand-me-downs that a friend had given her. It was full of old sequined square-dance dresses and matching shoes, including an eye-popping hot-pink outfit that I immediately wore to school.

I didn't care if my classmates stared or made fun. How could they not stare? When I put on that dress, I thought I looked like a beautiful princess. It was better than being me.

In sixth grade, I had only one so-called normal dress, a black and white polka-dot pinafore with a ribbon around the waist. My mom bought it on special at Sears and I loved it as soon as she brought it home. I wore it as much as possible, along with the colorful outfits that I got in the annual delivery of hand-me-downs. During recess one day a girl came up to me and put me down for wearing the same outfit nearly every day. I can still hear her high-pitched voice: *"You only have one out-fit! What's wrong with you?"*

I walked away, hurt and humiliated. I felt like she had glimpsed a part of the reality I tried to hide, my family's lack of money. The last thing I wanted was for someone to know the truth about me. As for the truth about the way I dressed, I was unable to express such complex feelings then, but slipping into those colorful outfits let me flee into a world of imagination, a place where I was freed from reality and kept from feeling like everyone else.

I was also the class clown and one of those girls who was good at sports. I was built like a barrel, but with skinny legs that carried me across the ball field and track as fast as, if not faster than, most of the boys. I ignored my classmates when they referred to me as fatso and Belimpa. *Ha-ha-ha*, I laughed. *You can't hurt me*. But they did.

I signed up for anything and everything that would get me out of the house. Brownies, Girl Scouts, ice-skating, sports—I did it all. At age ten I developed an interest in music. It was another escape, maybe the best and easiest I ever discovered. I spend countless hours at my friend Christina Badala's house, listening to music. We laid on her floor with our ears next to her stereo speakers. We tuned in to the popular AM radio station 93 KHJ, following it as if it was our religion. We thought of DJs Charlie Tuna, the Real Don Steele, and Humble Harv as evangelists who taught us about the Stylistics, Cat Stevens, and the Animals.

The first album I owned was *Pet Sounds,* the Beach Boys' classic. I won it at a bobby sox softball tournament. At the time, I liked the photo on the cover more than the actual collection of songs. I needed time to grow into the rest of Brian Wilson's masterpiece. It was a little out-there for a ten-year-old. Now it's one of my all-time favorites.

I didn't have enough money to buy more albums until high school. But every so often I scraped together enough change for a 45. My favorite was the 5th Dimension's version of "Aquarius." It was the first single I bought, and I like it today as much as I did back then.

In those days, I was into *The Brady Bunch, The Partridge Family,* and *Here Come the Brides*. I wanted to be Marcia Brady, and I had crushes on David Cassidy and Bobby Sherman. What can I say? I rode around on a Sting-Ray bike and had pigtails. I wasn't Miss Sophisticate.

But all that began to change in August 1969 when Charles Manson and his followers murdered director Roman Polanski's beautiful and young pregnant wife, Sharon Tate, and numerous others. By the time they went on trial the following summer, I was hooked on the macabre drama and obsessively followed the headline accounts of their horrific crimes.

At one time, the Manson family had lived in Topanga Canyon, which wasn't too far from our house. Their Helter Skelter bloodbath also wasn't that far away from us, maybe a twenty-five-minute drive. Both locations were close enough that my parents and our neighbors thought there might be more murderous hippies roaming the streets, or copycats, and they started locking their doors. Before the murders, they didn't think about it.

I couldn't get enough of Manson and his so-called family. I was fascinated when I learned about Manson's foray into pop music: that his evil had been inspired by the Beatles song "Helter Skelter," and his life had also intersected with Beach Boys drummer Dennis Wilson.

I got out my copy of *Pet Sounds* and looked at Wilson, wondering how he could have gotten involved with Manson. Later, I learned he had picked up two girls who were hitchhiking, and they turned out to be members of Manson's family. Soon Manson and a bunch of girls were living in Wilson's house. He introduced Manson to the Beach Boys producer Terry Melcher, who rented his home to Polanski, and that was where the murders took place.

It was weird, creepy, scary, terrible, and about the most interesting stuff I had ever come across. My mom scolded me when she saw me reading the stories in the paper. She didn't approve of my fascination with Manson. She probably feared I was being brainwashed when I stared at his picture. His gaze was powerful; those eyes certainly did cast a spell, and I can understand now how he was able to lure weak-minded women under his influence.

I especially got into the trial of Susan Atkins, a dark-haired flower child who was convicted of participating in eight of the murders. My mom forbade me to follow her story. She said it was too much for a child. But I snuck the paper into my room at night and read all the articles about her.

A year later, another murder was in the headlines. It was New Year's Day 1972, and Pete Duel, who costarred with Ben Murphy on the hit series *Alias Smith and Jones,* was found dead of a gunshot wound in his canyon home. I loved that show, and he was one of my favorite actors. Although his death was later ruled a suicide, I assumed it was a Manson-type slaughter of another actor.

I wanted to see the scene myself, and without telling my mom, I took off on my bicycle, intending to ride to his home. I didn't know that it was fifteen miles from my house, maybe more than that. It was also up in the hills. I pedaled most of the day, but never got close. I had no idea where I was going.

That was one of the last times I spent all day riding my bike. All of a sudden it seemed like something a kid would do, and I didn't feel like a kid anymore. I didn't feel like an adult either. I didn't know what I felt like, other than different. I was changing. My hormones had kicked into gear and were reshaping me in ways that my mom never took time to explain.

I got my period, started to develop physically, and experienced moods when I just wanted to put on my headphones, listen to music, and be left alone. I traded in my bike and instead went over to my friend Christina's and hid out in her guest house, where we burned incense and talked about which Beatle we liked best.

I was walking across the street one day, heading to a neighbor's house, when a boy who lived on the block and another guy whom I recognized from school pointed at me and yelled, "Hey look! There goes fatso!" A year earlier, I might have ignored them or run over and beat them up. Now those same words felt like a mortal wound. I stopped and nearly lost my breath, and when I caught it again, I burst into tears and ran home.

My mom, rather than telling me that I looked wonderful the way I was and to ignore those nasty boys, suggested that I go on a diet and lose weight. She offered to help. She was always on a diet even though she didn't need to be, and so she put me on the same program. She gave me a calorie-counter book and told me to keep my daily intake under 1,200. Thus began a ritual familiar to many girls—endless days of starvation, frustration, and disappointment in myself when I went off my diet.

Around that same time, we moved from Burbank to a slightly larger place in Thousand Oaks. My dad had spent months building it. I was midway through seventh grade when we packed up—not a great time to change schools. But I tried to make the best of it when I entered Colina Junior High. I told myself it was an opportunity to get away from all the kids who called me Belimpa or fatso and reinvent myself.

I stuck to a diet, traded my princess dresses for cutoff overalls and knee socks (think early Linda Ronstadt), and twisted my hair into braids. I lost about forty pounds by the end of the school year. My friend Christina couldn't get over it. She saw me for the first time in months when I visited my grandparents, who had moved into our old house, and she just stared at me, amazed, impressed, and maybe a little jealous of my new look.

"Oh my God, Belinda," she said. "You're hot!"

At Colina, I joined the track team and ran the hundred-yard dash. I was interested in boys but never comfortable around them. When I did have a crush, I kept it to myself. I carried around too much shame and fear to ever share my feelings and risk rejection. Then there was another problem: What if the boy liked me? I couldn't imagine bringing someone home to meet my parents. My dad's drinking made life in the new house as unpredictable and chaotic as it had been in Burbank.

I barely confided in my new best friend, Jean Olson, an outgoing, good-looking girl whose boobs had miraculously arrived a couple years before the rest of us were out of training bras. They gave her a personality and a presence. I was barely a year or two past believing that storks delivered babies. I'm serious. Even though my mom popped out a baby every couple years, I was ignorant of how it happened—that is, until Jean set me straight about that, and more.

And some things I learned on my own. The following summer I went on my Girl Scout troop's annual overnight camping trip to the beach. Every year we went someplace up or down the coast. This time we camped at Carpinteria, a surfing village just south of Santa Barbara. There was a boys' camp down the beach from us, a pretty far way down, but not too far that we didn't wander over to see one another. One boy took a liking to me.

I enjoyed the attention. We chatted, flirted, and chased each other up and down the beach. It was extremely innocent fun. We didn't even attempt a kiss, though secretly I wished we had.

After we returned home, my mom got a call from the troop leader. She said I had not conducted myself in the manner appropriate to a Girl Scout and therefore was not welcome to return to the troop. Not welcome? That was a strange way of saying I was kicked out of Girl Scouts. Apparently she went into a little more detail with my mom, but none of it was true.

I was furious. Jean told me not to worry, and she was right. I didn't care about being kicked out of the troop or that the leader had told an outright lie about me. It simply paled next to the realization that a boy had found me attractive. I was confused by the whole thing—but in a great way.

I wished that had translated into self-confidence, but it didn't. However, I did feel a certain something, a difference in the way I approached the world and felt about myself. Now I see that I was at that point in a girl's life when she realizes she possesses certain powers that make her different, powers that will beguile the boys and turn even the strongest of them into jelly if used properly.

In other words, I was slowly but surely becoming a woman. It takes a lifetime to figure out what that means and how to put that wonderful gift of fate to good use. It doesn't come with an instruction book; at least it didn't when I was that age. Instead, I gathered information from girlfriends and books. I went from Jean telling me where babies really came from to stumbling upon books about witchcraft and trying to conjure up powers without making a fool of myself—or at least *too* much of a fool.

Jean was amused by my interest in black magic. Why wouldn't she have been? Her natural gifts had already taught her how to cast powerful spells simply by wearing a halter top. Jean also taught me how to smoke. Along with another girlfriend, Bonnie, we snuck down to the far corner of the football field between classes and puffed away while listening to Carly Simon albums on a portable tape player.

She also introduced me to booze when I slept over one weekend and we got plastered on Boone's Farm apple wine. The fun didn't stop there. The two of us used to watch the Dallas Cowboys run through their workouts at Cal Lutheran College. The team set up camp there every summer before the preseason. Jean liked to watch the good-looking, hard-bodied athletes practice, and she took me along for company. We wore halter tops and short-shorts, and were quite the Lolitas as the players ogled us.

I'm sure there were older, more age-appropriate women around scouting the players for extracurricular activities. For us, it was an amusing way to spend a summer day. It was harmless fun. Some of the players had probably wished it wasn't innocent. Bob Hayes, the Cowboys' Hall of Fame wide receiver, kept a protective eye on us. He made sure the younger players didn't get any ideas. He also lectured us about being good girls.

One night Jean and I ran away from home. Both of us had been punished for something that seems insignificant now, but was a big enough deal back then to get us grounded. We snuck out of our homes, met at the local Kmart, and decided to leave town. We walked out to the road and stuck out our thumbs. Who motored by? Bob Hayes. The World's Fastest Man slowed down, and then stopped when he recognized us.

He had Jean and I get into his car and then drove us back to our homes. He gave each of us a stern talking-to about being careful and safe.

But home was the last place I wanted to be. My dislike for being there had intensified from the initial confusion and uncertainty I experienced when my mom and dad split due to the hardships Walt's drinking caused, as well as from the nonstop burdens of helping my mother. She needed more and more help, too. Something happened to her around this time that was never explained. She grew weak and almost feeble. It was a gradual downhill slide that occurred over months, until one day she stopped getting out of bed.

She was usually able to prepare meals for us, but otherwise she stayed in bed and I had to pick up much of the slack in running the household and caring for the little ones. When I asked my dad what was wrong with Mom, he said she wasn't feeling well. He didn't offer any more information.

I was forced to figure things out on my own. From conversations that

I overheard, I learned she was taking lithium and occasionally seeing a doctor. Then there was talk about the possibility of putting her in a psychiatric hospital for an undetermined length of time. That really scared me. I had no idea what that entailed, but my imagination went straight to the worst: shock treatment, a lobotomy—losing my mother.

I don't know how or why, but she gradually emerged from her depression before she had to be hospitalized. It was still a long time before she returned to normal. As much as I loved her, her illness was one more reason I didn't want to spend much time at home. It debilitated her, but it also put an enormous load on my teenage shoulders.

I went through a stage where I lied about my family and told all sorts of tall tales whenever someone asked about my home life. I went so far as to say my father was actor Chuck Connors from the TV series *The Rifleman* and that I was related to Ohio State's All-American linebacker Randy Gradishar. I lied all of the time. I can't even remember all the stories that I told.

In a way, I went into survival mode by inventing my own reality. Instead of facing the reality of my life, I made myself into someone else. For a while, I went through a stage where I decided to be a bad girl. I dressed in dirty jeans and scuffed shoes and washed my hair in baby oil to make it look greasy. I'll never forget leaving for school one day when my dad's voice stopped me in my tracks as he snapped, "Where the hell are you going looking like that?"

I didn't want to tell him that. By ninth grade, I had my eye on two very cute boys, Jack Wild and Kyle Rodgers. Kyle's father, Pepper, coached the UCLA football team. Both guys were cool, California types. They wore their hair long and dressed in faded T-shirts and shorts. All the girls, including me, thought that they were hot.

Jean arranged for the four of us to get together one Saturday night in a vacant house in Westlake Village. I think we had some wine and played Truth or Dare. Then the game morphed into Spin the Bottle and I ended up in a wardrobe closet with both Jack and Kyle, though not at the same time. It was my first time making out, and, of course, I loved it. I secretly hoped Jack would be my boyfriend.

Sadly, after we were back in school, neither boy acknowledged our kisses or having even spent time with me. It was as if the bottle had never spun. Jack never gave me the time of day after that weekend. I was crushed. Given my lackluster self-esteem, I figured something was wrong with me.

I was like a lot of girls in that respect but very different in another: I began shoplifting. I learned from three girlfriends of mine, all of whom happened to be Chicano. Like me, they were poor. I went through a phase where I thought their accents and the music they liked were cool. I went so far as to eat *menudo,* a traditional Mexican soup, on Saturdays the way they did.

One of them was an especially tough girl who made no secret of the fact that she stole clothes and accessories. She said it was easy, and lo and behold, I tried it at the Thousand Oaks mall and it was. I made a rule: Never steal from people, just stores. Somehow I convinced myself that was okay because I couldn't afford the stuff I took. It was convoluted thinking, but it made sense to me.

I was just doing what my friends did. I gave myself free rein at numerous stores, including Judy's, the mall's most stylish young woman's store. It didn't seem bad even when I was caught taking tikis from a gift shop at Disneyland, but only because the park's security let me off with a warning. I wasn't as lucky at Thrifty Drugs. There, security caught me outside the store with a purse full of merchandise from the cosmetics counter.

That turned into a bad scene. They held me in the manager's office, said the police were on the way, and called my parents. I didn't fear the cops as much as I did my dad. I pissed my pants and then pretended to pass out. The store felt bad and let me off with a stern warning. My dad wasn't as forgiving. As soon as we got home, his belt came off and he let me have it.

He said it was time I learned a lesson and grew up. Well, I learned a lesson, but growing up was going to take more time—not just years, but decades.

three

BENEATH THE BLUE SKY

THE SUMMER after graduating junior high, I continued to blossom into what one of my friends called "a cute surfer chick." I didn't surf and I wasn't sure about the cute part, but I gladly accepted her description and went out and spent most of my savings from babysitting on a new wardrobe from the surf shop at the Thousand Oaks mall. I also stole a few items from Judy's and started my freshman year at Newbury Park High School with a whole new look.

Success! Both guys and girls saw me as a fox, and I used that as leverage to become a cheerleader. I continued to sign up for as many after-school activities as possible, including the debate team. I wasn't your typical blond pom-pom girl. At the start of my sophomore year, I wanted to play basketball. Since there wasn't a girls' team, I asked the boys' varsity coach if I could try out for his team.

No such precedent had been set, but I made a good pitch, telling him that I was a guard and my favorite NBA player was the Los Angeles Lakers' All-Star guard Gail Goodrich. It worked. He gave me a shot, letting me play second-string guard in the summer league, and as far as I know, that made me the first girl in California to play high school sports for a boys' team.

I don't think I was a token player either. I kept pace and still remember making a half-court pass that drew oohs and ahs from the crowd, as if they were amazed a girl could make that kind of play against boys.

By the start of school, I'd had enough and quit the team. The practice schedule didn't appeal to me. I wanted to spend more time being social, and a short time into the semester it paid off. I had my first boyfriend,

Scott Russell, one of three well-known surfing brothers from Ventura County. He was a sophomore too. We made out in his car and at the beach. He surfed every day, and like a good surfer's girlfriend, I watched.

On one of the few occasions I went into the water, I got caught in the waves and nearly drowned. The waves were unusually big that day. I didn't know which way was up or down and thought I was going to die. Then Scott raced in, grabbed my arm, and swam me back to shore. As far as I was concerned, he saved my life.

But Scott dropped me toward the end of the year because I wouldn't go all the way.

I went to the prom with Rick Pond, a nice boy with a huge nose and piercing blue eyes. He was crazy about me. My mom made a gorgeous dress from slinky Qiana fabric I had picked out. I was nervous about Rick coming to the house to pick me up, but everyone was on good behavior and excited about my first big dress-up party.

Rick brought a corsage and pinned it on with my mom's help, though inside I was dying a dozen deaths from having his hand so close to my boob as my entire family watched. Unfortunately for Rick, I wasn't as attracted to him as he was to me, at least in terms of being an item, and eventually did the right thing, working up the nerve to make it clear he wasn't a boyfriend. To his credit, he stayed friendly.

I started my junior year as one of the head cheerleaders—a song leader, actually—and dated a basketball player, a football player, and even Scott, who came around again probably thinking he could get me to go all the way now that we were older. He was wrong. I was too uptight and insecure to share that kind of intimacy. It was easier to be admired but unattainable.

I might have remained an icy blond surfer chick through the rest of high school and gone on to college or junior college if not for the art class I took that year. It changed my life. The teacher was a cool, young hippie type who had long hair in the style of the Monkees' Peter Tork. He had a stereo in the room and let the students play albums as we worked on projects.

It turned out the students in that class had phenomenal taste in clothes and music. As I should've expected, they were far more interesting than the jocks and cheerleaders with whom I'd been hanging out. That first week a Mexican girl who wore the most beautiful jewelry and looked like a Gypsy captured my attention. I'd never seen her at school. Where had she been? I loved that look.

Then I met another girl, Theresa "Terri" Ryan, who became better known a few years later as the Germs bassist Lorna Doom. We clicked instantly. She had incredible taste in music. She was into the New York Dolls, the Velvet Underground, Nico, and Roxy Music. I hadn't heard of any of these bands. I felt like she was changing my life. She was.

She was also into Queen, especially the band's guitarist Brian May. She loved him. She took me to see Queen when they came through town in support of their 1974 album, *Queen II*. If I don't count seeing Glen Campbell at the Hollywood Bowl, Queen was my first rock concert. I left the show in love with the band's lead singer, Freddie Mercury. I had never seen anyone perform with such energy and passion.

Who looked like that?

Who sounded like that?

In order to go to more concerts, and to get around in general, I bought my first car, a Plymouth Satellite. It cost me $150. It was too good a deal to pass up, and my friends were impressed that I was able to get it so inexpensively. Then they saw why—from the driver's side, the car looked to be in mint condition, but if you walked around to the other side, you looked straight into its guts. The passenger side of the chassis was missing. It should have been in the junk heap, not on the road. But I didn't care. It got me around.

On most afternoons, you could have found it parked in front of the record store, my new favorite hangout. I was obsessed with looking through the bins and discovering new albums. I read liner notes with the kind of attention I should have given my schoolwork. Among those albums, though, I began to find myself. And redefine myself. I spent hours staring at covers, learning about new bands, trading gossip and opinions about songs and records, and developing a sensibility that hadn't existed before. It was like getting a makeover, but from the inside out.

I would go home and look at my record collection the way I did my old clothes. Albums from Tony Orlando & Dawn, Bobby Sherman, and Neil Diamond didn't fit anymore. I'd outgrown them.

It was a phenomenal period to discover music. I felt like my whole life changed the day I came across the cover of Iggy and the Stooges' *Raw Power*. Time stopped as I lifted the album from the bin and stared at the cover, a photo of a pale, painfully thin, shirtless guy staring off into the distance. He was hanging onto a standup microphone as if it was preventing him from falling over. The effect was ghoulish, dangerous, frightening, beautiful, and about a thousand other things all at the same time. I thought, What is *this*?

I didn't have the money to buy the album. But then someone brought that album to art class and I got to hear "Gimme Danger," "Your Pretty Face Is Going to Hell," "Penetration," "Search and Destroy," and "Death Trip." I looked around and saw that most of the other kids in class were reacting like me: grinning as the raw, sludgy loud music shook the floor, the walls, our desks, our chairs, and our brains.

It wasn't ladylike. It wasn't slutty either. It was new and different. And as I told Theresa, I loved it.

The two of us also saw Roxy Music, Thin Lizzy, Bad Company, ELO, and the Kinks. At the record store, Theresa always had her nose in one of the British music magazines, like *Melody Maker* and *New Musical Express,* or *NME.* I marveled at how she knew everything going on in London's underground music scene as well as who was hot and cool in the States months before anyone else had heard of them, including the Babies, Blondie, and the Enemies.

As much as I was drawn to this new world, I kept one foot planted in everything that was familiar. I still went to church on Sundays with my family, was known around the neighborhood as a dependable babysitter, maintained a B average, and enjoyed being a song leader. I also landed a plum job as an ice-cream scooper at Swensen's, a parlor whose owner, a guy named Ed, was known for hiring the cutest girls.

Working there brought immediate status, but there was a downside to spending that much time around ice cream. By the end of the summer, I had gained forty pounds. I also cut my hair off and gave myself an Afro with a Toni home perm. I have one comment: Yikes!

Call it a transitional period. Everything else seemed to be in flux—why not me?

Ed eventually sold the store to two women whom I didn't like. As a result, I began pocketing money that I should have been ringing up and putting in the register. After catching on, they took me aside one day before my shift and said it was time for me to go. I understood and appreciated the way they kept my dismissal low-key.

By then I was a senior and ready to shed my suburban skin for a whole new scene, Hollywood. I had dumped my Plymouth for a ratty old Datsun, the "Thrash Datsun" as I called it, that Theresa and I took to all the hottest Hollywood clubs: the Roxy, the Whisky, and the Starwood. I knew the girls from my old cheerleader clique wondered what was up with me when I stepped down from my position as the school's senior mascot, but it didn't go with the new life I was cultivating in Hollywood. When they whispered that I was changing, they were right.

Theresa and I joined the regulars who hung out at night in the Sunset Strip parking lot between the Rainbow and the Roxy. That spot was the late-night nerve center of L.A.'s rock scene. Between eleven P.M. and two A.M., rock stars and wannabes, groupies and insiders gathered there and waited for something to happen, though looking back I realize the party itself was in the parking lot and that just by being there we were where it was happening.

If only we'd known. But everybody who was anybody in music hit the Rainbow. It was the place for exchanging news and information, seeing stars, finding drugs, and finding out where the best party was that night.

If you were a poseur, this was where you posed. If you wanted to pass around a joint or score quaaludes, you showed up there. The lot was always filled with shiny Rolls-Royces and Excaliburs, clues that a VIP was having a good time inside. It was also the best pickup spot in the entire city. Everyone was on, as if playing a part in their own movie.

I was into guys who dressed like rock stars, guys who wore satin pants, platform shoes, and had big pineapple hairdos. As for me, I tied up my jeans at the bottom and teetered around on high platforms that made me feel as if I'd stepped into Hollywood straight from London's Kings Road. I ripped my T-shirts and wore them in layers, and put a beret on the top of my head. I also smoked colored Sherman cigarettes. Little details were key.

While I looked the part, I never felt as much a part of the scene as when I met the Who's drummer Keith Moon. I was inside the Rainbow and noticed he was with a black hooker whom I knew from the parking lot. As I passed their table, she grabbed my arm and pulled me into their booth. The three of us shared a pizza. I'm sure I didn't eat.

At seventeen, I was beside myself, sitting with a true rock star and trying to maintain my cool. I smoked my Shermans and let Keith buy me a drink. No one was terribly strict about carding kids then, and certainly the waitresses weren't going to stop Keith from buying drinks for the women at his table, even if one of them was still in high school.

They wanted to keep partying at wherever he was staying. I'm pretty sure they intimated or asked outright if I wanted to go back with them. I didn't, and I made some excuse why I had to leave. I went back outside and faded into the crowd, kind of pinching myself after socializing with rock royalty but still playing it very cool, like it was no big deal.

I had a similar encounter with Bon Scott, the lead singer of AC/DC. That also took place late at night inside the Rainbow. But he was whacked out of his mind. Keith had been inebriated, but Bon was wasted. He grabbed my shirt as I walked past him and said something along the lines of "My, aren't you lovely, let's have sex."

I wasn't remotely ready or interested in anything like that, even with a rock star. Besides, he was out of it. Who knows how much more of the night he saw before passing out. I bet not much. In any event, I said a couple of words to him in response, just enough to get him to relax his grip on my shirt, and then I spun away and disappeared into the restaurant, letting him fish for another girl.

By mid-year, I gave up on college. It wasn't an easy decision because the parents of one of my Mormon girlfriends had generously helped figure out a way I could get a partial scholarship to a Mormon junior college in Utah. But after I got a taste of the Hollywood scene, I couldn't envision myself leaving town.

I had a job at the House of Fabrics but knew that wasn't a career and began to think of life after graduation. I thought I might like to become a hairdresser and enrolled in night classes at the Newbury School of Beauty. What a crazy, wild place! The girls enrolled there were as funny as they were terrifically naughty and bad. They were chain-smoking, hard-partying, delinquent drama queens who shocked me with stories of their escapades.

And I wasn't exactly a bore. Through a few girlfriends who liked to go belly-dancing at Middle Eastern clubs, I got involved with a bunch of Iranian men. They were newly arrived in L.A., part of the influx of Iranian immigrants settling in the city around that time. From what I saw, they enjoyed leaving their restrictive culture back home and turned into wild men.

Freddie was one such guy. He was a hairdresser in his early fifties. He hit on me when I was on a cigarette break outside the House of Fabrics at the Conejo mall. I almost burst out laughing at the site of his toupee, something I never understood. He was a hairdresser with an awful and obvious rug on his head. Ugh.

Why did I say yes when he asked me out? It was probably because I was so amused by his look: in addition to his toupee, he wore jumpsuits and carried a man purse. We dated for about a week or two. He used to pick me up after beauty school and call me his "beautiful French fry." I called him "Papa." He was focused nonstop on getting into my pants. He would've had an easier time breaking into Fort Knox.

A few hours with Freddie was like a wrestling match. I finally stopped returning his phone calls after he gave me a painting of palm trees and camels on black velvet and talked about treating me like a princess if he could take me to Tehran. I didn't want to go to Tehran with Freddie, let alone be with him anymore.

I then started going out with Reza, a struggling Iranian artist who was even fresher off the plane than Freddie. We met at a different Middle Eastern nightclub. Reza, in his mid-twenties, had an enormous nose.

A comic would say it arrived five minutes before he did. He also wore thick cologne. Maybe that's why his nose never bothered me. I couldn't get past his scent. In all seriousness, I didn't mind either.

We danced all night after we met. He was a great dancer. After we had gone out a couple more times, Reza proposed to me—and of course I said yes. I was never serious and refused to take the ring he offered me, but Reza thought he had snagged a wife. I had the toughest time thinking of a way to get out of that jam. I felt bad when I came to my senses and realized my silliness had gotten out of hand. I worked up my nerve and broke off the engagement—and then told Reza I didn't want to see him anymore.

I had to watch myself. I couldn't lead guys like that on and not eventually get into trouble.

My parents never knew about any of these shenanigans. They wouldn't have understood. Actually, they would've asked where I found the time between school and work to have these wild romances. Honestly, I can't imagine how I made the time or found the energy. It helped that I was eighteen. I didn't have to sleep. I didn't even think of sleep.

Not long after I broke up with Reza, my schedule opened up unexpectedly when I was fired from the House of Fabrics. The manager caught me leaving with yards of fabric hidden under my clothes. He didn't even ask for an explanation; he just said I didn't have to come back. It was mortifying.

It was then that I quit beauty school and signed up for secretarial classes, where I learned to type and take shorthand. With graduation coming up, I was going to need a way to support myself. I had no idea what I wanted to do and figured I better have some skills.

four

LUXURY LIVING

AFTER GRADUATION, I went straight to the Roxy to see one of the guys from Heart play in a side project. I didn't care as much about the show inside as I did the one outside. I flitted around the parking lot with my crazy girlfriends, feeling like I was finally out of school and free to do whatever I wanted.

I *wanted* to go to Rome and ride around on scooters with cute Italian boys and smoke cigarettes on the Via Veneto. I had recently seen Federico Fellini's *La Dolce Vita* and left the theater imagining myself as Anita Ekberg, who had played a Swedish-American movie star pursued through Rome by a journalist (Marcello Mastroianni) on a search for meaning in life amid the city's wealth and decadence.

Inspired, I had saved money for months and just had to sell my car to put me over the top. But my plans were derailed when I lost control of my car on the freeway while switching radio stations and smashed into the back of a truck. My Thrash Datsun actually flipped over. Just to show how focused I was on getting to Rome, as I was in midair, instead of thinking I was about to die or be seriously injured, I thought, Oh shit, now I'm not going to be able to sell my car.

Miraculously I wasn't hurt. But my car was irreparably damaged, along with my travel plans and immediate future. It was summer 1976, and I figured I might as well have a good time in Hollywood. Without school, I stayed out later and partied harder. My parents, who were still raising five other children ranging in age from sixteen to two, charged me $60 a month to live at home. I assumed that meant I could come and go as I pleased.

Wrong. A short time after my eighteenth birthday, I returned home from the Rainbow at three A.M. to grab some albums and clothes, maybe some other things, too, before going to my boyfriend's place. Stacey, who was actually more of a friend than a boyfriend, was in my car as I pulled into the driveway. In his satin pants and platform shoes, he looked as if he had stepped off of a New York Dolls album cover.

I had him wait outside while I grabbed my stuff. But as I hurried back through the house my mom intercepted me in the living room and said I wasn't going anywhere.

"Sorry, I have to go," I said, and pushed through the door, leaving her in her nightgown to watch from the window as I backed out and drove away.

My parents were more upset when I didn't return until early the next evening. We had it out, and soon after, Theresa and I got a small, very cheap one-bedroom apartment in Hollywood. Other than our beds, we didn't have any furniture. We didn't have food either. I ate instant oatmeal with margarine and Sweet'N Low three times a day. I didn't care. Along with cool clothes and shoes, all that mattered was location—and our place was within walking distance of all the clubs.

Our arrival was perfectly timed. In fall 1976, Rodney Bingenheimer, also known as the "Mayor of the Sunset Strip," began hosting a Sunday-night program on KROQ, a tiny Pasadena-based radio station with an underground sensibility. It was a hub for new music, and Rodney's show, *Rodney on the ROQ,* was at the leading edge of all that was new, different, punk, and straight from England.

Rodney's background prepared him to be ahead of music's curve. He had been Sonny and Cher's publicist, a stand-in for Davy Jones on the hit series *The Monkees,* and more recently proprietor of his eponymously named club, Rodney Bingenheimer's English Disco, which was so hip the Stooges and David Bowie went there when they were in town. As Bowie once said, Rodney knew more cool, cutting-edge music than anyone.

I thought of Hollywood as one great big outdoor club with its own soundtrack. Theresa and I began our nights at the Rainbow and as soon as we heard about a party, we sped through the Hollywood Hills, looking for the address. As young, attractive girls, doors opened easily for us. Once inside, I needed a couple drinks to get loose enough to enjoy myself. A quaalude also helped. At the time, my drug use was strictly recreational.

But still, a girl had to be careful. The city was full of predators. There were old letches like "What's Happening" Bob, a guy in his sixties known for laying his slimy hands on girls as he drilled his smile uncomfortably close and asked, "What's happening?" And there was Paul with the purple Excalibur, who had a similarly sleazy act.

I learned my lessons like everyone else. I remember flitting through a club one night when a good-looking guy pulled me aside and within minutes had me telling him my life story. A classic Hollywood smoothie, he put his hand on my shoulder as if to balance himself, stepped back, and said I had a beauty that was unlike any he had ever seen. He said I could be in *Playboy* magazine if I wanted.

At that point, he had my head spinning. I had never been flattered like that before.

"Really?" I said. "You think so?"

He nodded. "Why don't you come to my place and let me take pictures of you?" he asked.

Moments later, I was following him to his house. Halfway through the photo session, as some of my clothes came off, he came on to me. I cringe as I think back on how stupidly and predictably that scene unfolded. I was so ignorant. Luckily for me, I sobered up in time to realize the whole thing was bullshit and I got the hell out of there, scolding myself for being so gullible and naïve.

I supported myself with secretarial work that I got through temporary agencies. I started out at Home Savings and Loan and typically moved on to another job after a ninety-day probation period. The cash was good, it was convenient, and I never got attached enough to feel guilty about coming in at nine with my eyes still half-closed and my head not yet cleared from the previous night.

By afternoon, I was sneaking personal phone calls, making plans for later that night. As always, though, my evening centered around the

Rainbow's parking lot. I had a feeling that rock stars and Hollywood A-listers went through the same thing during the day, calling around to find out where the parties were going to be, who was playing in which club, and eventually ending up at the Rainbow, too.

Inevitably, I saw everyone who was anyone, including Robert Plant, Ron Wood, Rod Stewart, Alice Cooper, and Linda Ronstadt. The difference was they got out of fancy cars while I had walked down Sunset and hung out with other kids, smoking, whiffing amyl nitrate, gossiping, laughing, and fantasizing about being a star myself.

I was at work one day in early 1977 when Theresa called me with breaking news. Queen was in town. She was breathless from the excitement. They were staying at the Beverly Hilton hotel, she said, and she asked if I wanted to go there with her and try to meet the band. Of course I did, I said. I didn't even have to think about it.

That night, we dressed up and went to the hotel. Theresa had found out what Freddie Mercury's room number was, and we headed straight for it after making it through the lobby and into the elevator without getting stopped. We laughed nervously and wondered what we would say if Freddie actually answered the door and invited us in.

Outside his room, we encountered two other freaks on a similar mission to meet Freddie. They told us their names, Bobby Breahm and Georg Ruthenberg. They were our age and from West Los Angeles. They immediately pegged us as a couple of girls from the Valley. It didn't matter.

"Is this Freddie's room?" I asked.

They nodded and added that they had been camped there for a while and hadn't seen him come or go.

"Or heard anything going on inside," one of them added.

Theresa and I turned toward the door and knocked. We waited and then hit it again. We probably knocked about a dozen times without anyone ever coming to the door. In retrospect, I know from personal experience that this didn't mean he wasn't in there. I've been in plenty of hotel rooms over the course of my career and heard fans in the hallway debating whether or not to knock on my door, and then knock over and over again. I never open the door.

So for all we knew, Freddie could have been inside the room and just didn't want to be bothered by four fanatical kids. Eventually we sat down in the hallway and forgot all about Freddie. Instead we got to know one another. We talked for hours about music and emerged at the end of night as friends. Bobby and Georg said they were going to start a band and asked if we wanted to be in it. Theresa and I said yes.

At the time, L.A.'s punk scene was barely a blip in the city's more commercially oriented music world. Disco was the fad of the day and although I saw a Bee Gees show that is still the best concert I've ever seen, the music and the silk-jacket scene didn't resonate with me. Nor did it grab anyone in my immediate crowd.

We were different from even most of the kids at the Rainbow. I'd say 99.9 percent of them wanted to be rock stars. Only a handful of freaks and misfits thought of themselves as punks. I'd say there were only fifty people in all of L.A. like us who were paying attention to the Sex Pistols in London, the bands at New York's CBGB, and the new era that dawned when Rodney played the Ramones' first album.

We read *NME* and *Melody Maker,* not *Rolling Stone.* We knew that Malcolm McLaren had spotted Johnny Rotten, aka Johnny Lydon, on Kings Road wearing a Pink Floyd T-shirt over which he had written "I HATE," and so we wrote on our T-shirts. When Rodney declared he was "anti–the Eagles," we nodded in agreement and ventured out of the shadows, realizing we were part of the same intense tribe—a tribe that would soon ignite a full-fledged revolution.

We stayed in touch with Bobby and Georg and eventually got around to making good on the idea of forming a band. We jammed in Georg's garage and started messing around with lyrics. It was fun. Georg was the only one who played an instrument, but actual proficiency was not a requirement in a punk band. Theresa, who dyed her hair platinum blond, picked up the bass. I sat down on drums, and Bobby, as we assumed he would, stepped to the front as the lead singer.

We went at it with a noisy recklessness and disregard that was so much fun we didn't care what we sounded like, though we thought we sounded pretty good, or at least good enough. In the spirit of Johnny Rotten, we adopted *noms de punk.* Bobby became Darby Crash. Georg became Pat Smear. Theresa came up with Lorna Doom. And I chose Dottie Danger.

Why Dottie Danger? It sounded cute and angry at the same time.

Darby and Pat had been down this road before. They'd started a band after being kicked out of high school. They called it Sophistifuck and the Revlon Spam Queens—a great name. But when they couldn't get all those letters on a T-shirt, they renamed themselves the Germs.

We got really into the band as we practiced, picked up some steam, and set our sights on doing something Darby and Pat hadn't done in their previous incarnation as the Germs—perform a show, a real show at a club.

We didn't possess anything close to the skill and polish of bands that were headlining clubs in L.A., bands like the Ramones, Blondie, Television, the Quick, and Joan Jett. But we still got booked at the Orpheum Theatre in April 1977. We printed flyers and posted them around town.

However, as the date drew near, I got very sick and was diagnosed with mononucleosis. I had to drop out of the band and move back home with my parents for three months. Becky Barton, another girl from my high school art class, took my place. She called herself Donna Rhia. Hilarious.

I still attended the show. I wouldn't have missed it even if I had been hospitalized. As I think about it, wearing a hospital gown might have been very punk. Anyway, as I recall, about eight people showed up to hear the band, which was typical of hard-core punk shows at the time. They drew fans who were early adapters and very plugged in or friends of the band. People didn't just casually go check out a punk band, not one like the Germs.

You had to *want* to see Darby.

Among all his screaming and histrionics, he stuck the microphone in a jar of peanut butter and covered his body in red licorice. As Pat recalled, they were thrown off the stage after five minutes.

But we thought that was a huge success. The band had played in public! We felt validated and real. The Germs were considered legit and later on were regarded as L.A.'s first homegrown punk band. I had been disappointed that I wasn't able to participate as originally planned. I was also bummed about living at home again. I seemed to have regressed.

Little did I know I was about to rev up.

After recovering from mono, I stayed connected to the Germs as their publicist, which meant I put flyers up in record stores. I also announced the band before shows and stood off to the side of the stage, handing Darby his peanut butter, licorice, and salad dressing. I wished there had been a place for me, but another opportunity arose when my friend Connie Clarksville called and asked if I wanted to sing backup for Black Randy and the Metrosquad.

Someone had dropped out and they needed a fill-in. I was glad to help, and even happier when I found out I could take my place onstage wearing a dashiki and a beehive wig. It was the best dress-up party I'd ever been invited to. Black Randy's show was like a circus, and part of the performance was the assemblage of this crazy horde of musicians, singers, and dancers, all of whom contributed in some way to his reworking of James Brown's "Say It Loud (I'm Black and I'm Proud)," as well as funny and funky originals he wrote about drugs, prostitutes, and whatever else crossed his mind. He had one song about Ugandan dictator Idi Amin.

Randy was an acquired taste, both brilliant and self-destructive. Like Darby, he did heroin, which I didn't like being around. Drugs, like the geographical divides that made for Hollywood punks, beach punks, and South Bay punks, created their own culture, look, and rituals. From what I experienced, there were two basic groups: those who did heroin and those who were into dropping acid and partying. The junkies were dark, violent, and scary. Those who preferred acid, like me, were more sociable, fun, and interested in a good time.

And I had a good time. Once I was healthy again, I moved out of my parents' house and went back to Hollywood. Without my own place, I relied on friends letting me crash on their couches or in most cases, their floors. I didn't care where I slept as much as I did about getting into hot shows featuring the Plugz, the Deadbeats, and the Screamers.

In July, Devo played at the Starwood, and the Ohio art school grads were so good they subsequently ended up being the house band at the Whisky.

The Masque emerged as the center of L.A.'s punk scene. It was literally an underground club—a hole-in-the-wall basement located beneath the Pussycat adult theater. By the time it closed in 1979, the little stage featured X, the Weirdos, the Germs, the Dils, and almost every other local punk band of note. Equally famous were its concrete walls, which were covered in graffiti that many considered made it one of the great, if not sacred, shrines to the origins of the punk movement.

The Roxy and Whisky were still popular, as was the Starwood, but the bands that played those clubs were by and large big, or on their way up. The Masque was a big cold room filled with weirdos, misfits, and iconoclasts. If you were a punk, you fit into one of those categories, or you simply checked "all of the above." I was one of the regulars and notable for the way my close-cropped hair changed colors almost as often as the club changed bands.

Part of the fun I had was being able to dress up in whatever kind of outfit I thought about putting together. I preferred avant garde designers like Kenzo, but if I managed to splurge occasionally at Fred Segal or Neo 80, one of the few punk stores, it usually left me flat broke, and then I relied on my mom to make me clothes for work or I scrounged through thrift stores. I had an eye, though, so everything worked for me—or so I thought. I remember wearing a paisley dress and two-toned cowboy boots to work and then changing into a fifties-style prom dress with torn stockings and stilettos. I famously showed up once at a party wearing a Hefty trash bag.

I often topped off my getup with a faux-diamond-encrusted tiara. Why not step into the role of punk princess? I thought.

No sooner did I do that than a prince came into my life—Karlos Kaballeros. Karlos was the drummer for the Dickies, a band whose music I loved. He was also my type—dark, handsome, and Latin. I knew of him and the band before, but we actually met one night at a party in the Hollywood Hills. He thought he was laying a cool line on me (and he was) when he said I reminded him of a punk Kim Novak.

Hearing that, I immediately acted out the sultry scene from the movie *Picnic* when Kim clapped her hands and swiveled her hips in a slow dance that put William Holden under her spell.

It had the same effect on Karlos. He became my first real boyfriend, my first romantic boyfriend, too. He was also my first rock star. The Dickies were on the verge of being signed to a major record label, and that made them hot stuff around town. Despite the buzz, though, they were still as broke as everyone else. Karlos was like me in that he didn't have a place of his own. After the parties were over the two of us would curl up together on friends' floor spaces or couches.

We had a pretty bohemian romance. We were broke, rarely sober, and always on the go. Our lives were about music. We went to shows, found parties, and made a few trips to San Francisco for concerts at Mabuhay Gardens, or the Fab Mab as everyone called it, in the city's rather skeezy North Beach district. We ate at Johnny's Steakhouse on Hollywood Boulevard, flicked our cigs as we walked down the Strip, and shared bottles of cheap wine along with our innermost dreams until we passed out on each other.

After a couple months together, I sensed something strange going on with Karlos. It was a subtle change that made me think he wasn't being forthright with me about our relationship. I didn't say anything, but one night when we were meeting at the Whisky, I saw him walk in and got a sense that he was going to break up with me. And strangely enough, he did.

He found me in the club, gave me a kiss on the forehead, and started to make small talk. I asked if something was bothering him, and after stammering for a moment, he said something along the lines of "I'm not good enough for you." I understood where that was going and thought it was a pathetically weak way of telling me that he had found someone else. Regardless, I was crushed. When I asked what was behind his decision, if there was someone else or something else, he said there was nothing to discuss.

I saw him a few nights later at a club. He was with another guy and they were about to leave on their motorcycles. For a moment, I thought about going over to them and having some words with Karlos. But, as hard as it was, I decided to leave it. Whatever I said wouldn't make me feel better. He didn't want me anymore.

I had a hard time for months. Everyplace I went reminded me of him—or of us. I cried as I rode the bus to and from work; the city seemed so cold, empty, and lonely. I remember bursting into tears when I heard Rod Stewart's version of "The First Cut Is the Deepest."

Four or five years went by before I saw Karlos again. I was in the VIP balcony at the Starwood, checking out Mötley Crüe, when some guy began giving me a very hard time. We exchanged words and suddenly he cocked his arm to hit me. I saw it happening in slow motion, the way I had years earlier when my car flipped over on the freeway. Then from out of nowhere Karlos appeared, blocked the guy's arm, and beat the crap out of him in my defense.

I was extremely grateful, slightly embarrassed, and pleased to see that he still cared.

five

WE'RE HERE NOW

MOOCHING A PLACE to sleep every night got old. I reconnected with Theresa, and we rented an apartment in the Canterbury, a large, run-down apartment building from the thirties on Cherokee. It was a terrible neighborhood, but only a block from the Masque, which was why, aside from it being cheap, it seemed like everyone we knew lived in the building.

If someone had blown up the Canterbury, and God knows someone might have tried, most of Hollywood's punk scene would have been destroyed. I heard rumors the Canterbury's landlord was also a pimp and oversaw a theft ring. True or not, he was a dodgy guy—but perfect as the ringmaster for the characters who called the Canterbury home.

All the punks had apartments throughout the building, including my friend Connie, who had gotten me into Black Randy. She was also a former beauty school student and sold drinks at the Masque. She had lived at the Canterbury for years and liked to say she predated the punks, having moved in when the renters were merely drag queens and pimps.

Connie gave haircuts to anyone who wanted one and boasted about having hundreds of clients. Clients? To me, they were weirdos like myself who wandered into her apartment. Later, she was a roadie for the Go-Go's. I always thought she was a riot. Once when we were bored, she pushed me down Sunset in a wheelchair while I pretended to be spastic. The more people we unnerved, the funnier we thought it was.

Alice Bag was another major force of feminine creativity and vision who also sang backup with Black Randy and went on to lead her own bodacious but short-lived group, the Bags. She was another one of those marvels who were incredibly smart, opinionated, and prescient. She knew of music before anyone else did and swore by the Ramones until she heard the Weirdos, who memorably and famously told *Slash* magazine, "We're not punks. We're weirdos."

Alice was among the most committed to music and life on the fringe of art and acceptance. In every era, including the punk era, there are those who get notoriety and those who are just as instrumental and inspiring, if not more so, but for some reason don't get the fame—Alice was one of those people. We were good friends. We got drunk together pretty frequently, shopped the thrift stores, talked endlessly, and hung out. I also remember making out with her on a bench as we waited for a bus on Vine Street. In those days making out with someone of your own sex was fashionable.

The Canterbury was a great big interconnected stew of crazies devoted to two things, partying and music, though it was hard to tell where one ended and the other began. You could stand in the courtyard at almost any time of the day or night and hear different music blasting out of every window—and believe me, that was the least of it.

I was carried out or passed out more times than I can recall. Others were way wilder. I don't even want to think about the strange bedfellows you would have found if you peeked inside those windows. It was insane, in a great way.

Theresa and I had a studio apartment with a kitchen. It came with a disgustingly dirty and worn plaid sofa—the piece that qualified it as "furnished." We also shared a Murphy bed. One day, in a burst of inspiration, I set out to paint the bathroom bloodred, but I ran out of steam halfway through and never finished.

I probably went out and never picked the brush up again. I expended more energy making sure I was at all the hot shows, whether the bill was the Screamers, the Ramones, and Blondie or the Weasels, the Bags, the Eyes, and the Quick.

The Germs were also busy and productive that summer and into the fall of 1977, their most notable gigs being at the Whisky in September with the Weirdos and the Bags and then the next month when they opened for Devo and Blondie. I can still be heard on a vintage piece of video on YouTube introducing the band.

The parties that followed the shows were as important to us insiders as the shows themselves. They gave everyone a chance to mingle, talk about the performances, compare what we'd seen and heard to every other band on the planet, and hook up. I was a huge fan of Devo, but I was always intimidated around Mark Mothersbaugh and the other guys. It wasn't for any reason other than that they were smart college graduates who had a well-thought-out vision, and I feared not understanding whatever it was they were talking about.

I also got a kick out of the Weirdos, especially the Denney brothers, John and Dix, who were fun on- and offstage. But I remember seeing the Stranglers when they rolled into town from the UK and getting a sense from their attitude and apparent aggressiveness that they were probably too much for a carefree party girl like me.

I underestimated myself. One night I dropped some acid with Germs drummer Don Bolles and a group of friends. There were probably ten of us who decided to trip together that night. After ingesting the LSD, we walked en masse from the Canterbury to Hollywood Forever Cemetery, which was a decent walk when you were straight, but a flat-out adventure while tripping.

Once there, we crawled underneath the main gates and spent a couple hours exploring the grounds. We found the graves of Hollywood legends Rudolph Valentino and Tyrone Power as well as Virginia Rappe's plot. Rappe was the silent film actress Fatty Arbuckle was accused of killing, a dark tragedy that had intrigued me for many years. We also goofed around in one of the old mausoleums, shaking a couple urns as if they were maracas.

As several of us were sticking flowers in our hair and joking around, we heard a deep, stern voice on a loudspeaker cut through our laughter and say, "Everyone stop whatever you're doing and come out with your hands up." It was the cops. I looked out toward where I heard the voice and saw several squad cars with their lights flashing just like on the old TV series *Adam-12*.

Oh crap, I thought as I was hit by a sick feeling I hadn't felt since I was caught shoplifting from Thrifty. As my friends slowly marched out to face the police, though, I decided I wasn't going with them. I didn't want to get arrested, not while still blazing on acid. Instead I hid behind a tombstone, not knowing how much of the fear I felt was because I was high and how much was because I was really scared.

After all the others were outside the gate and standing nervously in the glare of a spotlight from one of the black and white police cruisers, the cops issued several more orders to come out. I didn't know if some-one had said I was still in there, but I didn't move—not even when they shined a powerful spotlight from another car in my direction, panning it across the grounds, searching for me.

I don't think I breathed until they finally left. I guess they felt like they were hauling in enough weird-looking kids for the night and didn't need one more girl with short platinum-colored hair. I continued to sit in the dark for some time, waiting until I felt certain the coast was clear. Then I sprinted through the lightless night as fast as I could, running breathlessly across the tombstones toward the cemetery's other gate. I crawled under and walked back to the Canterbury.

On Santa Monica Boulevard, about halfway there, I bumped into Don Bolles, who had escaped, too. We looked at each other and shook our heads in disbelief. All the others had been taken to jail. Later in the week, a couple of the girls told me that they had spent several days in Sybil Brand, the women's jail. They were pissed, but they'd had no choice. No one had any money to bail them out.

The year wound down with shows at the Whisky from the Deadbeats, the Mumps, Elvis Costello, Talking Heads, the Ramones, the Screamers, and the Dickies (which I continued to see despite the heartache I felt watching Karlos). After one show, I met a guy who said he heard that Natalie Wood's sister, Lana Wood, was having a party at her house, and he suggested we crash it.

Why not? We found her house, bypassed the valet parking out front in favor of parking on our own up the street, and walked straight into the party, where we tried to keep our cool and look like we belonged while gawking at stars. I remember elbowing my friend and saying, "Look, there's Jack Haley Jr." He had no idea.

Crashing fancy parties became something I did fairly often. It was cheap entertainment. I got dressed up, drank champagne, and tried to look posh. The Chateau Marmont hotel was my favorite place to crash events. One night I stumbled into a hoity-toity celebration for a famous New York artist. After a glass or two of champagne, I ran out and broke all the lightbulbs in the hallway as I passed them.

Looking back, my life at that time stands out as surreal, colorful, vibrant, reckless, and irresponsible. I didn't have any money but felt like I owned the town. Occasionally I was onstage as a backup singer, other times I was in the audience, but I was living the dream all the time. It was wonderful. The humdrum monotony of temp jobs in the daytime was minor compared to the thrilling anticipation of something wonderful happening at night.

I didn't want to miss anything. No one did.

Word spread that the Sex Pistols were going to play at the Winterland Ballroom on January 14 in San Francisco. Only seven months had passed since "God Save the Queen" had been released like a firebomb across the airwaves. I had listened to it with Darby and Bobby; they had played it over and over, as if they were tattooing it in their brains. It provided our revolution with an anarchist anthem.

The Pistols' incendiary album *Never Mind the Bollocks, Here's the Sex Pistols* soon followed, and it was pretty obvious from those songs, along with what I'd read, that Johnny Rotten, Sid Vicious, and the boys were like a fast-moving cyclone and I'd better do everything I could to see them before they blew apart.

A bunch of us felt the same way, like we needed to do whatever we could to get up to San Francisco. I went up with Theresa and a group that included Connie and others. She recalls us checking into a Chinatown hotel, trashing the room, and then being unable to find another place to stay, all of which is likely true. I just don't remember any of it. I was probably on acid.

My memory of this trip kicks in right before the show, when I ran into other L.A. punks, such as photographer Jenny Lens, Hellin Killer, Margot Olaverra, and Jane Wiedlin, then known as Jane Drano, a cute, outgoing girl who was around the Masque and Canterbury from the beginning. All of us were excited to be there, and the show more than lived up to any expectations we had of the world's greatest punk band.

It was a miracle the Sex Pistols even made it onto the stage after a three-week tour across the southern U.S. that filled the underground with talk of new highs and lows of self-destructive behavior. It was all part of their larger-than-life reputation, which, in a way, transcended anything they played that night, though as I recall, the show we saw was brilliant.

I still get goose bumps when I picture Sid Vicious poised at the edge of the stage, in his leather pants, billowy white shirt, and black vest, grasping the microphone with both hands. I remember his hair sticking straight up and the violent way he thrashed through the band's songs. By the end of the night, he was shirtless, and his skinny white torso was full of gashes that were dripping with blood, while Johnny Rotten was kneeling onstage, chanting, "This is no fun. This is no fun."

Those words turned out to be prophetic. Within the week, Johnny Rotten announced the band had broken up and little more than a year later Sid Vicious was dead of a heroin overdose.

It was amazing. Inspired by the Sex Pistols show and determined to see punk rock in the place it originated, Theresa and I saved our money until we could afford tickets to London and spent two weeks there seeing shows, shopping, and looking for cute boys. We shared a room in a small, old hotel in Paddington, and aside from just the fact that we were in London, the most memorable part of the trip was when I woke up from a sound sleep one night and saw a ghost.

I didn't just *see* the ghost. I had woken up because it was holding me down. I saw and felt it on top of me. I tried to scream but it wouldn't let me open my mouth. It started to choke me, and just when I began to panic that I was going to pass out, it disappeared.

In the morning, I told Theresa what had happened and when she gave me the kind of disbelieving look you would expect, I simply said, "Believe what you want, but it was real."

Back home, I was hanging out one night with Jane Wiedlin and Margot Olaverra at a party in Venice. The house was little and crowded with people, and at one point the three of us found ourselves sitting on the curb, with beers and cigarettes. We talked about the Sex Pistols' show in San Francisco, which was still fresh in our minds, and I added stories from my trip to London, and eventually we were talking about starting our own band.

Margot had been trying to get something together for months. She had, in fact, started learning to play bass and had already recruited another girl, Elissa Bello, to play drums.

Jane and I jumped in without having to think about it. Jane said she wanted to play guitar. I'd wanted to play bass, but since Margot had already claimed that role, I was left with one option—the lead singer. I laughingly admitted that my only previous experience as a singer was as a backup with Black Randy, which half the residents at the Canterbury seemed to have done, and before that, as a little girl singing along to *The Sound of Music* soundtrack.

But my lack of experience didn't matter. None of the others had much either. The beautiful thing about punk was that you only needed to have the guts to try and the enthusiasm to think you could pull it off. We had both the guts and the enthusiasm, plus some additional craziness, and as we sat on the curb, we talked one another into a froth of excitement. Everybody we knew was in a band. Why not us?

We sealed the deal by telling each other that at the least we could be as bad as everyone else, but the unique thing that happened and separated us from the pack from the start was that we also agreed that we didn't *have* to be bad—and we could probably be better than most, and definitely cuter.

I remember the looks we gave one another and the back-and-forth before we got up. It was like making a pact.

"Is this for real?"

"Yes."

"Are we serious?"

"Yes."

"Really serious?"

"There's no flaking out, right?"

"Okay, if we're a band, when's rehearsal?"

As far as I was concerned, we were going to be big. I had no doubt.

*   *   *

Our first rehearsal was at Margot's apartment off Robertson Boulevard. We were pretty scattered and lost. We didn't even know how to start; we barely figured out how to set up our instruments. We banged around, tried to write songs, and then went to Denny's for dinner. We were situated in a booth, a mix of kicky hair styles and colors wrapped in cigarette smoke. All of us were in agreement that our first rehearsal had surpassed expectations. Hey, we'd shown up and done it. But we were missing something key—a name for the band.

We tossed suggestions back and forth, and continued the discussion for a few days before we whittled the choices down to two, the Misfits and the Go-Go's. Both were good names. We nearly chose the Misfits and went so far as to print up a flyer. But someone looked up "go-go" in the dictionary and found that it meant something like "uninhibited and free," and we liked that. Everyone agreed it fit. And from that moment on, we were the Go-Go's.

We rehearsed in the basement at the Canterbury, then shuttled between there and one of the several tiny rehearsal rooms at the Masque, which we shared with other bands, including the Motels and X. Both bands gave us pointers. With our purple and fuchsia hair, we were a sight as we wheeled our amps down the street from the Canterbury to the club, which was beneath the Pussycat porn theater on Hollywood Boulevard.

We came up with two songs, "Overrun," a fashionably angry romp that I wrote, and "Robert Hilburn," a tongue-in-cheek ode to the *Los Angeles Times*'s rock music critic written by Jane, who from the outset revealed herself to be an incredibly prolific and clever songwriter, something that was even more impressive considering she didn't know anything about writing songs and learned the chords by putting masking tape with numbers on her guitar frets.

That was the amazing thing about the band. We did everything by instinct—and it usually turned out to be right.

The best move we made was realizing that we needed help. We needed someone to guide us through the basics, starting with how to plug in our equipment. We really were that clueless.

Margot suggested that we invite Charlotte Caffey to join the group. All of us thought it was a brilliant idea. Charlotte was a California blonde with a sensibility that was more pop than punk. It was probably because she actually had some music training. I didn't know her personally, but I knew who she was. She had played bass with the Keys and more recently with the Eyes, a band that I really liked. She also dated the Dickies' singer, Leonard Phillips. And most important, she knew how to do all the things we didn't.

Margot and I approached her one night backstage at the Starwood and asked if she wanted to join us in our new band, the Go-Go's. It's funny to think that we hadn't even played a gig but we were already talking as if there was nothing more real and happening than our band. Even funnier is that Charlotte said yes without pausing to think about it.

I thought that was a little bizarre, since she was already in a group. But later Charlotte explained that she had been intrigued with the way Margot and I looked, and she figured we'd be fun girls to hang out with. She was also ready to leave the Eyes.

We told her who was in the group and that she would play lead guitar, which she said sounded great. What she left out was that she didn't know how to play lead guitar. But she learned.

Our first performance was a going-away party for the Dickies at the Masque on May 31, 1978. They were leaving for a monthlong tour of the UK. The club was packed. People were right in our face as we played both of our songs and repeated "Overrun" as our encore. According to Connie, I was so nervous I peed my pants. I don't recall, but I'm not denying it happened either.

Afterward, everyone said we were great. We knew our limitations, but we agreed. We had the time of our lives, too.

At the Masque, a band would play, finish, and then four other people in the crowd would get up and play. Almost everyone there was in a band or wanted to be in a band or knew the people in one of the bands. We played the Masque again a week or so later on a lineup that included the Bags and the Plugz. It felt like another triumph. I thought we were great, even better than before.

A few days later, I was with Jane, heading downstairs to rehearsal at the Canterbury. Charlotte had traveled to the UK with her boyfriend. Jane and I were talking about the previous two shows, reliving every moment and detail, from the performance to the people we saw watching us. We were bursting with ideas and enthusiasm and dreams of a big future.

I said, "You know we are going to be rich and famous," which was such an uncool thing for punks to admit, but Jane agreed, adding, "Yeah, we are."

After Charlotte returned from the UK, we rehearsed and wrote with even more purpose and passion. We had fun and spurred one another on to work hard. A group dynamic quickly emerged. It was one of those things where, when I think back, I can see so clearly that our five personalities immediately added up to something that was greater than any of us as individuals could have ever been. It was the right chemistry.

In other words, as we rehearsed and played, worked up our ideas and shared our dreams, and just hung out—because that's what you did when you were in a band—we clicked as friends and had a fantastic time. And it translated onstage. The Go-Go's were a "new, fun group" that "you can't help but love," noted a punk magazine review after our third show, by which time we had a dozen songs. And the review concluded, "In all, a dynamic set of female rockers."

I came off the stage that night feeling like we had played our best show yet. The review proved it.

But then I popped a cassette of that show into the tape player of a friend's car. Until then, I had never heard myself sing. I was horrified. I sounded terrible. I could carry a tune, but barely. I also screamed more than I sang.

I hit the Stop button, put my hands over my face, and thought, Oh my God, I need to take some vocal lessons.

I scraped together enough money to take lessons from a well-regarded vocal teacher, an older woman who lived in a charming home off Sunset, on Alta Loma, where she taught me scales and warm-up exercises. She also told me stories about performers, including her own experiences as a singer, and she treated me with a seriousness that even more than the things she taught me let me feel like I had it in me to be a real singer.

As I told her, I was willing to work at it.

six

WE GOT THE BEAT

WITH OUR day jobs, we all lived schizophrenic lives. Margot worked at House of Pies. Charlotte clocked in at Kaiser Permanente medical center. Elissa held down various waitress jobs. And Jane, who had studied fashion design, worked in a factory downtown making patterns. I think she even wrote a few song lyrics on those patterns.

None of us had any money beyond what we needed to get by, but we didn't care. We talked about getting rich and famous as if it wasn't a fantasy. As long as we had enough for rent, food, and the occasional trip to the secondhand shop, we didn't worry.

I had a bank account but gave it up when keeping a minimum balance became nearly impossible after portioning out my paycheck from working at Petersen Publishing on essentials like clothes, shoes, hair, rent, bus fare, and nighttime fun. From then on, I kept my cash assets in a Barbie thermos. I carried it everywhere, too. During shows, I set it on the drum riser. I didn't want anyone taking my last few dollars.

Margot had a similar quirk. At some point in the evening, whether we were playing or partying, she would end up on the stage in whatever club we were in, shouting, "Where is my purse? Somebody stole my purse!" Then she cried. Then she got mad at everyone, grabbed the microphone, and shouted, "Motherfuckers, give me back my purse!"

People got so used to it they rolled their eyes and said, "There she goes again." As far as I know, her purse was never stolen. She was never able to remember where she had put it before she started to party. She always found it, though, and all ended well.

We played two shows in October, one early in the month at the

Whisky and a second on Halloween at the Hollywood Roosevelt with the Germs, Satin Tones, and Mau Maus. With everyone dressed in costumes (not much of a change from our everyday appearance) and ingesting copious amounts of booze, quaaludes, hallucinogens, and God only knows what else, the atmosphere was especially festive. Being at the Roosevelt, it was also old-Hollywood and tatty, which I liked.

And we seemed to be liked right back. A review noted, "Well, I can say that I have heard of them [the Go-Go's], but I still can't say that I've seen them, the band being totally obscured by a wall of sweaty, haphazardly costumed bodies. They have a strong sound, but I have no idea what their songs are about."

They were about us—our lives. They weren't specifically feminine or different from songs an all-guys band might write. They were unique to what us girls saw and felt. Also, part of the reason people liked us was because we were a crazy, fun, energetic mess onstage. Quite simply, we were a good time—raw, but the kind of girls you wanted to see again.

We worked hard and continued to mesh as a group. Charlotte, Jane, and I developed an almost telepathic understanding of each other based on ambition, backgrounds, and senses of humor. When we met to rehearse, no one took the lead. We tossed out ideas, tried each other's songs, and got better.

Slash magazine ran our first print interview/feature, and in it, Jane described herself as an "ex-Catholic, ex-cowgirl, ex–fashion designer." Charlotte said that she possessed an IQ of 165 and declared herself a genius whose fantasy was "to be gang-raped by seven Mister Rogers clones." I described myself as a reject from a "strict Southern Baptist home" who liked "huge sweatshirts, rabbit feet, the Hollywood cemetery, rosaries, penguins, the Marquis de Sade, and gin rummy."

Elissa and Margot were less outgoing and out-there but no less passionate than the rest of us, though Elissa was difficult and defensive in rehearsals and periodically a no-show, something you can't be in a band, and she and Margot regularly clashed. It was a tough subject to broach, but all of us knew Elissa's days were numbered.

In early January 1979, we played the Starwood, before that club quit booking punk bands in favor of hair bands like Mötley Crüe and Van

Halen. I remember Alex and Eddie Van Halen crashing a few punk gigs and taking over the stage with a sense of good-natured mayhem.

In his memoir, David Lee Roth said he screwed one of the Go-Go's. Not true—unless there was some hanky-panky I didn't know about. He may have exaggerated a close encounter the two of us had one night outside the Whisky following a Van Halen show. He was entertaining a gaggle of girls on the sidewalk, and I was walking to the Rainbow from my apartment. As I passed by, he grabbed me and we made out on the corner.

Till that moment, we had never met. I'm not even sure that should be counted as a meeting.

Such craziness was more routine than you'd think. Margot and I were doing acid one night and talking about the drive we had planned the next day to see a punk show, including Black Randy, in Pismo Beach. Around two A.M. I suggested we scrap the drive and hitchhike there. Margot said why not, and soon we were standing on the side of the Hollywood Freeway with our thumbs out.

Within minutes, we caught a ride to Thousand Oaks—about fifteen miles, but also the off-ramp nearest my parents' house!

As we waited for another ride, I freaked out.

"What if my dad drives by right now and sees me?" I said. "I'm blazing on acid and hitchhiking. I'll be totally dead."

Margot laughed.

"He's not going to drive by at two thirty in the morning," she said.

Margot and I got as far as Solvang. Then someone gave us a lift into Pismo Beach, where we slept on the sidewalk outside the club until everyone else arrived that afternoon.

In February, the Go-Go's played two nights at the Mabuhay in San Francisco, our first out-of-town gigs and also at a club that gave us some word-of-mouth credibility. Poet-musician Jim Carroll, author of *The Basketball Diaries,* came to one of our shows with his crew of friends. His presence gave us some street cred, and I got zonked with him and his pals afterward.

Back in L.A. we opened at the Whisky for Lydia Lunch, another poet/street icon around whom I always felt intimidated just because I thought she was so damn smart. Being around people like that often made me feel insecure about my own abilities or at least caused me to question what I was doing and wonder whether I was really any good at it, which, as I eventually learned, was ultimately a self-defeating and damaging way to go about life.

Our next show was with the Circle Jerks at Blackie's, and during the show a fight broke out between the Hollywood punks and the beach punks. Each gig was eventful like that; there was, it seemed, never a dull moment—or a dull person.

As the punk culture spread, certain areas of Hollywood looked like they were straight out of the movie *Mad Max* via London's Kings Road, and the transformation created tension in certain parts of the city. Even I grew to see there was a dark side to some punks, particularly the groups that were into heroin and those who were into violence.

By and large, though, there was tension between the punks and the police just like there had been ten years earlier between the hippies and the police. Even a lightweight like me felt it when I walked down Sunset Boulevard and saw the cops eyeing me and my friends for no reason other than we looked and dressed different from most people.

That tension erupted on March 17, a night that became infamous in L.A.'s punk history as the Elks Lodge Massacre. There was a well-publicized punk show at the Elks Lodge across from MacArthur Park just west of downtown. That it was Saint Patrick's Day added to the partytime atmosphere. We were on the bill that included the Plugz, the Zeros, the Wipers, and the Alley Cats. It was an all-ages show, and about eight hundred people turned out.

We played after the Zeros and were followed by the Plugz, who had gotten halfway through their set when all hell broke loose. I was hanging around and talking to friends, but not anywhere near the activity that allegedly caused the problem. According to what I heard and read, around eleven P.M. someone threw a beer bottle against a wall outside the lodge, prompting the manager to call the cops. The LAPD responded by sending in an army of cops in full-on riot gear, and they stormed the place. One account said they'd been ordered to "charge the hall and clear the ballroom."

As soon as the cops arrived, I got the hell out of there. I could feel the ominous change in the air, and I knew better than to hang around. Most of those who did were beaten up. The police ended up putting out a story that they'd had plainclothes officers on the site earlier in the evening and they'd witnessed people fighting in stairwells and throwing beer bottles. One cop even went on Rodney's radio show that night and blamed the punks for causing the melee. The officer in charge told the *Los Angeles Times* they'd gone into the lodge only because it was "a real life-or-death situation."

I saw none of that. The mayhem started when the police showed up and kids were dragged from the hall and out onto the street, clubbed, and hauled away. There was a press conference the next day at the Masque where a bunch of punks presented the other side and accused the LAPD of causing the "massacre."

As I recall, Jane, Charlotte, Margot, and Elissa had, like me, managed to get away before the violence started. However, our manager, Ginger Canzoneri, was beaten with a nightstick. It was scary, dangerous, and one of those very unfortunate events now relegated to a footnote.

Around this time we were having trouble with Elissa, who was proving unreliable, and we were quietly looking for a new drummer. We put out word through the grapevine and somehow it reached Gina Schock. Gina was a talented, serious, and trained drummer from Baltimore who had come to L.A. with Edie and the Eggs, an art-house group fronted by Edith Massey, a favorite actress of cult movie director John Waters.

Gina saw us play at the Whisky and sent word that she was impressed— and thought we could be even better with her as our drummer. Something about that attitude appealed to us, and we invited her to one of our rehearsals. Obviously we made sure Elissa wasn't there, but that wasn't hard since part of our problem with Elissa was that she frequently missed rehearsals and didn't seem to be taking the band seriously enough.

When Gina walked in, I saw her frizzy hair and overalls and thought, wow, she doesn't look like a punk rocker. She definitely didn't look like a Go-Go. But that could be rectified with a trip to the thrift store and some hair dye, and it wasn't nearly as important as how she played. It turned out Gina played phenomenally well, and we invited her to join the band.

We broke the news to Elissa, who was understandably upset and ended up telling people that she'd been booted because she was dating a girl whose ex was our manager, and blah blah blah. It wasn't true. Elissa was fired because she wasn't reliable and it became obvious we needed a drummer with serious talent and attitude. Gina filled that role.

It was a really hard thing to do and forced us to deal with the gossip she put out there, but we got over it, and Gina really did, as she had promised, make us sound dramatically better. She pulled us all together. We finally sounded like we were playing the same song. As we went into summer, we made a significant leap musically. Our songs got tighter and though they still had a punk edge they sounded more pop.

Above all else, with Gina on drums, we really did have the beat; it wasn't only apparent to us.

A *Los Angeles Times* review of our July show at the Hong Kong Café noted that six months earlier all the group "had going for it was an all-girl novelty status and lots of enthusiasm. [But] it's since grown into a fine rock band. Friday's show introduced a better repertoire of material, a new drummer (Gina Schock—a feisty addition), and reveals the group to be steadily gaining control of its instruments. Guitar leads are still a bit ragged, but no matter—if it has managed to come this far in six months, its future seems more than good."

The review went on to say the band's "ace-in-the-hole is its attitude, refreshingly free of the chip-on-shoulder butch stance commonly assumed by women rockers. The Go-Go's don't trade their girlish charms, but neither do they deny them. They are young and cute and enjoy being cute.

"The focal point of the five-girl crew is singer Belinda Carlisle, an energetic beauty with bee-stung lips and a Monroe-esque vulnerability. Carlisle's voice is adequate, but her charm as a performer lies in revealing that she cares. You like her for that."

We played there again two months later with the Bags, Fear, Extremes, and Gear, and a review in the local punk magazine *Flipside* said we delivered "an excellent set even if Belinda was drunk off her ass." I was guilty as charged. Unaware that we were playing two sets, I took a quaalude after the first show and then slurred my way through the second set while sitting in a chair.

Hey, those things happened.

Once, to spice up a long drive to San Francisco in a rental van, I took a big dose of speed and put the pedal to the metal. Somewhere in the middle of California, a cop pulled me over and I broke into a fit of uncontrollable nervous laughter. Obviously it wasn't funny, but I was imagining how the cop was going to react when he came over and saw that in addition to being high, I was dressed in a hot-pink, Indian-style dress with fringe, pink moccasins, and a pink headband.

I turned to the girls in the back and asked, "What if he makes me get out of the car?"

"He might," someone said.

"Then I'm probably going to piss my pants," I said, laughing.

Fortunately, as the cop checked my ID, I kept it together. He was a pleasant guy and allowed me to stay in the car even after glancing in the back at my snickering cohorts. In the end, he advised me to stick to the speed limit and let me off with a warning.

seven

MADNESS

IN DECEMBER 1979, we opened at the Whisky for Madness, an English ska band whose recently released first album, *One Step Beyond,* was earning them raves and a handful of hits, including "One Step Beyond...," "The Prince," "My Girl," and "Night Boat to Cairo." They hit the town with a unique sound and the fun attitude of English boys out for a good time.

At sound check, I clicked with the group's lead singer, Graham McPherson, who went by the name Suggs. By showtime, we were flirting and having a good time watching each other onstage. Afterward, everyone from both bands went back to their hotel, the Tropicana, and partied pretty hard. I woke up the next morning in a chaise longue next to the pool. Suggs and several others were asleep in nearby chaises.

I shook my head, then checked my watch and suddenly bolted upright. I had to go to work!

After Madness left town, Suggs wrote me a few letters and sent me some English cigarettes. I knew he liked me, but I didn't let myself imagine anything developing since I knew from following the bands in the English magazines that he was involved with punk beauty Betty Bright. Still.

A few months later, Madness returned to L.A. and I don't know why I let myself, but I hoped Suggs would try to start something. He didn't. I heard he might have had a dalliance with a cute waitress, but that was mere rumor and I didn't want to turn my quaint romantic fantasy into a disappointment. Better to maintain the memory of a fun flirtation and not let it get messy.

That decision was probably smart, too, because Madness liked us and before they left town they invited the Go-Go's to open for them on their UK tour that spring and summer. We jumped at the opportunity.

We knew going to the UK was one of the necessary ingredients on the way to success. It gave U.S. bands credibility. We saved for months before we could even think about affording to get there, but the prospect of touring the UK inspired one of the Go-Go's most creative and prolific phases. During the first three months of 1980, we played at least every other week in L.A. and San Francisco, and Jane and Charlotte, separately and together, went on a writing tear that produced "How Much More," "Lust to Love," and "We Got the Beat," which Charlotte wrote in about two minutes while watching a rerun of the old TV series *The Twilight Zone*.

I loved those songs the first time I heard them and thought they were going to be hits. They sounded even better when Paul Wexler, the son of Atlantic Records cofounder Jerry Wexler, helped us record a four-song EP so we would have something to sell when we went overseas.

We flew to London in April, which was on schedule, but only after Ginger, showing more dedication than her job as manager required, sold everything she had, including her Mercedes, to make sure we could get overseas. Once there, we faced another issue, namely figuring out where to stay.

We arrived without a predetermined destination. We didn't have a travel agent and couldn't afford nice hotels. Those days were far off and merely a fantasy then. We crammed into a couple small and cheap hotel rooms while Ginger frantically searched for a home base. After a few days, she managed to rent a shabby but charming five-bedroom house in Belsize Park.

We turned the house into a crash pad for girls. Besides the eight of us (the band, Ginger, and our two roadies, Connie and Lydia), we sublet a room to some models from Los Angeles, a girl in the Belle Stars, and another from a local punk band. Everyone shared a bedroom, except for Lydia, who lucked into a single when her roommate, Connie, went back to the States.

Lydia occasionally made extra dough by renting her room to those of us who wanted, or needed, privacy for the night. Boys were always prowling around the house, but we didn't have money to do anything. It was not fun being broke. Even beer was a luxury. When we toured with Madness, we waited for them to finish their preshow dinner and then dug through the trash for the scraps they threw out.

I still managed to gain thirty pounds over the next two months thanks to the Nutella I smeared on white bread every morning. And the beer and booze I drank every day when the entire city seemed to hit the pub. The good times often carried over to the house, which seemed to turn into party central. Big surprise, right? It was a house full of girls.

There was one particular party that was memorable because it got out of hand when all of London—from skinheads to celebrities—seemed to come. I don't know how it happened, but well over a hundred people showed up and the crowd spilled out onto the street. I saw Ozzy Osbourne and tennis star Ilie Nastase, and since we didn't know either of them, I wouldn't have believed it was actually them if I hadn't read about it later in one of the London papers.

In addition to the celebrities, we invited all types and were unaware that you didn't mix punks, skinheads, and rockabilly boys. But they all converged at our house and after enough beer they beat the crap out of one another. We woke up the next day and found the house trashed. It looked like a battlefield.

Little did we know it was like a warm-up for our tour. We played rough clubs across Northern England, including Leeds, Newcastle, Coventry, and Liverpool. The conditions were difficult and trying. The weather was dreary and we were broke, lonely, exhausted, and uncomfortable. Worse, we had to deal with the hard-core skinheads at the clubs where we played. They got drunk, fought, and taunted us as we performed.

Apparently that's what they did. They were young, angry neo-Nazi extremists who hated everyone, including us—and that was before we played the first song. Once they saw we were five little girls from Los Angeles, they yelled vile things and called us terrible names. They spit on us too. They called it "gobbing." I later read that the practice began at a Damned concert when someone threw a beer at Rat Scabies, and he grabbed the guy and spit in his face. I also heard it may have originated with the Sex Pistols.

Regardless, gobbing caught on—and it caught us by surprise. Keep in mind that the clubs we were playing were more like large rooms in a bar, or next to the bar. The stages were slightly elevated platforms, and the audience was a few feet away. They may as well have been part of the show, and with their gobbing, they were.

They ran up to the stage, coughed up a wad of spit, and hocked it at us. It was unnerving, and getting hit with spit was downright gross. I never saw the gobs coming, but I felt my stomach turn after they hit. There were stories about performers getting sick after being hit in the eye or accidently swallowing someone else's spit. We came offstage covered in snot, and I cried afterward, as did the other girls.

On the bright side, though, Stiff Records—the prestigious label that launched Elvis Costello, the Damned, the Pogues, and Nick Lowe— released "We Got the Beat" as a single in the UK. They did it as a favor to Madness, but we didn't care how it got done. On May 9, the label issued a press release that touted us as "5 girls from Hollywood aged 19 through 21, who play as good as they look."

"We Got the Beat" took off in the clubs and became an underground dance hit. Suddenly the Go-Go's were making a splash. The Specials asked us to record background vocals for them, and we were nominated for Most Improved Band at the Club 88 Awards. We finished up our stay in London with a June show at the Embassy club that inspired a writer for *Sounds* magazine to observe we "broke down the barriers of music biz supercooldom to the extent that people more accustomed to posing were actually moved to shake bits of their bodies in time with the music."

He praised "We Got the Beat," "Automatic," and "Tonight." "Doing their thang each night in a motley collection of mini-skirts, Doc Martens and what looked like a job-lot of footless tights, they gave the impression that the five of them could have been thrown together as much by their unconventional [for L.A.] looks and non-conformist fashion tastes as by any shared interest in music...But the point is, it all seemed disarmingly natural and uncontrived—the looks and the music."

He went on to praise our musicianship, especially Gina "for keeping the set so tight and powerful," and added that Jane, Charlotte, and I deserved "top marks for the best and most consistent unison singing I've heard outside a studio automatic-double-tracking machine."

It was a positive end to a long, hard trip. In a short time, we had grown up, toughened up and accomplished more than we expected—indeed, more than we knew.

Our homecoming gig at the Starwood was an instant sellout. While we had been overseas, Rodney had talked about the Go-Go's as if we were stars in London, and he played "We Got the Beat" until it caught on here, too. As a result, lines for our show wrapped around the block. Our shows had always been crowded, but this was insane. We gave an inspired performance to the hometown crowd that included many friends and some of our earliest fans.

Two weeks later, we flew to New York for shows at the Mudd Club. It was our first time playing in the city and another sign that the Go-Go's were gaining some serious buzz. Like London, New York was home to many of the bands we admired, among them the Ramones, Blondie, and the New York Dolls. We wanted to do well.

It was a hot, humid, and terribly uncomfortable summer day when we arrived. It felt like the hot air was coming straight up off the asphalt and then sticking to our skin. After renting a truck for our equipment, we didn't have any money for a hotel, so Ginger arranged for all of us to share an apartment in the Village. Then we got there and found it didn't have any running water or working plumbing.

After some frantic, pissed-off calls to Mudd Club management, Ginger got several of us placed at the bartender's apartment and a couple of us were farmed out to other employees. Once onstage, we forgot all about our makeshift accomodations. *New York Times* music critic Robert Palmer praised our opening show and said we played "tighter, more kinetic rock and roll than most all-male bands," adding, "They have an original, intelligent perspective on the rock and roll tradition and their place in it."

We partied the same way offstage. The first couple nights in New York were typical of the Go-Go's, full of wild, reckless, carefree fun—and then I got out of control. After our second show at Danceteria, I got drunker than I had ever been in my life and had to be carried outside. I projectile-vomited all the way back to the place where we were staying and I stayed in bed for two days with a hangover that still ranks as the worst of my life.

After impressing all the right people, we returned home with a lot of heat and momentum. All the labels knew about us, and I am positive we would have been signed right away or perhaps even earlier if we had had a guy or two in the band, especially as a lead singer. Joe Smith, the head of Capitol Records at the time, personally told us that even though he adored us, he couldn't sign the Go-Go's because no female band had a track record worth investing in.

Yet we were the cool band in town and execs and A&R men from all the labels came to our shows that summer, including a big one in August at the Whisky with Oingo Boingo and the Surf Punks. We were also filmed for *Urgh! A Music War,* a British documentary on punk and new wave bands that featured Joan Jett, the Dead Kennedys, the Police, XTC, Devo, UB40, and Echo & the Bunnymen, among the who's who.

As I recall, we were shot performing "We Got the Beat" in the back of a truck as it cruised down Sunset. I wore a red Chinese dress and weighed about 175 pounds—excess baggage from London and New York. At the time, Ginger was offering all of us ten dollars for every pound we lost.

Miles Copeland, the founder of IRS Records, was working on the movie. At thirty-six, he was a music-industry powerhouse and visionary who had started his label when none of the established companies would sign the Police, which he managed. His younger brother Stewart was the group's drummer, too. Now IRS was also home to the Buzzcocks, the Dead Kennedys, the Cramps, R.E.M., and Oingo Boingo.

We sensed that Miles was going to sign us. He had been sniffing around the band for a long time. Ginger had been in discussions with him off and on. We liked him. But as we wondered when it might happen, other questions about the band took precedence.

eight

GOOD FOR GONE

THE CLOSEST I came to any kind of normalcy was that fall when Connie and I shared an apartment on Hollywood Boulevard and I worked in the photo department at Peterson Publishing. For some reason, my boss, Jack Cook, tolerated me coming in late, hungover, and with purple hair. He asked about the band with seemingly genuine interest and ignored me when I was working out details with clubs instead of answering the phones.

Then craziness took over when my friend Pleasant Gehman invited me to take the empty bedroom in her two-bedroom apartment at Disgraceland, an aptly named building in the heart of Hollywood. The landlord was Jayne Mansfield's ex-husband, former Mr. Universe Mickey Hargitay, and the array of characters who passed through this place made it the most famous crash pad in the punk universe.

I had gone there a year earlier with Suggs, looking for a party, and had been shocked by the conditions in which Pleasant and her roommates existed. Clothes were piled as high as people, food had been left on every possible surface, the walls were filled with random scribbles and band posters, and it was as dirty as you would expect from a party pad that had the same hours as a 7-Eleven. It never closed.

I don't know what about me had changed when I moved in, but I embraced the pigsty as my palace, too. In a small part, I might have thought of living there as a rite of passage or—believe it or not—a measure of prestige. It could have been convenience, too. But thinking back I believe it was all about being close to Pleasant, a singer, poet, artist, journalist, and later on a belly dancer. She was like a punk Gertrude Stein: charismatic, brilliant, and fun.

I met her one night on the roof at the Continental Hyatt hotel; both of us were looking for Nils Lofgren, who had played at the Roxy. I recognized an original when I saw one. Pleasant glammed herself up like a 1950s-style Lolita, in a little T-shirt, with heart-shaped glasses and big, lush bee-stung lips. Nobody looked like her. Or lived like her.

She shared Disgraceland's front bedroom with her boyfriend Levi Dexter, who led the English rockabilly band Levi and the Rockats. I took the back bedroom and immediately painted it bright blue, and then added gold stars on the walls. I parked my Puch moped in the living room. Pleasant's friend Ann McLean slept in the closet. A couple times we put on rubber gloves and tried to clean the place, but it was futile.

Soon after I settled in, I began a two-year relationship with the Blasters' drummer, Bill Bateman—aka Buster. We'd crossed paths at clubs and parties, but it wasn't until Pleasant set up a situation one night at the Troubadour that Buster and I were able to talk more intimately and get to know each other. He had on a striped shirt and wore a bandana around his neck. I thought he looked cute, and I liked him even more as we talked.

I thought he liked me, too. It was one of those setups where everything clicked except for one detail. I didn't like his hair. As I told Pleasant, there was too much of it. He needed a new do.

Well, the next time I saw him, Buster had a nice clip. Imagine that. I guess he had somehow gotten the message. I let him know that I approved, and from then on we were a couple.

He was one of the nicest people I'd ever met. Buster lived in Downey, where he and Phil Alvin had started the Blasters before recruiting Phil's brother, Dave, who turned out to be one of the greatest songwriters to emerge from L.A. during that era. Buster showed me around the town, including the original McDonald's restaurant and the two side-by-side apartment buildings that Karen and Richard Carpenter had built. They were named Close to You and We've Only Just Begun.

Buster also took me to the butcher shops where he bought large meat bones, which he then boiled, fried, and occasionally used in lieu of drumsticks. I thought that was cool.

Most of the time we went to shows and stayed at my place. I had traded my moped to a friend going to Europe for her white Cadillac, which was the ultimate cruisemobile. Buster and I felt like the first couple of Hollywood as we rolled down the Strip in the wide-body as a Jolly Roger flag flapped from the antenna. One of my favorite memories from that time is of Buster sitting on the windowsill of my bedroom, watching me put on makeup as he drank a beer from a bottle that was wrapped in a little brown grocery bag. And then for some reason he threw his head back and laughed at me.

We had a problem within the Go-Go's that wasn't a laughing matter. It had to do with Margot. She was still a committed punk and felt that we were selling out with pop-sounding music. She was against anything that sounded too polished and commercial. But that was the direction in which we were headed, and it created serious tension within the band.

It was even more problematic in that Margot was the one who originally helped put the Go-Go's together. Jane and I were with her that night on the curb in Venice, but she lit the match that started the fire. That's also why she gradually drifted into a very bad headspace. She had a different vision for the band, and on top of that she didn't cope well with the demands of our schedule. She didn't take care of herself and missed rehearsals, and when she was there she was contrary and argumentative.

One day, as we struggled with the bridge to a new song, she stopped playing, which brought the song to a halt, and looked at us with a frustration that I found impossible to read. Then it became apparent that she simply didn't like what we were doing.

"Why can't we play songs like X?" she said.

I felt like she left rehearsals and bitched about us to her friends, like Exene Cervenka of X, who seemed to turn against us, especially me.

I already felt like Exene thought I was a stupid, silly girl anyway. The thing with Margot, I was sure, made it worse.

In the fall, Margot was arrested at the Starwood for buying cocaine. She stayed in the West Hollywood sheriff's jail until her pal D. J. Bonebrake from X got her out the next morning. We came down hard on her for that screwup. That might have seemed hypocritical; none of us was an angel. The truth was, this gave us a problem we could substitute for the real issue—we weren't on the same page. We were working hard and on the verge of signing a deal. We were playing six sold-out shows at the Whisky over New Year's, three nights with two sets each night, and we didn't want to worry that Margot might jeopardize all of our hard work.

We needed a solution to the problem. After many private conversations, the consensus was that we were either going to remove Margot or she was going to remove herself.

And that's what happened.

In December, Margot was diagnosed with hepatitis A. It was another sign that she wasn't taking care of herself. We had to go to a clinic and get hepatitis shots, which put me in a foul mood. But we turned the situation into an opportunity to make a lineup change before the very important Whisky gigs.

Margot was upset. She insisted she was well enough to play the Whisky shows. While explaining that that wasn't our only concern, we auditioned replacements, including Kathy Valentine. Kathy had been playing professionally since her teens in Austin, Texas. At sixteen, she had moved to London, and then three years later she'd come to L.A. and cofounded the Textones. She knew one of our roadies and immediately fit right in.

There was one glitch. Kathy had never played bass. But as soon as we asked her to fill in for Margot, she spent nearly a week learning the new instrument and all of our songs. Onstage, she played as if she had been doing it for years. I looked at her at one point and thought, We have to keep her. Kathy was of the same mind-set, and fully intended to stay.

After the Whisky shows, we met privately and agreed Kathy was a better fit for where we wanted, and *needed*, to go. In January, Ginger was charged with the messy job of firing Margot. She was told that since she was the manager she had to do it. It was a chickenhearted move on our part, but none of us could handle the dirty work.

Margot responded as expected. She protested, cried, begged, and denied any of the problems we raised really existed. Ginger kept responding, "It was the band's decision." And later Ginger told me, "It was really sad and awful." I believed her.

With Kathy on board, we were a unified group. We eliminated the tension and added a talented new songwriter all in the same move. We played through the chill of January, February, and March, performing sold-out shows with the sixties surf band the Ventures in L.A., and then hitting clubs up and down the coast. By spring, we were in agreement about Kathy; she felt like the missing piece. The picture seemed whole.

It was around this time that Pleasant and I worked as secretaries for Marshall Berle, comedian Milton Berle's nephew. He managed rock bands (he was working with Ratt, after being fired by Van Halen) and didn't mind that we were blitzed on acid as we answered his phones. Sometimes Milton's brother Phil came in to flirt with us. It was a fun place to work.

The office was above a witchcraft store on La Cienega Boulevard, which we frequented, as we did a similar shop on Santa Monica Boulevard. I built a small altar in my room at Disgraceland. Even though Pleasant and I had serious boyfriends, we would cast spells on boys we liked. We would put a small amount of our period blood in a vial and surreptitiously drop it into the drink of whichever unsuspecting boys we were crushing on that night. It was something we had read in a book, and every time we did it, I laughed hysterically, thinking, If only they knew.

For our gigs in March, my mom outdid herself making outfits for me to wear onstage. Since I had an eye but couldn't afford anything, I sketched several outfits, bought fabric, and gave it to my mom, who worked magic with her sewing machine. And voila! I had an ultra-cool, totally original balloon dress made from a pink and purple giraffe print. I wore a purple faux-fur coat over it. The point was to look like a million bucks. And Jane was an original, too. She always looked cute.

Our getups turned a lot of heads. One of those heads we turned belonged to Miles Copeland, who was already a fan. In April, following months of back-and-forth between Miles and Ginger, he finally signed us to IRS Records. We were very excited to finally get a deal and have the chance to make an album, but in private we shared disappointment that we weren't getting a million-dollar advance from a big label, which had been our dream and probably would have happened if our band hadn't been all female.

The opinion of Capitol Records honcho Joe Smith echoed loud and clear: female bands didn't work, and the return on investment wasn't worth it. But none of that mattered after we came to an agreement with Miles. At that point, we said a collective Screw it, screw everyone, we'll show the entire industry.

We officially signed on April 1, 1981, and celebrated over dinner and drinks—lots of drinks—at Kelbo's, a kitschy Polynesian restaurant in West Los Angeles. It was like a great first date, one where all of us knew we were going to see one another again and have a long and significant relationship.

After dinner, we went with Miles to the premiere of the movie he was creative consultant for, *Urgh!: A Music War,* and I was impossible. I had done a bunch of coke at the restaurant and taken a quaalude before we left. Buster was out of town and I brought a cute skateboarder for company. We sat right in front of Miles and made out through the entire movie.

At one point during the film, I got up to go to the bathroom and glanced over at my new boss. I felt his steel-blue eyes cut through me like a carving knife. Too wasted to care, I smiled and waved.

He probably wondered what he had invested in. No, on second thought, he knew exactly what he was doing. He was going to make a Go-Go's album and I think he had the same feeling the rest of us did— that it was going to be great.

nine

LET'S HAVE A PARTY

PER MILES'S DECREE, we made arrangements to record our album in New York City. Before I left, Pleasant came up with the crazy idea of switching boyfriends because hers was in New York for work and Buster was in L.A. She reasoned that we could keep an eye on them, and it wouldn't be cheating since we had agreed to it. We didn't plan on telling the boys, and then we would switch back when I returned.

I thought it was weird, but I shrugged and said, Oh well, let's see what happens. It turned out absolutely nothing happened. It required scheming, work, and time, and once I arrived in New York I was way too busy.

We shared suites at the Wellington Hotel on Seventh Avenue. Charlotte and Jane paired up in one room, and Kathy, Gina, and I unpacked in the other. We made an agreement that whoever brought a guest for the evening had to pull their mattress into the foyer. Gina always got a good night's sleep.

I don't remember sleeping much, but it wasn't because I was busy in the bedroom. We were in New York, and it was a twenty-four-hour playground. Kathy and I sat up one night at the kitchen table, talking about the boys we'd seen at clubs, and as we traded notes and stories, we got the idea of forming our own organization: the Booty Club, or as we officially dubbed it, the Booty Club Internationale (note the "e" on the end of *Internationale,* which we thought made it more sophisticated and European).

We were so entertained by the idea of having our own girls' club that we actually made up business cards that night and then went out the next day and had them laminated. Our idea was that if we were flirting with a cute guy, we'd flash the card and say, "Hi, I'm a member of the Booty Club Internationale." I don't think any of us ever used the cards, but we kept them in our wallets. They made us laugh. They still make me laugh.

While sitting at the kitchen table that night we also discovered that we could see directly into an apartment in the building that was across from us, only a few feet away. We looked over at the window all the time, and after a while we saw that an older couple lived there, a man and a woman. But we could only see their torsos. He walked around in his underwear and T-shirt, and she was always in a slip. We were dying to see what they looked like, so one day we threw an orange at their window. They heard the noise, bent down, and we saw their faces. They looked like our grandparents. From then on, though, we threw all sorts of trash at their window, then eventually inside their window, and watched them try to figure out where the stuff had come from. Little did they know it was the naughty girls from across the way.

And we were sort of naughty—at least I was. Before leaving L.A., some of us had started to get into cocaine, though none more than me. I finally had enough money coming in to afford such an occasional indulgence. The funny thing was, I only knew one person who dealt it—a guy in a photo lab on Santa Monica Boulevard. I had to have him FedEx it to me in New York.

One day I got a package with a half gram in it and later that night I went with Kathy to the Mudd Club, where we were having a good time when John Belushi sidled up alongside us. John was one of my favorite comedians, and he was an equally big fan of the Go-Go's. He had seen us play the previous December at the Whisky and partied with us a bit backstage afterward. After Kathy and I traded hellos with him and explained why we were in New York, I asked if he wanted a hit of my coke.

Because of his reaction, I almost felt like I had insulted him. First his eyes widened, then he pulled Kathy and me close so we could hear him better, and then he proceeded to give us a stern lecture on the evils of drug use, fame, and the sycophant-filled world of show business. I was shocked. I felt kind of embarrassed and stupid for having offered him coke.

A week later, the phone in my hotel room rang at one in the morning.

It was John. He said he was in the lobby and asked if he could come up. I said, "Sure, we're up." A moment later, I let him in and then stood back, shocked, as he blew past me like a blast of wind and circled the room. He was wild-eyed and obviously wired. He took a huge vial of coke out of his pocket, dumped it on his hand, and looked at me and Kathy and the other girls with the face of a toxic teddy bear.

"Do you want some?" he asked.

We knew John had serious issues with drugs. If we hadn't known, we certainly saw them laid out in thick, messy lines on our dining room table. We obviously weren't Girl Scouts, but he was in a different league, and it scared us. We declined his offer to get high, and we said no when he invited us out to hit the clubs. None of us felt comfortable being part of that craziness.

After he left, I turned to the girls and said, "Didn't he just lecture us about not doing drugs and avoiding that whole scene?"

It was strange and stranger still in retrospect. John left our place and eventually found a cabdriver who drove him around for a couple of days as he hit clubs and late-night clubs and God knows where else.

If it wasn't the start of his rapid decline, it was part of it. I could tell he was in trouble.

That said, our producers, Rob Freeman and Richard Gottehrer, had their hands full with us. We were either drinking and partying in the studio or hungover from the night before. Kathy and I went to clubs every night and stayed out until all hours. When the clubs closed around two A.M., we rounded up whoever was left and went to the after-hours joints, where we sang, played drinking games, and flirted until we crawled out at around eight in the morning.

I don't even remember when we worked. But we did—and we had fun. We were probably relaxed because we had such a wealth of good material. With what I know now after having recorded so many albums, I realize there's nothing like that first album. You have years to work on that material—to write and hone as many songs as you can create—to get rid of the bad ones, perfect the good ones, and treasure the great ones.

We actually had too many songs. One of my favorites, "Fun with Ropes," didn't end up making the album. We left those important choices mainly up to Rob, who had worked with Blondie, and Richard, who had written the pop classics "My Boyfriend's Back" and "I Want Candy" in the sixties. They had taste and knew what they were doing.

The album, which I had already titled *Beauty and the Beat,* came together pretty easily. I remember everyone having trouble laying down the basic tracks for "We Got the Beat," which we were redoing from the UK version. Everyone's timing was a little off. We took a break, ordered in pizza, and tried it again. We nailed it on the first take. Food always worked with us.

The album's biggest hit, "Our Lips Are Sealed," was a gem that we'd played for a year. Jane had gotten involved with the Specials' lead singer, Terry Hall, when we'd been in London, but he had a girlfriend. After we left, he sent Jane a letter about their complicated situation. She set some of the lines from that letter to music, added some lyrics of her own (she's a genius), and voila, she had "Our Lips Are Sealed." I knew it was a hit as soon as I heard it, and I was right. The song only got better the more we played it.

The entire album was like a time capsule: "Tonight" captured the vibe of being on Hollywood Boulevard; "Lust to Love," which Jane wrote, was immediately one of my favorite Go-Go's songs; "Automatic" was about Jane's boyfriend Dean, who was in the Rockats; "You Can't Walk in Your Sleep," a Charlotte and Jane collaboration, was about Jane's problem with insomnia and occasional tendency to sleepwalk; Kathy brought in the song "Can't Stop the World," which she had originally intended for the Textones, but it was such a natural for us. Finally, "Skidmarks on My Heart," which I cowrote with Charlotte, was about my brother, who was going through a hard time; my cat; and my first car, the one missing the passenger side.

Like the title, I came up with the concept for the album's front and back cover before we ever left L.A. I thought putting us in face masks and wearing only towels was a look that would be timeless. Take away our identities and clothes and we were women who would be just as current in twenty-five years as we were then. And I think I was right. The back cover, showing all of us in a bubble bath, was supposed to be pure girly fun, and it was—except we shot the photo in our hotel room and the Mr. Bubble in the tub gave all of us an infection.

We were back in L.A. and rehearsing for upcoming gigs in one of the large rooms at Studio Instrument Rentals, or SIR, a Hollywood production facility, when the label messengered a copy of the finished album to us. We ran out excitedly to the parking lot and listened to it from start to finish in someone's car. Our hopes were so high and before we pushed the Play button we were all shushing one another. Then the drums kicked into the first cut, "Our Lips Are Sealed," and we quieted down. We let the next ten tracks play without too many comments either way, and finally, after about thirty-five minutes, we just looked at one another for reactions.

We weren't happy—or as happy as we had hoped. In the studio, we had thought we were making a great punk album. On hearing the final version, it sounded more pop than we had anticipated.

We weren't going for anything as hard as Margot had wanted, but we'd had more of an edge in mind. Everyone had little criticisms. In my case, I was horrified by my vocals. They had been sped up and I found it painful to hear myself race through those songs.

Don't get me wrong. We recognized the album's charm. But we still wanted it remixed.

We took our case to Miles, who said no. As he explained, he got exactly the record he had wanted from us. He loved it. Then, of course, as a wider audience responded positively to the album, all of us began to change our opinion and think, Oh, it's not *that* bad. Later on, we upgraded it again. On June 12, "Our Lips Are Sealed" was released as the first single. We promoted it with an in-store appearance at the Licorice Pizza record store on Sunset Boulevard, and thanks to nonstop promotion from Rodney, plus advertising, the store was already mobbed when we pulled up in a limo. We stayed all afternoon, signing autographs for every single person.

I was in Buster's car the first time I heard the new single on the radio. We were on Sunset, and he turned up the volume. As much as I didn't like my vocals, I couldn't stop grinning, moving, or singing along with the radio. I was on the radio: I felt like a rock star.

We celebrated the single with a sold-out show at the Roxy, and then a month later, at the end of July, we played one show in Palo Alto and immediately followed that with a much bigger bash at home. "*Cute.* That's what I thought two years ago when I first saw the Go-Go's," wrote critic Robert Hilburn in the *Los Angeles Times*. "*Great.* That's what I thought after seeing the Go-Go's concert Friday night at the sold-out Hollywood Palladium. The quintet not only has more spirit than ever, but its musicianship is also vastly improved..."

For me, though, that show was as much a good-bye as it was a triumph in front of the hometown fans. I had moved with Ann McLean into the Trianon Apartments from Disgraceland, where, sadly, I felt a little too exposed and unprotected. I didn't know how to deal with losing my anonymity. I just knew it made me uncomfortable. But I had no time to think about that or anything else.

In August, we hit the road for a month of shows back east. We rented a big white van and piled in, all of us: band members, roadies, and equipment. We turned the van into a pit on wheels; I mean, we defaced it in every possible way, letting trash and stink pile up and writing on the walls as we drove from Boston to Philadelphia and into Canada, opening on an all-IRS lineup featuring us and Oingo Boingo and topped by the Police, who provided our first up-close exposure to real rock stars, with their big entourages, bodyguards, fancy coaches, and private jet.

Sting was nice but aloof and seemed to be reading a Sartre book whenever he had free time. Gina palled around with Stewart, and Charlotte had a brief fling with Andy Summers. All of us attended Miles's wedding in New York and jammed at the beautiful reception he had at Tavern on the Green in Central Park. We also played a show at the Ritz, where I spotted the Who's Pete Townshend and other rock royalty checking us out. Even though I was not starstruck, I regretted not having been able to hang out with them.

In September, as reviews and mentions of us appeared in *People* and *Rolling Stone* magazines, we returned to L.A. and watched with a mix of curiosity and amazement as our video for "Our Lips Are Sealed" hit

MTV, the brand-new music TV network that had launched only the month before. I was clueless about the impact it would have on music, fashion, and pop culture.

Just to show where my head was at, I thought making a music video was a stupid idea. I had grumbled about it being a waste of time and asked why I had to do it. It just seemed ridiculous, and so I gave it a half-assed effort. I couldn't even be bothered to get out of the car when, after tooling around in the convertible, we pulled up in front of Trashy Lingerie and Jane did her solo, singing, "Hush, my darling." If you look close, you can see me hiding; I'm bent down but the top of my head shows.

We also tried to amuse ourselves by getting arrested. That's how we ended up frolicking in the water fountain at the intersection of Wilshire and Santa Monica boulevards. We thought if we jumped in, a cop would see us, stop, and there'd be a confrontation, which we would capture on tape. But nobody came to arrest us. Cars just slowed and some guys honked and whistled at us.

When I think back on those early days of MTV, all I remember seeing is a lot of the Split Enz hit "I Got You." I noticed them because of a funny thing that happened a year earlier when I was living at Disgraceland. It was the night we were having one of the more infamous parties in that place's history, an event we had dubbed the Forbidden Foods Party. It was girls only—no boys allowed. About thirty of us got together, and the two requirements for admission were that you had to wear a negligee and bring the most fattening food you could find.

We were in the middle of this party, drinking from a giant bowl of alcoholic punch, dancing around, eating, and acting crazy, when there was a knock at the door. We opened it and Neil Finn and some of the guys from Split Enz were standing there. They said they had just come to town and heard there was a party, so they showed up. It made perfect sense to me. What do you do when you get to town? You find out where the party is and go. So I told them to come on in and enjoy themselves.

How could they not? There were thirty girls prancing around half-naked, eating pizza, French fries, cannolis, and cream puffs. They didn't know what hit them. To this day, whenever I see Neil, he says, "Do you remember that party?" And there's always a twinkle in his eye.

In October, we flew to Rockford, Illinois, to open for the Rolling Stones, which was incredible just to say out loud. It was also weird, thrilling, and probably the most nerve-wracking gig I had played to that point—not because of the size of the crowd as much as knowing Mick Jagger, Keith Richards, and the rest of the legendary band were watching us. Only a few years earlier I was in high school and listening to their albums.

Unfortunately, I didn't have any interaction with them other than see-ing Mick stretching before the show. But that's how those shows could be; you could have several bands backstage and they never saw one another because of their different preperformance rituals.

Then we flew back to L.A. and performed several concerts up and down the coast before finishing up with three star-studded nights at the Greek Theatre. Talk about a great venue. The theater was outdoors and nestled in the hills of Griffith Park, and the number of stars in the sky seemed to match the number of stars in the audience. One night I looked out and saw Steve Martin in the front row. The next I saw Al Pacino. Midway through that second show I also spotted Rod Stewart and between songs I turned to Jane, made sure she saw the celebrities, and said, "This is really freaking me out."

As cool as I tried to look in the spotlight, I couldn't get over the fact that these people, these stars, were coming out to see anything I was part of. I couldn't reconcile the larger picture that people were interested in me. But they were; interview requests streamed in. I put on a funny face for *People* magazine, which photographed me goof-ing around with Buster for a profile on the band in October. The next month, I mused more seriously to the *Boston Globe,* saying that while success hadn't changed me, I was "afraid of [others'] perspectives of me changing. I can't exactly go out of my head and go dance and have a great time because I'm constantly being judged."

True, but it didn't really inhibit my behavior. In November, we guested on *Saturday Night Live,* along with Bernadette Peters and Billy Joel. The appearance was a significant moment for us. *Beauty and the Beat* was number 20 on the Billboard 200 chart and climbing; the exposure on a show that defined hot to America's youth was going to keep that momentum going. And in terms of pop culture, playing on *SNL* was huge; in fact, it blew my mind to think that we were big enough to be on the show.

But Kathy, Charlotte, and I got ripped. We had sat around the studio all day, drinking the free booze, and when it was finally time to go on, we gave one of our worst performances ever. We played "We Got the Beat," and we destroyed it. It didn't even sound like a song. I knew it was bad, but excused myself from embarrassment by telling myself, Hey, we're rock stars. We're supposed to party. Wasn't that the way it was done?

As far as I was concerned, it was. A couple of drinks and sometimes a hit of coke was the way I got ready. What was the big deal? A dancer stretched, a rock star partied. That's the way I rationalized my behavior. More than twenty years passed before I faced the fact that I never went onstage sober not because I was a rock star but because deep down I was scared shitless—scared that I wasn't any good and the audience would see me as the fake I feared I might be.

The rock-and-roll lifestyle was lenient. By the time we returned from a brief end-of-November swing through the East Coast and played a small show at Palos Verdes High (which was videotaped and released as *Totally Go-Go's*), I was doing coke regularly and not thinking twice about it.

Well, that's not exactly true. I thought a lot about it—how much I loved it. From the first time I did coke at the Canterbury, when a friend of Margot's gave me a little bit to try, I couldn't wait to do more. It sent me into happyland, far away from whatever else was on my mind. It always made me feel better no matter what else was bothering me.

I relied on it to keep me up and going despite our demanding schedule. In January, we hit Sweden and London, where we stayed at Miles's stately manor in St. John's Wood. It was a formal home, and Miles made us swear to following one unbreakable rule—no boys. His booming voice had barely ceased echoing through the estate before Kathy and I went out and brought two guys back to our rooms in the basement.

We didn't do anything with them. We just wanted to disobey Miles. It was like a sport.

We also brought Lords of the New Church lead singer, Stiv Bators, back to Miles's place after we played a few dates with his band. Years later, we found out Stiv had gone from bedroom to bedroom, smelling our underwear in a self-styled game of Guess-which-Go-Go stays in this room.

I can't say we were much better. In January 1982, we were in Atlanta and I was at dinner with one of our roadies at the local Holiday Inn, listening to him tell me in *Penthouse Forum*–type detail about his and our other roadies' adventures from the previous night. They had gone to a couple bars and each of them had brought women back to the hotel and, according to him, engaged in various sexual activities that sounded too wild to believe.

When I refused to believe what they said happened, the roadie with whom I was having dinner called another crew guy over to the table and had the tale corroborated.

I wasn't a prude, but whoa, I was shocked by what he said they had done. I wanted to know how these guys were able to convince women to do such things. What I really wanted to know was who these young women were; they met strangers in a bar and a few hours later were in a hotel room doing things that porn stars might have found hard-core.

"What's going on out there?" I asked. "What's the secret?"

"Alcohol," our roadie said with a shrug.

My curiosity turned into quite a topic of conversation. Later that night, long after our show, I was back in my hotel room when I got a call that the most freakish of the roadies was extremely wasted in his room and with the same girl from the night before, and did I want to join most everybody else on the tour in watching them go at it. Of course I did, and I hurried over there and joined the crowd. Someone videotaped it, too.

Wasted, he had no idea he was being watched or taped, and she didn't care. That tape was pirated and passed around among bands for years as an example of extreme rock-and-roll debauchery. For a long time, we thought it was funny. In retrospect, I came to regret it existed and didn't want it to be part of the Go-Go's legend.

In February, we were back on tour with the Police, which was always lovely because of the luxurious way in which they traveled and their generosity to us. They saw us as little sisters. They were at the top of rock's mountain and we were their younger labelmates on the way up. Sting brought a bottle of champagne into our dressing room one night to celebrate our success. It was nice. Those gestures went a long way and helped us forget that we drove from city to city in our white van while they traveled in a private jet.

After a show in Denver, though, they offered us a ride back to L.A. on their jet. The temperature was near zero so we were grateful not to have to make the twenty-four-hour drive back to L.A. Instead we'd get home in a couple hours. As I watched the ground crew deice the wings, I thought about how nice it was going to be to get back home. Then we taxied out on the runway and suddenly one of the engines burst into flames. There was a loud pop, and then I heard someone yell, "Fire!"

To me, it was like a starter's gun when I used to run track. I jumped up, grabbed my thrift-store fur coat and trampled Miles, Andy, and even Sting on my way to the door.

They made fun of me for months. But, as I told the guys, the lesson was clear. You don't want to be near me if I'm in a panic because I'm going to run over you. I don't care if you are the world's biggest rock stars.

We were doing pretty well ourselves. Success was amazing. I loved my bandmates like sisters. We didn't have any of the jealousies or bullshit that came later. The grueling schedule created unusual demands and stresses, but the times were filled with excitement.

The hardest part of our success in those days, at least for me, was going back home. I always wanted to get off the road and sleep in my own bed, but whenever I got there I found myself feeling sad, lonely, and isolated. I didn't fit easily back into our scene. My old haunts and old friends weren't that accepting; no one wanted to have anything to do with me. I didn't feel like I had changed, but everyone else did.

In a sense, they were right. Like the other girls, I was seeing the world, meeting new people, and having incredible experiences that were hard to relate to unless you were there and involved. So yeah, I guess I had changed. My mistake was thinking I could go back home and find things were the same as I had left them. That's not the way it worked.

EVERYTHING BUT PARTY TIME

IN 1982, the Go-Go's were nominated for a Grammy as Best New Artist. At the February event, we were up against Adam and the Ants, James Ingram, Luther Vandross, and Sheena Easton. We were thrilled, and I'm pretty sure we wanted to win, though I remember being more concerned about what I was going to wear to the awards show, which I thought of as the world's glitziest prom.

And as with my high school prom, my mom made my dress, a fabulous, princess-style gown with big gold-lamé puffed sleeves, a matching skirt, and a hot-pink bodice. I looked like Cinderella at the ball.

But unlike Cinderella, I started doing coke in the morning and I was out of my head by the time Buster and I stepped out of our limo and hit the red carpet, which was lined with television crews, reporters, and photographers. Maurice Gibb of the Bee Gees, who was doing interviews for *Good Morning America,* actually took me aside before talking to me and told me to wipe my nose. That was embarrassing.

Inside, I spotted *Dallas* actress Charlene Tilton, who was there with her country-singer husband, Johnny Lee. I introduced myself and said that I used to get her mail when I lived at Disgraceland, though I told her the actual address of the building rather than using its nickname. She said she'd never lived there and her husband quickly pulled her away.

"Wow, that was rude," I said to Buster. "I don't care what she says. I still got her mail."

I was checking out other stars when Moon Unit Zappa, who was famous for contributing to her father's satiric hit "Valley Girl," came up to me and introduced herself. I told her that I was a real-life Valley girl, and we laughed.

"I love your dress," she said.

"My mom made it," I said.

Moon stepped back so I could see her dress. "My mom made mine too."

As for the awards, Kim Carnes won Record of the Year for "Bette Davis Eyes," and John Lennon's album *Double Fantasy* was honored as Album of the Year, which provided the night's most emotional moment when Yoko Ono came out to accept with her six-year-old son, Sean, and delivered a poignant speech on behalf of her slain husband, saying they both were proud to have made good music that contributed in a positive way to the planet.

Quincy Jones won five awards that night. Al Jarreau took home three. And the Go-Go's? None. We lost to Sheena Easton as Best New Artist, which didn't bum us out as much as it caused us to lose interest in the rest of the show, and so at the next commercial break we got up and left, which, as we later learned from the network, was a no-no.

But we didn't know any better, and we were eager to join our boyfriends who had been hanging out backstage with Jerry Lee Lewis and other stars, having a grand time. We joined them and then hit the official Grammy ball at the Biltmore Hotel, where we sat at a table for a few hours, drank, and gawked at Ted Nugent, Joe Cocker, Tina Turner, Rick James, and other stars.

I packed the next day for a trip to Japan, where the Go-Go's were booked for a TV ad for Daihatsu. I had never been to Tokyo, and it was wild. Between the time change and the neon lights I saw from my hotel window, I felt like my senses were overloaded. The city looked like a giant club, and over the next couple of days, we treated the work that brought us there as secondary to exploring Tokyo.

Before leaving L.A., I had returned a piece of furniture that I'd borrowed from a friend and met his neighbor, Jack, a great-looking guy who modeled in Japan. My friend had warned me not to get any ideas; Jack was gay. It turned out he was going to be in Tokyo at the same time I was, and after I got my bearings I looked him up.

Jack knew the city, especially the nighttime scene, and he escorted me to several of the edgiest clubs. At one club, he introduced me to Isao, a makeup artist, who immediately led me onto the dance floor and stayed near me the rest of the trip. Isao had an exotic style, look, and energy unlike that of anyone I had ever met. I couldn't figure out if he was straight or gay, but I was drawn to him without really knowing why, and as he put the moves on me, I let myself be seduced.

I didn't know if I was attracted to him, merely curious, or getting myself in trouble. I had partied so hard over the past few months and crossed so many time zones that I didn't have clear judgment when it came to people or my boundaries. He was like a new drug, a new escape.

Indeed, I couldn't stop thinking about him when I got back home, and as soon as the Go-Go's took a much-needed break in March and April to work on our next album, I told Buster that I was going back to Japan to hang out with my new friends, Jack and Isao. We had planned for the break to be our time together, so he got pissed off when I left and probably knew that our days as a couple were numbered.

I didn't care—and didn't want to talk about it.

It wasn't one of my finer moments.

During breaks in the Go-Go's writing and recording sessions, I made several trips to Japan. I traveled back and forth as if the long flight was a short commute. It wasn't, and those trips cost a fortune. They were one of many examples that showed I wasn't exercising good judgment. Isao was another example. In Tokyo, I actually spent most of my time with Jack, drinking greyhounds and shopping in Harajuku, but once it was nighttime and the neon lights were flashing throughout Tokyo, I found myself hitting the clubs with Isao.

My strange friend led me from one club to another. I got the sense he was quite a playboy. Everyone knew him. I followed him around as if I would be lost without him, which was true. When we went out, I had no idea where I was. I was lost, figuratively and literally. That scared me.

Our affair lasted for a while, but it was dependent on me going to

Japan. It never matched the intensity of those initial months, and then, as could have been predicted, it devolved into one drama after another as I gradually and painfully found out Isao had numerous model girlfriends from the West that he didn't tell me about.

I probably got what I deserved, considering I was doing sort of the same thing to Buster. Even though he was the easiest-going person I knew, we were on different schedules, both of us consumed by the often-conflicting demands of our bands. It took serious commitment to make that kind of relationship work, and while Buster may have been ready, and in fact wanted to get engaged, I wasn't capable of such deep responsibility to another person, let alone myself.

At the beginning of March, I was at SIR with the girls and taking a break from rehearsal when I got a phone call from John Belushi's wife, Judy, asking if I had seen John. She knew our social circles sometimes crossed at night. She said he was in L.A. and had gone AWOL on her, and she was concerned. I hadn't seen him, and none of the other girls had either.

Less than a week later, on March 5, John was wheeled out of the Chateau Marmont hotel on a coroner's gurney. He had died of an overdose of heroin and cocaine at thirty-three years old.

The following day, we were back at SIR and talking about John's death and comparing notes about what we had either heard on the news or from other people, when Ginger walked in with a bottle of champagne. Our album, *Beauty and the Beat,* had hit number one on the *Billboard* album chart. We popped the cork and screamed. It was the first time in rock-and-roll history that an all-girl group who had written and played their own songs had an album that went all the way to the top.

We toasted one another and talked about the past few years and everything that we'd gone through since day one. After partying all afternoon, I went back to my apartment and continued to celebrate by myself until the good times unraveled in a frightening breakdown.

Seated at my dining room table, bent over several lines of coke and puffing on cigarettes, I had no idea I was about to come unhinged. In theory, I was rewarding myself in private for being part of the Go-Go's history-making accomplishment. My face was all over the press, and there were few girls in the world who wouldn't have wanted to trade places with me, and yet at that moment I would've been the first to ask them why.

After doing a couple more lines, I looked at a stack of magazines and newspapers on the table. All of them had stories about the Go-Go's. I sifted through a couple and thought how awful it would be if people only knew the truth about me, the truth as far as I was concerned—namely, that I was a fake and didn't feel like I deserved any of my success. I had no sense of self-worth, and worse, I felt like I was on the verge of being found out.

The combination of being high, fearful, and anxious triggered something in me, and suddenly I felt a surge of panic and then it was as if the floor gave out beneath me. I had a full-on panic attack.

For a while, I thought I might die. Gradually the extreme anxiety subsided, but I was still gripped by a powerful fear that I had walked into a trap, that my newfound notoriety as evidenced in all those magazines and papers was going to backfire on me in a big way. I stayed inside and went out only if I had to. I shuddered anytime someone honked or recognized me. I had the same feeling I got as a kid when I wanted to run away from home. But now, where was I going to go? I couldn't run away from myself.

Or could I?

I pulled the curtains in my apartment and binged on coke for days. I didn't go outside and refused to answer the phone.

Unbeknownst to me, the town was swept up by rumors that I had died. I don't know who started them. If I had been aware, I would have stopped them. Immediately. Ginger eventually got in touch with me, though, and mentioned that all of the girls had been trying to get ahold of me. Without filling me in, she sent word to the record company that I was okay, and soon IRS released an oblique statement to the press that the Go-Go's were alive and well and working on the band's second album.

I didn't need to comment further once I heard what was being said. But many years later I looked back at that moment in time through more sober eyes and saw some truth in the rumor.

With the success of *Beauty and the Beat,* the Go-Go's turned into more of a serious business than it had initially begun. We lost our anonymity and privacy. We also began to lose the relationships we had with one another. At photo sessions, I heard one of the girls behind me say, "Does she always have to be in the middle? Can't someone else stand in front?" I saw eyes roll if reporters asked me too many questions.

On top of the jealousies, there was serious pressure. As we worked on our second album, we knew Miles wanted another megasmash. While that was understandable, and our hopes for a follow-up also matched his, the reality was such that we'd had more than two years to come up with material for *Beauty and the Beat* and now we were being given only a couple of months to write songs for the next album.

It was a tall order even for writers as talented and prolific as Jane, Charlotte, and Kathy, especially when the vibe among us was much different from how it had been in the beginning.

With Richard Gottehrer producing again, we proceeded as if we were repeating the same formula we had followed with the first album. We alternated between different recording studios: Sunset Sound, Studio 55, and Indigo Ranch, which was a beautiful rustic outpost located on the old John Barrymore estate at the top of Malibu's Carbon Canyon.

Richard set us up there, hoping the isolation would let us work without the distractions of the city. It didn't happen. We went into town at all hours of the day and night, depending on what was going on in town. Despite the distractions, we delivered new material that I thought captured the Go-Go's brand of pop punk, including "He's So Strange," which was left over from the first album, and "Girl of 100 Lists," which I thought was Jane being typically clever even though some of the other girls thought it was wimpy.

I worked with Charlotte on "I Think It's Me," a song about a crush I once had on the Flyboys' singer John Curry. Charlotte and Jane wrote "Get Up and Go," which ended up having a hideous video with me wearing an off-the-shoulder sweatshirt and headband, a look that predated

Flashdance—yuck. "The Way You Dance" was about a cute guy we had met on tour in Philadelphia; I wrote the lyrics to "Beatnik Beach," about *The Lloyd Thaxton Show*, a dance/music TV show from the sixties; and "It's Everything but Partytime," a Jane and Gina collaboration, revealed the pressure we were starting to feel.

We weren't against exposing a good amount of ourselves, as evidenced by the *Rolling Stone* cover of the five us of wearing white underwear. We looked like five virginal high school girls dancing together at a slumber party. Yet the reader knew better, and if they didn't, they were set straight by the headline, "Go-Go's Put Out."

I laughed at the cover and loved it when the magazine came out. A quarter of a century later, it's still a strong image that captures the spirit and irony of the times, and it's all due to the inspired eye of legendary photographer Annie Leibovitz.

We were excited to be photographed by her, but didn't discuss what she had in mind beforehand. We had put the finishing touches on *Vacation* in May, and then spent the next month rehearsing for a new tour and doing gobs of press; we had the energy of a boulder rolling downhill when we encountered Annie, who was her own force of nature.

We walked into the studio, expecting to find a stylist with various wardrobe choices for each of us. But we didn't see any clothing racks packed with the latest designer outfits. Nor did we see a stylist waiting to help us. It was just Annie and her crew.

"I have an idea," Annie said. "And I want you to hear me out before you say anything."

As she explained the concept, I glanced at the other girls, all of whom were busy shooting one another looks, and I thought of Annie's stature and who else she had worked with, and all the famous *Rolling Stone* covers she had done, including her famous last shoot with John Lennon and Yoko Ono—the one with a naked John curled up against Yoko in bed. That one in particular gave me the chills since John was shot and killed right after that session.

More than an artist, Annie was part of rock history, an iconographer as much as she was a photographer, and I knew what it meant to be photographed by her. However, I still didn't want to get undressed for her. I didn't want to pose in my underwear. I didn't explain why, but if I had, I would've said that I could still hear the boys on the playground calling me Belimpa and fatso. So no thanks.

The other girls also balked. Annie's who she is, in part, because she doesn't take no for an answer, and she chipped away at our resistance. Tall, smart, cool, and confident, she patiently stood her ground and said, "No, no, no, I think it's going to be really great."

Eventually we changed our minds. As Annie understood, we had to go through a process of trusting her. And once we got in the underwear and saw the first Polaroid test shots, we understood what she was going for and we enjoyed ourselves. The result—well, it spoke for itself.

After the photo session, Buster picked me up and we went to Fat-burger. I wolfed down a chili burger with fries.

Unlike *Beauty and the Beat,* I liked *Vacation* when I first heard a mastered version of the entire album. I thought it was a good, strong, fun effort with one caveat: I hated the way my voice sounded. I could hear where I had difficulty singing and felt guilty that I had spent too much time partying and hadn't given it my all. But there was no time for regret or redos.

In May, we jetted to Italy for a one-off show at a club in Milan. It was a long way to go for one show, but the performance was incidental to the sights I saw, starting with the club's promoter, who had the tightest black leather pants I had ever seen on a human being, male or female. As I discreetly pointed out to the girls throughout the show, you could see *everything.* Far more exciting, at least for me, were the stores. I spent all my money on clothes and bags and enjoyed every morsel of food I ate except for one meal where my host smiled after I tasted a platter of different-tasting meat.

"What is it?" I asked.

"Camel," he said.

"What?"

"Camel."

I fared much better a few weeks later when we played five shows in

Japan, where I caught up with my friend Jack and barely slept over six days. From there, we went to Australia, where I fell down the stairs as I came offstage and broke my foot. I actually heard the bone break. We canceled our final show and flew directly to Honolulu, where I recuperated before our shows there by doing coke in my penthouse suite and waited for Buster to arrive.

Buster was disappointed when he saw the condition I was in. From the outside, I looked great. I was tan from Australia and a few days in Hawaii. On the inside, though, I was a mess. It made connecting with Buster on any meaningful level almost impossible. Then again, I didn't want to connect with anyone, including myself.

I had been running away from my life since I snuck out of my window as a teenager and then moved to Hollywood. Being in a rock band was perfect for someone like me. Stardom made it even easier. I lived in airports and hotels, where bills were paid and beds were made for me. I wasn't easily reachable. Except for sound checks and shows, I didn't have to be responsible to anyone other than myself. Drugs and booze were plentiful, easily accessible, and considered part of the job. It was a very indulgent and dangerous way to live.

In August, we began a trek up the West Coast. Our album, four weeks after its release, had achieved gold-record status, meaning it had sold more than 500,000 copies, and moved into the top 10, along with its first single, "Vacation." We weren't setting the world on fire, but we were happening in a big way. We were working hard and living in our own little Go-Go's bubble. There was the real world, and then there was our world in which strange and exciting things happened.

One night I received an unexpected call in my hotel room from a young man who said his name, Mike Marshall, and then paused in a way where I could tell he expected me to recognize who he was. I didn't.

"I play for the Los Angeles Dodgers," he said.

I still didn't recognize his name, but I knew the Dodgers. As a girl who was never able to get the football player in high school, I realized I had something even better on the line: a professional ballplayer. Not just any old ballplayer either. He was an L.A. Dodger. In a deep voice, he explained that a mutual acquaintance in show business had given him my number. He paid me a number of compliments, said he was a fan of the band's music, and explained that he had a feeling we would get along if we met.

I don't know if it was boredom or intrigue, or a combination of both, but I was interested. When I asked him to tell me about being a Dodger, he explained he was considered a good player, and that he'd actually won the minor league Triple Crown the year before and was now in the major leagues, which was pretty exciting.

"So are you good?" I asked teasingly.

"I hit a home run my first time up to bat at Dodger Stadium," he said.

"Yeah, but are you good?"

This first call turned into a nightly occurrence that I looked forward to. I liked the back-and-forth volley with this strange man. Without him knowing, I tooted up during the call and spewed what I described as my coke rap. It's what I did when I was in my hotel room and bored, with nothing to do after shows except drugs.

Our conversations quickly moved past playful flirtations and turned into more intimate explorations. It was like a game of Truth or Dare—a drug in and of itself.

I had no idea what Mike looked like or that his teammates had nick-named him Moose for his thick, lumbering physique. He was a Dodger; that was intriguing enough. Although he knew what I looked like, I probably held the same allure for him: I was a rock star. It was like being in high school again.

I looked forward to his calls as we traveled from Berkeley to Denver, Calgary, and Edmonton. By the time we hit Vancouver and Seattle, Mike and I wanted to meet, and the fact that we hadn't but were talking more and more intimately heightened the anticipation. We finally arranged to rendezvous before our show in Santa Cruz. When I saw him for the first time, I didn't think he was handsome or cute. I don't know what image I had in mind, but he reminded me of Lurch, the butler on the old TV series *The Addams Family*.

However, as I repeatedly told my friends later on, almost as if I needed to convince myself, he was a Dodger. And, as I would tell my therapist much later on, I was on drugs and making poor choices.

After weeks of anticipation, we had a hot and heavy time in Santa Cruz. After two solid days together, Mike asked me to move in with him. Just one problem there—neither of us had our own place. There was also an even bigger problem—I already had a boyfriend.

Buster had been checking in with me regularly, asking about the tour and waiting for me to return home. The Go-Go's had a big show coming up at the Hollywood Bowl and his group, the Blasters, was the opening act. We had been looking forward to it being a grand, triumphant night. As Southern California kids, we knew the significance of playing the Hollywood Bowl.

Now the thought of it made me queasy. I dreaded what I was about to do to him.

Buster was as nice as any human being I'd ever met. Probably the nicest. I'd never heard him utter an unkind word about anyone, including me, a feat that should have earned him the boyfriend's equivalent of a Nobel Prize, considering the way I sometimes treated him. He had lost his temper with me only once in the two-plus years we had been together. He had come to Disgraceland one night to pick me up. But he arrived too early, and unfortunately I had another boy in my room. In a scene straight out of a bad movie, I pushed the other guy out the window and was then a complete bitch to Buster as he tried to figure out why I was behaving so strangely.

This time I wasn't as secretive. I called Buster from a pay phone in Santa Barbara and broke up with him. Without telling him about Mike, I said, "I don't want to be with you anymore."

Buster was totally blindsided. I couldn't have been colder or more callous. It was one of the shittiest breakups on record. I still hate myself for the way I treated him. Years later, after I got sober, I made amends to him in a letter. But at the time it went down, it was a mess—the kind only a drug addict can make.

I wouldn't have called myself an addict then.

Now I know better.

Two nights after the breakup, we played the Hollywood Bowl. I stayed clear of Buster. I couldn't face him because I was ashamed of the way I had broken up with him. I had even told him to keep my white Cadillac. Everyone in the punk scene seemed to be at the Bowl, and most of them were backstage. They knew what had gone down between Buster and me, and more embarrassingly, *how* it had gone down.

I felt their hatred. No one spoke to me, and I didn't want to look anyone in the eye. I wanted to get onstage, where I could look at Mike, who was using tickets I had given him. He sat front and center. It was like rubbing salt into a wound. But I didn't care.

The trouble was, I didn't care about much of anything.

SPEEDING

MIKE AND I went looking for apartments together. He found a place in Marina del Rey. My taste ran more to Hollywood, but then again I still had a lot of tour ahead of me.

It was September 1982, and the Go-Go's played a show almost every night across the Midwest and South. We had upgraded to a more comfortable tour bus from our cramped white van. If there was still anything glamorous or romantic about traveling to a new city every day, I didn't see it. The travel and the sameness of each day was a grind that made me feel suspended in a netherworld where many times I found myself saying, "Be careful what you wish for."

The five of us spent way too much time with one another, waking up and seeing one another through blurry, sleep-crusted eyes, falling into bed as we rolled across dark highways, gossiping, eavesdropping on conversations, compromising on which movies or TV shows we watched, getting wasted, and nitpicking at one another like girlfriends whose inside jokes had gone stale.

Mike came out for some dates and brought along his hard-partying teammate Bob Welch, who was a great guy, though not without his own troubles. He and Charlotte took a liking to each other.

In the middle of the month, somewhere between the Carolinas and Georgia, I suffered my worst panic attack since I had broken down in my apartment after the Go-Go's first album went number one. I walked into my hotel room after a long trip on the bus and too much coke the night before. I went into the bathroom, turned on the light—a harsh, unforgiving light—and glanced at myself in the mirror. It wasn't a pretty sight.

I saw the truth: a twenty-four-year-old girl who was doing too many drugs, who didn't have any center of gravity, who felt massive regret, sorrow, and pain, and I knew deep down that I wasn't compatible with Mike.

I had everything I'd ever wanted, and it wasn't right.

Ugh.

It was too much truth all at once. I started to cry.

"What am I going to do?" I said to myself. "What am I going to do?"

I repeated the question over and over until I felt like I was drowning—and that's when the anxiety hit, only I had no idea what it was or what was happening to me. I broke out in a chilly sweat and felt like I was hyperventilating. I feared I might be having a heart attack. By showtime, it had passed and I was able to push beyond the panic-stricken hours I had spent in my hotel room, wondering if I was going to overdose.

I think I figured out the catalyst for the attack. A few days earlier, I had received word through our record company's office that a man claiming to be my father wanted to meet me at our show in Baton Rouge. Apparently he had told local press there that he was my father, explaining he had been shown a photo of me as a little girl in the *Vacation* tour program and it matched a photo he kept in his wallet.

Ginger and the others were aware I hadn't seen my father since I was five or six years old. I think there was mention of that in the newspaper story, too. Anyway, they looked at me to see whether this man was real or a nutcase. Before I heard if his name was, in fact, Harold Carlisle, I already knew it was my dad. When I was fourteen years old, I had picked up the phone at home in Thousand Oaks and heard a strange man's voice ask if Joanie was home. No one called my mom Joanie. I instantly knew it was my father. Ten years later, I had the exact same feeling.

Reluctantly, I agreed to meet him after the show. Then I had to work through the anger I began to feel toward him for handling a matter as private as our reunion in such a public forum. I didn't like the way he had made a big stink out of it in the paper. On the bus, as we arrived in Baton Rouge, I kept saying, "It just isn't cool."

I was angry with him for more than talking to the press. I harbored long-standing feelings of resentment and hurt toward him for disappearing without any explanation when I was little, never sending child support to my mom or making contact on birthdays and holidays to see if I was alive. I also chafed at the nerve he had coming back into my life now that I was famous.

How could I trust any of his motives?

I ran through various scenarios of what seeing him would be like. Each one gave me the creeps. I wished I hadn't said yes.

My stomach was in a knot through the show, especially toward the end when I began to think about confronting my father. He had brought his new family, a wife and two daughters. Afterward, as they were ushered backstage, I locked myself in our dressing room and snorted coke till I rendered myself emotionally numb and stupid enough to face him, not that I was any good at expressing my emotions anyway.

At our reunion, I was friendly to everyone, probably too friendly and trying too hard in order to compensate for being loaded. My father took me aside and tried to deliver what he must have thought was a heartfelt explanation of why he left—basically his side of the story. As soon as he began to blame my mother, I tuned him out. I pled exhaustion and ended the evening.

However, they wanted to see me again before we left and so all of us met the next morning for breakfast and hung out for a spell afterward. This time, I was hungover instead of high, but still pleasant. As we parted, my father's daughters, the ones with whom he replaced me, said they loved me.

"I love you!" they called.

Waving good-bye as they got in their car and drove away, I thought, How can these people love me? They don't even know me.

At the end of October, after playing sold-out venues every night from Houston to St. Louis to New York's Madison Square Garden, we took our brand of new wave merriment to Amsterdam. I couldn't wait. Even if we were still working, I was ready for an escape that would let me feel far away from home.

I arrived with the intention of having a great time. But I was run-down and needed to rejuvenate. So, soon after checking into our hotel, the Sonesta, I corralled Charlotte into going to the health club with me. I thought a soak in the hot tubs and a massage would do the trick.

At the time, the Sonesta was a luxurious hotel—and very European, especially the spa. At the desk, the attendant informed us of the club's policy: We had to take off all our clothes. Though this is common in Europe, we were still surprised. Charlotte and I looked at each other and said what the hell. Then we stripped off our clothes and ran out to find a hot tub to ourselves, hoping the other women we saw wouldn't stare.

We didn't even consider the spa might be co-ed—that is, until a French man in his fifties sauntered up to our hot tub. He arrived just as we were starting to relax and gazed down discerningly at us. (We also looked up discerningly.) After a moment, he joined us.

"So where are you girls from?" he said in heavily accented English.

"America," we said.

"I'm going to guess how old you are," he said. "Twenty-five or twenty-six?"

Charlotte nodded.

"How'd you know?" I asked.

"I can tell by your bodies," he said.

I didn't know whether he was creepy or not. Either way, I didn't want to get out of the water. Neither did Charlotte. It was safe to chat while keeping a careful eye on the bubbles to make sure as much as possible stayed covered up. It became an endurance contest: Which of us could tolerate the hot water the longest, the two of us or our new friend, whom we nicknamed Jeff Jetsetter.

As we began to shrivel up like vegetables in a pot of simmering soup, Jeff invited us up to his room that night.

"I have a big penthouse," he said.

Charlotte and I traded looks that spoke volumes. We were at a loss for how to politely say thanks, but no thanks. Sensing our wariness, he quickly added, "I also have champagne and cocaine."

"Cocaine?" I said.

He nodded.

"How much do you have?" I asked.

He smiled. "A lot."

"Okay, we'll come up," I said.

With a satisfied nod, he stepped out of the hot tub and said he'd see us later. When the coast was clear, Charlotte said that was weird. I shrugged. Weird was relative. We were in Amsterdam.

Later that night, the five of us went up to Jeff Jetsetter's penthouse. It was magnificent. As promised, he had a ton of blow. He was extremely generous, too, but before long I saw what Jeff had in mind. He put it right out there. He wanted to have sex with us. I was equally blunt, as were the others. It wasn't going to happen.

Buoyed by drugs, booze, and his intense desire to get laid, he refused to give up. He tried charm, jokes, gestures, and direct invitations. He brought out a suitcase full of sex toys. He thought he was being romantic. We thought he was bizarre, and we got completely grossed out. We said as much. He didn't care. I finally said, "We aren't going to screw you. Just give us the drugs."

Something clearly got lost in the translation. That or he was just thick. It turned into a pretty comical scene. He kept going into the palatial bathroom, filling up the tub with bubble bath, and lighting candles. He came out each time grinning mischievously, perhaps hopefully, announcing it was almost ready for us. Then one of us went in there, blew out the candles, emptied the tub, and turned on the lights. We were terrible. This went on for two days.

By the second night, the party broke up and I found myself with a couple of the other girls prowling Amsterdam's seedier clubs. We had descended into the underbelly of the after-hours scene. We were working our way through a pretty hard-core club when I spotted Jeff Jetsetter. He was there with a rich Texas oil guy and a couple of hookers of dubious gender. We traded hellos, and of course he invited us to have a drink and sex with them.

Again, we declined. Never mind the place was an extremely weird scene. The sun had already started to come up and we had a show that night at the Paradiso.

Jeff Jetsetter showed up there, too. Somehow he looked fresh while I was a haggard facsimile of myself from not having slept for three days. Through the first part of the show, I felt like I was standing in a tunnel. I couldn't make anything out, not the music or the audience. As I began singing "Fading Fast," I lost my hearing altogether. I sang anyway, but I couldn't get my key. My voice was all over the place. Jane glared at me, pissed off that I was *that* bad.

We were a worn-out bunch on the flight back to the States. Charlotte filled up seven vomit bags. I felt like we weren't ending the tour as much as we were escaping with our lives.

At the end of November, the Go-Go's went on extended hiatus. After nearly seven months on the road, we needed a break. We had worked nonstop for several years. *Vacation,* though certified gold, didn't live up to the massive expectations our debut album created and left us scarred. Egos, publishing issues, and drug use also took their toll on us. A *New York Sunday News* magazine cover was right on with its headline "For the Go-Go's, it's not easy being rock's sweethearts."

Many years later I laughed to myself when I saw that the band Metallica had hired a therapist to help them through issues they were having with one another. We should have done the same thing.

The petty jealousies and comments that we once overlooked or laughed off grew more frequent and caustic. More serious, too. Whereas in the early days we might have sniped about boys, it was now apt to be about business. Songwriting royalties enabled some of the girls to make a lot more money than the others. Charlotte, for instance, bought a large house in Los Feliz while others were still trying to scrape together enough money for cars and condos. The arrangements affected the dynamics within the group and tested friendships.

I never approached the issue myself. I felt guilty about being such a mess. I knew I wasn't entitled to more of a piece of the pie.

Ginger, who had begun managing the band out of her apartment, opened up an office on Hollywood Boulevard, and then, as the business grew even larger and more complex, brought in high-powered manager

Irving Azoff and his company, Front Line Management. It was the beginning of the end for Ginger, who half-jokingly described her departure to me as "being strong-armed by the music industry." After receiving a Grammy nomination for her work designing our *Vacation* album cover, she moved back to New York, ending our ties to the all-girls, do-it-yourself ethos that had driven us since we were part of the punk scene.

With our new high-powered management behind us, the band got into a pissing match with IRS over royalties we claimed were due us from our first album. They claimed they didn't have the money to pay us, and we settled for $1 million, which was really settling. Margot also sued the Go-Go's, claiming she was owed money for her contributions. As I recall, we settled with her for around $30,000.

Who would have thought a curbside conversation at a late-night party in Venice could have led to all of this?

I guess I did, in some way.

In February, I joined Mike for spring training at the Dodgers' complex in Vero Beach, Florida. There was nothing for me to do. While he worked out with the team, I went to Bible study sessions with the other Dodger wives and girlfriends, which I found as torturous as Sunday school when I was a kid. I had no idea what I was doing in those sessions—or in Florida, period.

By the time we returned to L.A., our relationship was fodder for gossip columns and tabloids. Writers dug up old photos of Marilyn Monroe and Joe DiMaggio, Hollywood and baseball's most famous couple. They had wed in January 1954 and nine months later Monroe filed for divorce, citing mental cruelty.

My relationship with Mike followed a similar course, minus the marriage. Once the season began, Mike turned into a different person and living with him was difficult. He blamed me for his strikeouts, groundouts, errors, and anything else that went wrong. I fretted about what kind of mood he would wake up in in the mornings. I was constantly afraid of doing something that would upset him. I walked on eggshells; sometimes it felt like it was a minefield.

One time he lost his temper after smelling cigarette smoke in his car and berated and bullied me all night until I reluctantly admitted I had smoked in it, which he forbade. In many ways, my life with Mike reminded me of growing up with my dad when he drank. Mike wasn't an alcoholic, but he created a volatility that, although unhealthy, was very familiar ground to me. A few times I reminded myself of my mother as I yelled back at him.

Meanwhile, Mike had no idea I was a druggie, something that obviously contributed to the tension in our relationship. I was hiding a pretty big and serious secret. Shortly after we settled into the Marina del Rey apartment, I was at my lawyer's office and asked one of his assistants if they knew of a coke dealer in the Marina. I needed a connection closer than Hollywood. My lawyer's assistant made a call and gave me a slip of paper with a number on it and said it was okay for me to call.

I went home and it turned out that the dealer lived on the floor directly below mine. I couldn't believe my good fortune.

"You're in the same building as me?" I said.

"Yeah, the same one," he said. "I've seen you here."

He told me his apartment number.

"I'll be right there," I said.

Mike never picked up on the frequent visits I made downstairs. He was too into himself to notice I was high out of my mind. As he slept, I sat on the floor of his walk-in closet, snorting lines till the sun came up. On game days, I showed up at Dodger Stadium just before the opening pitch, and I was always loaded. I have no idea how I made those drives back and forth without an accident.

At the stadium, I sat in the section reserved for the players' wives and girlfriends. These were women with the big hair, jewelry, and designer outfits. They had their own social pecking order. I was not a part of their hierarchy. It was like being a guest at a club where they don't allow those of your skin type or religion. In my case, I was a nonconformist, drugged-out rock star. I was a celebrity in my own right, not dependent on Mike in any way. They also hated me for all the attention I received from dating Mike. I just clearly didn't belong—and none of them wanted me around.

Not that I cared. I had nothing in common with them, plus I was coked up to my eyeballs and focused on Mike's play on the field only so I could gauge how he was going to treat me at home.

I've been told our relationship helped inspire playwright Neil Simon to pen the movie *The Slugger's Wife*. If he had only known the truth!

Miserable, I sought out Jack, my model friend from Japan, who had moved back to L.A and was working at the China Club in Hollywood, and I spent quite a bit of time partying there. I noticed who was with whom and looked for other, more interesting opportunities. One came along in May when I took a small part in the movie *Swing Shift*, director Jonathan Demme's romantic comedy about Rosie the Riveter–type women who took over factory jobs when the men went to Europe to fight World War II. The film starred Goldie Hawn and Kurt Russell.

I hit it off with Jonathan, who was at the opposite end of the spectrum from Mike. In his late thirties, Jonathan was brilliant, clever, funny, way hip, knowledgeable about music, and adorable. One day on the set, as I stood amid the clutter of cameras and lights, he came up alongside me and with a playful twinkle in his eye that was pure Jonathan, he said, "So how does somebody get a date with you?"

"Just ask," I said.

twelve

THIS OLD FEELING

I BEGAN SEEING Jonathan on the sly. I had a great time with him. He was smart, talented, and funny. We shared common interests and knew some of the same people. All these things made me ask myself, Why was I with Mike? Friends of mine, those who hadn't dropped me because they were put off by Mike, asked the same thing: What do you see in him?

My gay friend and sometime assistant, Jack, had the best line. One day, after Mike made some off-putting comment about him when he'd called (like "it's your fag friend"), Jack simply said, "Honey, I don't get it. He's not even cute."

But like many women, I was unable to step outside of the hold he had on me. In fact, I got deeper into it. Against my business manager's advice, I let Mike talk me into buying a condo in the Marina and we moved into it after his lease on the rental was up. At that point, splitting with him would have required too much energy, something I didn't have to spare.

After *Swing Shift,* I was cast in the Long Beach Civic Light Opera's production of *Grease.* I thought it would be fun and different to act in a play, and would broaden me as a performer. I don't know what was wrong with me. Even though I was secretly insecure, I tested myself, maybe even tortured myself a little, by putting myself in this situation.

But it was okay. I starred opposite Barry Williams, who was best known from his years on *The Brady Bunch.* Working with him was surreal. I had grown up wishing I could be Marcia Brady, and now I got to kiss Greg Brady every night. He was a really upbeat, hardworking guy, and loved musical theater.

Jonathan saw the play numerous times. For some reason, he always cracked up during the same scene at the beginning of the play when, after the T-Birds and Pink Ladies complained that the new school year meant the return of bad food, I said, "You want my coleslaw?" Maybe I pronounced it in a funny way.

Sadly, Jonathan eventually gave up on me. Though we had a great time together, he saw that I wasn't going to leave Mike, not for him, not for something that was healthy and made sense. I have a hunch that Jonathan also realized he was competing not only against a Dodger but also against another equally fucked-up relationship of mine—with cocaine.

As much as I didn't want to acknowledge it, I was now an addict. Early in the production, I asked a young woman on the crew who was helping me get situated in my dressing room if she knew anyone who had coke (I could always sniff out who knew where the drugs were). She said, "Well, I happen to be a coke dealer." From that day on, I never gave another performance of the play sober.

Since the reviews were all positive, I thought I was getting away with it. After each show, I went to the drug dealer's house in Long Beach and stayed until the sun began to come up the next morning. If Mike was in town, I made sure to get home before he woke up. By the time the play ended, I weighed about five pounds. I thought I looked phenomenal, like I had finally lost the baby fat that made me Belimpa. I lived in a pair of size 2 hot-pink leather pants that I wore with a black top. I remember catching sight of myself in a window, seeing the way my clothes hung on my stick-thin frame, and thinking I was the picture of elegance.

For fun, Jack and I dressed up in crazy outfits and paraded up and down Sunset Boulevard, like two peacocks on display. We were completely tweaked. That's when people began whispering about me doing too much coke. My sister was the only one honest enough to say something to my face. I had taken her to a Dodgers game, and as we entered the VIP section, she turned to me and said, "Belinda, I hate to say this, but you look really old."

I was just shy of turning twenty-five.

*   *   *

That summer, Charlotte, Jane, Kathy, and Gina all began writing songs for our third album, *Talk Show*. Jane lectured me on the importance of my writing and getting songwriter credits on the album so I would make money, and Charlotte came over to my house numerous times to write with me, but I was too scattered to be creative. I couldn't focus enough to find the words and melodies that I knew were somewhere inside me.

It was no secret why. On some tapes we made of us trying to work, I could hear myself in the background snorting coke. On other tapes, I was on the phone arguing with Mike.

Mike was a problem. I had promised myself that I was going to break up with him. I knew there was nothing there but negative energy. The issue was that I couldn't pull the trigger, I couldn't find the wherewithal to escape. It was like a trap. As I made a salad one night, he yelled at me for cutting the lettuce instead of tearing it. I stood there with lettuce leaves in each hand and thought, What's wrong with me that I can't leave this guy?

As usually happens in such situations, I started a friendship with someone else, in this case Jimmie Vaughan of the Fabulous Thunderbirds. Now I kept two secrets from Mike, a dealer downstairs and a guy across town. Instead of doing the right thing, I kept complicating the situation.

I knew I was in a bad place. I was aware that I wrote a lot of checks that year that said "Pay to the order of cash." I finally reached out to Michael Des Barres, the British rocker-turned-actor who had helped a few wayward Hollywood souls like myself get sober. He'd been through it himself. We met at the Border Grill restaurant on Melrose and he talked to me about addiction and sobriety in an understanding and gentle manner.

I realized from the stories he told about his own life and how he related to me that he knew me better than I knew myself—or at least what I was willing to admit to myself. He brought out a book of daily reflections, which he signed and gave to me. I still keep it on my bedside table.

Michael urged me to start attending AA meetings, and though I promised I would, I never went to any meetings. I'm sure I had a million excuses. I just wasn't ready for abstinence. I wasn't ready to face any of my issues. I came up with my own solution. I thought I could learn how to use in moderation, rather than give it up completely.

Of course, it didn't work, and I was still using heavily in early September when the Go-Go's played a handful of dates in the Southwest. We brought in ex-Rockat Tim Scott to play guitar for Charlotte, who was struggling with carpal tunnel syndrome. We performed one of our biggest gigs ever at Anaheim Stadium when we opened for David Bowie. I was a massive Bowie fan, and I could have used the opportunity to seek him out and watch from the side of the stage. But I was too insecure and really more interested in partying in my dressing room. I didn't even want to mix with our old pals from Madness, who were the first act on the bill.

I went straight home after the show, and for the life of me I couldn't figure out why I was going there. The place was empty. Mike and I had broken up. He had finished the baseball season and moved to the Valley. When the girls and some of my other friends like Jack heard about the breakup, they called—not to console me with soothing advice but to offer their congratulations for getting out of a toxic relationship. All of them wanted to celebrate.

I rewarded myself with a trip to Rome. I thought it was a perfect time to indulge the *La Dolce Vita* fantasy I had harbored since my senior year of high school. I wanted to ride through the city on scooters, smoke cigarettes at cafés, and pretend I was Anita Ekberg. I flew there and lasted exactly twenty-four hours.

As a young, blond American girl on her own, I was pestered nonstop. I wouldn't have minded getting complimented, hit on, or even pinched one or two times. But twenty-five times before lunch was too much. I realized this plan of mine was a disaster and flew to London, where I was scheduled to meet up with the girls anyway and start recording the next Go-Go's album, *Talk Show*.

Earlier, we had decided to make the record in London. It was an opportunity for all of us to leave our demons at home and work as a band. On the previous album, we had seen that working in even the most remote and inconvenient outpost in Malibu wasn't far enough away to remove us from trouble. Miles and the record company knew the band was struggling under the weight of our individual issues, a nice way of saying we were barely holding it together. On paper, London was a good plan.

In reality, it was a nightmare.

Martin Rushent, who had worked with Spandau Ballet, the Human League, and ex-Buzzcock Pete Shelley, was hired to produce and bring in fresh, new influences. He was a lovely, low-key Englishman whose success had brought him a measure of wealth, stature, and a particular way of working. Then he ran into the Go-Go's; we were like a storm hitting his verdant Tudor studio in Berkshire. We recorded from November through January 1984. But Martin preferred to work on tracks methodically with each girl individually, which allowed those of us not involved to take off for London or Los Angeles, or just to take off.

I made what was supposed to be a quick trip back to L.A. to deal with the last details of my breakup with Mike and see friends. I wasn't in good shape upon arrival and it only got worse when I found Mike had taken the washer and dryer when he moved out of my condo. I argued with him until he agreed to return my appliances and then I spent several days getting high by myself in the dark in my bleak, sparsely furnished apartment.

When it was time for me to return to London, I had the kind of trouble you'd expect from someone in my state. I missed two flights in a row. I got to the airport okay, but I was too high to navigate the terminal and get on the plane. I caught a cab home after both false starts. On the third try, I had a big wad of coke with me and I went into the bathroom to do a line and figure out how to deal with everything. Realizing I couldn't deal, I decided to go home.

As I waited for a cab, I was positive that plainclothes detectives had me under surveillance. Several walked slowly past me, turned, and made eye contact, which I assumed meant they wanted me to know that they were aware of me. How? Well, either they had hidden cameras in the bathroom or they had noticed that I was completely gone. There was also the possibility I was paranoid.

On my fourth attempt, I finally made it back to London. There, I found the girls in their own state of disarray. Charlotte vanished for a week, and none of us had a clue where she had gone. We were extremely concerned until she popped up again not much the worse for wear. Gina was constantly fatigued or sick and going through her own struggles. Then, in the middle of making the album, Jane decided she wanted to sing some of the songs, and she kind of flipped out when she was told no.

As I knew, the word "no" was a hard thing for any of us to hear. We were not told no that often, certainly not as much as we should have been. I understood Jane's problem. She was cute, full of personality, and she wrote some of our best songs; she had an ego like anyone else, yet she stood off to the side, and it bugged the crap out of her—until finally she blew.

Jane resented me for getting all the attention. She'd had moments like this before. Sometimes it was about boys, and sometimes, like this time, it was about the spotlight. I didn't think it was true, and in fact I knew reviewers paid as much, if not more, attention to the songs as to me. Unfortunately for her, the band was built around one lead singer, around that singer's look and sound, and that job belonged to me.

I suppose we could've talked it out, but that wasn't the way I handled problems. My way was to ignore them, to pretend they didn't exist. If I didn't confront Jane, she wouldn't confront me about any of my problems. And that's pretty much the way the Go-Go's functioned in general. No one busted anyone. And maybe that's why, despite all the crap and chaos going on in the band, the five of us still hung out together.

But that was about to change. One day Jane just couldn't take it anymore. She smashed the mirror in her hotel room and flew back to the States. When she returned, she had decided to leave the band and pursue a solo career, though she kept that news from us for a few more months.

In many ways, it's remarkable we were able to make an album given the nonstop drama. Even more remarkable, I think it's the best

Go-Go's album. There's no doubt that when we were in sync, the five of us had a special chemistry and spirit. Like on "Head over Heels," a great song, classic Go-Go's, and still among my favorites to perform. It perfectly captured our state of mind at that point in time. "Beneath the Blue Sky" was another favorite of mine, a beautiful song whose vocals were, unfortunately, too complicated for us to ever do live.

As for the others, well, Jane wrote "Forget That Day" about a guy she had met in Amsterdam, and "I'm the Only One," while a good song from Kathy, never felt to me like it belonged on a Go-Go's record. A number of songs probably shouldn't have been on the album but made it anyway because people insisted on publishing credits. And then there were those I didn't get. "Turn to You," for instance, was one of my least favorite songs (the video was even more hideous, I thought), and yet the *Rolling Stone* album review that would appear a few months later called that particular tune the "best in the bunch." Go figure.

By February, we were back in Los Angeles with an album that, despite all the personal ups and downs we went through while making it, generated a buoyant optimism at the record company. As we rehearsed for a new tour, we got behind it, too. On March 15, "Head over Heels" was released as the first single, and the next day IRS put out the entire LP. There was no chumming the water; this album was going to live or die on our shoulders. It didn't look promising.

A *Los Angeles Times* review a few days after the album's release called it "awkward," noted the absence of catchy pop hooks, and said "the songs demand more work from the listener, and the elaborate melodies certainly demand more of singer Belinda Carlisle." Unfortunately, I agreed. Deep down I knew that I had bitten off more than I could chew on that album. Unlike the other girls, I hadn't worked on my craft as hard as I should have.

I would develop into a decent singer later, but at the time I didn't improve as much as I would expect myself to if I was able to go back and do it over again. But my vocals were the least of our problems.

I didn't know what to do with my life. After we returned from London, a stewardess friend of mine set me up with her cousin, a nice, very religious, normal guy from Northern California with whom I spent time, but

I knew he was a fake boyfriend. I used him to fill a void. I had to have someone around. I never wanted to be alone. God forbid I face myself.

Then I decided I didn't want to be with anyone. With a long summer tour ahead of us, I thought it was a good time to be by myself, a free spirit not beholden to anything but my own whims and wiles. What a crock!

In reality, I sat in my condo with the lights off and the curtains drawn, doing lines and smoking cigarettes. But my well-being was secondary.

In mid-March, after months of declining energy and nagging illnesses, Gina saw a doctor and was diagnosed with a heart murmur. She wore a monitor on her chest during several rehearsals. I couldn't have been more mistaken in thinking it wasn't serious. Along with the other girls, I went with Gina to her doctor's office and sat with a slack jaw and a face pale with worry as her doctor explained that she had a marble-sized hole in her heart, a birth defect that had finally caught up with her, and needed open-heart surgery.

An operation was scheduled for ten days later. Then the five of us did what we did best—we went into denial.

We rented a Cadillac and a Jaguar, packed enough drugs and alcohol to ensure that we didn't think about Gina's upcoming surgery, and drove to Palm Springs. We checked into a bungalow at Two Bunch Palms, a rustic spa to the north of the desert outpost. But I don't recall booking any spa treatments. We slept during the day and partied at night. Gina didn't partake, of course, but the four of us did enough to keep her spirits high.

A week later, she went in for open-heart surgery and came through without a hitch. I visited her a few days later in the hospital. Despite the IVs and monitors, she looked healthier than she had in weeks. Color had returned to her face. When the nurse left the room, I sat down on the side of her bed and jokingly whispered, "I have some coke. Do you want any?"

thirteen

GET UP AND GO

BY SUMMER 1984, Gina was fully recovered, and the band was sharp and well rehearsed. I decided not to think about questions dealing with our future, like the one *Rolling Stone* writer Chris Connelly posed in his review of *Talk Show* when he asked if the album would revive the Go-Go's cooled career.

We were hopeful upon the album's release, but we knew where we stood when "Head over Heels," our first single, peaked at number 11, and the album itself didn't break the top 25. We didn't know if it would go gold, which meant selling half a million copies. We didn't need to be told it was a disappointment, and none of us talked about how it would affect the band, or at least we didn't talk about it openly. Perhaps that was because it already had affected us.

At the end of June, as we set out on tour, the Go-Go's were divided into two camps. There were the good girls, Jane, Kathy, and Gina; and then there were the bad girls, Charlotte and me. Drugs and sometimes people's egos were usually the issues that created such factions. Those were very much issues when we were on the road, as were uncertainty, disappointment, and ennui.

As a house divided, it was difficult and often tense since we knew we were all saying things about one another in private, yet we also knew there wasn't that much to say that we didn't already know.

Our best times were still onstage when we came together and then afterward when we hit the town. Like in New York. After playing Radio City Music Hall, there was a party for us at Private Eyes that drew all of Manhattan's in crowd, including Liza Minnelli and Andy Warhol, whose diary noted, "It was just the party of the year." I don't know why he would have said that; he also gushed about getting free drinks.

Most of our nights were pretty crazy, thanks largely to being on a monthlong tour with INXS. The Australian rockers weren't just an amazing band; they were pretty amazing partiers, too. They were riding high on the single "Original Sin" off their newly released album, *The Swing*. All of us clicked immediately. We were kindred spirits. I don't know if that was a good thing, but it made for fun on- and offstage.

That was particularly true in the case of INXS's lead singer, Michael Hutchence, and me. We were attracted to each other as soon as we met. He was a sexy, sensual man, with great eyes that didn't suck you in as much as they made you want to *jump* in. He had all the goods to make him a great lead singer: hot looks, an animal-like sexuality, a mysteriousness, and the ability to deliver to an arenaful of people and touch the person in the back row. That's raw power, and it was packaged perfectly. Imagine trying to deal with that force of personality when he's right across the table from you.

We talked backstage in his dressing room and in mine. We also sat on the stage and then shared tea at a table in the catering room backstage. He was full of conversation about any subject, yet when he listened I felt like there was no one else in the world talking but me.

I knew something was going to happen between us before there was any discussion or a move in that direction, and I warned myself in the strongest of terms that he wasn't the kind of person to get serious about. Once I was satisfied I could handle that, which was about two days into the tour, I gave in to Michael's charms and we hooked up.

We had fun, and I had to keep reminding myself not to let him get under my skin. He had a serious girlfriend, but he admitted that he also had many "friends" and preferred that arrangement. That was one more reminder that if I let him into my life he would be the death of me. I didn't need to have any more messes in my life.

We watched each other perform, partied after the shows, and eventually disappeared into one or the other's hotel room for the night. His charms were strong, and I quickly felt close to him. I felt like he understood me. He had that way about him, yet I constantly reminded myself to keep a distance and protect my heart. I was partying pretty hard at the time, harder than even Michael, and at one point the girls in the band asked him to speak to me after I lost my voice from doing too much coke.

He wasn't the kind of guy who was going to save anyone, but he tried. He talked to me about the responsibility the singer had to the band, the record label, and the fans. He was extremely thoughtful and insightful about the special place we occupied in the imaginations of our fans.

"They fantasize about much more than is really there, don't you think?" he asked.

"Very much," I said, and for a moment I considered confiding how little I thought of myself, and how frightened I was that people were going to find out that I was nothing more than an imposter.

It would have been very easy to go there, but I feared it would have been letting Michael too far inside me. Ultimately I knew that revealing myself to him would only result in disappointment. As a result, I thanked him for sharing his concern but kept on doing my thing, which disgusted my bandmates so much that at one point on the tour they actually quit talking to me. It didn't last long, and neither did my summer fling with Michael. At the end of July, we said good-bye and Michael and I had a sweet, romantic, and passionate last night together that was a little sad and something of a relief and, in retrospect, kind of interesting in that we promised to remain friends, which we did until his death.

There was also a much bigger, more important breakup in front of me.

Toward the end of the INXS tour, Jane informed us that she was leaving the group. She said she would stay through the tour's last stop in Texas in October, but then she was going out on her own. When asked why, she said that she'd simply had enough and needed to do her own thing. She had considered leaving before, she said, but stayed through this album and tour out of loyalty to the band.

I understood Jane's reasons. She was articulating frustrations that had built up over months, if not years. I had been acutely aware of her feelings when we had recorded our album in London, and frankly, by now, it was an old story, one I was sensitive to but couldn't do anything about.

I had plenty of sympathy for Jane, and I understood if she wanted to sing and write all the material on her own album. My big fear was the future of the Go-Go's, and likewise my future, which was tied to the band.

We'd been together for seven years. All of us had grown up and changed. We weren't kids anymore. Now we had lawyers and business managers. When we had gone to England to make *Talk Show,* I had feared it might be the beginning of the end of the Go-Go's, and with Jane's departure, it looked like the end had arrived.

We continued on through August, performing in Northern California and working our way to Los Angeles. When we got home, I learned Michael Hutchence was also in town and hoping to see me. I considered it, and knew we would have a good time if we got together. But I was feeling extremely vulnerable and didn't know if I could handle seeing him. In the end, I sent word that I was busy.

It was one of the rare times I said no. I heard he was upset, but I did what I had to for my own self-preservation.

In the meantime, Los Angeles was the place to be. The Summer Olympics had started on July 28 and the city was filled with athletes and parties. The air crackled with electricity, especially at night. I attended a night of events and a party at the invitation of Tom Hintnaus, an Olympic pole vaulter who was more famous as a Calvin Klein underwear model.

About a year earlier, he had posed in nothing but his tight white Calvins for an ad that became iconic in the gay community after it ran in *GQ* magazine and then whipped up a storm of controversy when it was unveiled as a billboard in Times Square. Soon after, Kathy and I were walking through Times Square. I stopped to admire his ripped body and said, "I want to go out with that guy."

Ironically, I met him a short time later at a party in Los Angeles and he followed up with an invite to the Olympics. Having failed to make the U.S. squad (he had been on the team in 1980, the year America boycotted the Moscow games), he used the fact that he was born in Brazil to sign on with their national team. We had a good time together and I liked hanging around the athletes. We played three shows at the Greek Theatre, and each night the front was filled with Olympians from different countries.

After the shows, I went carousing at the Olympic Village on the USC campus and had fun in a way that reminded me of high school. The village was the place to be. Some five thousand cute, athletic boys from around the world were staying there, and I saw or met most of them, including a yummy rower who competed with Tom for my attention as if I were one of the Olympic events. Having never been that girl in high school, I didn't mind.

We left Los Angeles days before the closing ceremonies. I celebrated my twenty-sixth birthday at Red Rocks Amphitheatre just west of Denver, though I felt like the partying had begun a few days earlier in Las Vegas. It seemed to continue over the next few weeks until I confronted the reality that these were the last shows the Go-Go's would play with Jane.

It was hard to imagine. From our very first two-and-a-half-song gig at the Masque, I had performed every Go-Go's show with Jane standing to my left. They amounted to hundreds of shows and many times that number of rehearsals. I couldn't begin to recount all the times she had laughed, frowned, and cursed at me. She had always been there. I went through the same roller coaster of conflicted emotions as the other girls, from anger and sadness to bewilderment and hopefulness that things would work out for all of us.

We met individually and in groups, with Jane and without her, with managers and lawyers and without them, and when all the tears were dried and the hard feelings sorted through and mended, we accomplished two things that I thought were absolutely crucial: We parted on good terms, wishing Jane good luck on the solo album she planned to release the following year. And Charlotte, Kathy, Gina, and I decided that the Go-Go's would continue.

We played our last show together in San Antonio. A story headlined "Go-Go's to Go On" appeared the next day in the *Los Angeles Times*. Jane followed with a letter to fans that asked for "understanding about [her] departure." She called her years with the band the best in her life, adding, "The other girls have been great about it and I wish them all the future success and happiness in the world. I hope that we will all look at this as a positive step towards more good music for everyone."

I hoped so, too. But after we returned to Los Angeles and began talking with our management about replacing Jane and preparing for our next gig, a spot in January's massive, multiday Rock in Rio festival, I didn't know if it would be possible to carry on. I didn't know whether we could sell the new Go-Go's to the fans—or if we could sell it to ourselves.

I set that uncertainty aside temporarily by focusing on my social life. I went on a few dates and for some odd reason received a flurry of calls from political types, guys with Washington, DC, connections. One guy was the son of a senator. Another was a lawyer who remarked that he had been part of a congressional hearing that was covered on the news and asked if I had seen him. Uh, no, I hadn't.

I didn't know how my name got on those politicos' list—who knows, maybe it was date-a-rock-star month in DC—but I thought it was funny.

Then, in early December, with 1984 coming to a close, my DJ friend Rodney Bingenheimer called out of the blue and said a guy with whom he was peripherally acquainted had contacted him about being set up with me. His name was Morgan Mason, and as Rodney explained, he came with an impressive pedigree and résumé. He was the oldest of two children of actor James Mason and his socialite wife, Pamela. As a child, he had appeared in several movies, including *The Sandpiper* with Elizabeth Taylor and Richard Burton. He had worked in Ronald Reagan's White House as deputy chief of protocol and special assistant to the president for political affairs. In 1982, he had left the White House and signed on as a vice president of the international PR firm Rogers & Cowan. He had also dated Joan Collins.

Being the son of famous parents didn't impress me. In Hollywood, "children of" were a dime a dozen and often the last people I would have wanted to date. His White House connection didn't impress me either, as I barely knew who Ronald Reagan was. I found the last bit about him having dated Joan Collins funny.

"Oh, I'm never going to get along with someone who went out with Joan Collins," I said. "Forget it."

"But he really wants to meet you," Rodney said.

"He's from a different world," I said.

After more back-and-forth peppered with laughter and gossip, during which Rodney revealed that Morgan was a notorious bachelor, I agreed to meet him at a party for a new Chinese restaurant in Beverly Hills. Actually, I didn't agree to meet him as much as I agreed to go to the party, knowing Morgan would also be there. I did so reluctantly, too, saying, "Fine, I'll go."

The party was on the seventeenth. That afternoon, I got a reading from a psychic that someone had given me as a gift. The appointment had been set up months earlier, while I was on tour. I enjoyed readings as a fun indulgence. The psychics I had seen in the past were usually more interesting than the readings. This particular one, a woman, fell into that category. She was a talker, with a warm manner and a gentle curiosity that had her quickly asking if I had a man in my life. When I said no, she raised her eyebrows as if she knew something I didn't.

"You are going on a date tonight, huh?" she asked.

"No," I said. "But I am going to a party."

"With a man?" she asked.

"I'm supposed to meet one there," I said.

"He's the one you're going to marry," she said.

I then raised my eyebrows. "Really?" I said.

She nodded.

"Honestly, I don't want to be with anyone now," I said.

She shrugged. "He's the one."

She made me think about this guy, Morgan. He was probably a nice guy, which didn't appeal to me at all. How could I possibly get along with anybody who had worked in Washington and dated Joan Collins?

He was clearly from the right side of the tracks, and I was from the wrong side. Nonetheless, I was curious.

It was after dark when I pulled up in front of Bao Wao with my actress friend Diane Duarte along for company (and who knew, maybe protection) and turned my car over to one of the valet parking attendants. We went inside pretending we were there for the scene, though in reality we were using our eyes like radar to scan the crowd for Morgan.

I wasn't there long before one of the junior publicists grabbed my arm and took me to meet Morgan. He was outfitted from head to toe in Brooks Brothers. He looked very straitlaced and unlike anyone I had ever dated. When we were introduced, he was utterly, almost rudely, dismissive and totally uninterested in me. Wasn't he the one who wanted to meet me? Yet he wasn't nice. I didn't get it.

I asked him for a cigarette and he nonchalantly tossed one at me. "Here," he said, before turning his back and disappearing into the crowd. I thought, How dare he! It was like a scene from a 1940s movie. As Diane and I left the restaurant, I didn't think I would ever see him again. Why would I?

A couple days later, Diane and I were having a girlfriends' lunch at La Scala Boutique, the casual offshoot of the older, fancier Beverly Hills restaurant La Scala, which was famous for the Leon chopped salad, named after the restaurant's owner, Jean Leon. I spotted Morgan at one of the back booths. I nudged Diane, who looked along with me in his direction. He turned and saw us. His glance was barely perceptible, but both of us saw it.

A few minutes later, he got up and came over to our table. He was in another beautiful suit, with his hair perfect. He was extremely dapper and self-confident. He asked, "What's going on?" and dropped his business card on the table. I shrugged. "Nothing." He smiled and said, "Well, if anything is going on, you have my card."

As soon as he was gone, I turned to Diane and made a face as if I had just tasted sour milk.

"Ewwwww!" I said. "He's just so arrogant."

But I guess, at least in retrospect, Morgan knew what he was doing, because I couldn't stop thinking about him. I had tickets to a Hall and Oates concert on December 21 at the Forum and wanted to invite him, but I was too nervous to call. I had Diane call him and pretend she was me. She left a message with my number. He called right back and said he would love to go.

Two nights later, Morgan picked me up in a limo. I was still living in the hideous condo left over from my Mike Marshall debacle and felt like I had to explain why I lived there when it wasn't really me. But within seconds the long black chariot was whisking us to the Forum and the two of us were talking as if we had been friends for years. We got along ridiculously well. It was instantaneous and one of the biggest surprises of my life.

We had a blast at the show, which was great, and then flashed our VIP passes to get into the after-party at Wolfgang Puck's restaurant Spago. After five minutes, Morgan suggested grabbing dinner on our own and he spirited me away to a cozy corner booth at Trader Vic's, a landmark Beverly Hills hideaway, where we ordered giant Scorpion drinks and pretty much decided we wanted to get married and spend the rest of our lives with each other.

fourteen

HEAD OVER HEELS

I MOVED IN with Morgan the next day. Everyone thought it was crazy. They thought we were crazy. Morgan and I said they didn't understand. We thought it was the most natural thing in the world. We were in love.

Of course, he didn't have any idea that he had gotten himself involved with a cocaine addict. He looked at me through a haze of affection. It blinded him to reality, a reality that I strove to conceal. I showed him the very best of me, the person I wished I was, the person I might have been if not for the whole secret life I had going on as a drug addict.

I was able to hide my coke addiction, but it took major effort and tons of lies. I was slow in moving my stuff from the Marina on purpose. I used my condo as a hideout, a secret den where I could go and get high in safety. At night, after Morgan fell asleep, I snuck out and went to my old place and got high. I always left little notes on the bed for Morgan, saying that I went out to get Pepto-Bismol.

If he hadn't been a sound sleeper, and if both of us hadn't been extremely busy, I wouldn't have gotten away with that charade. It was the end of December, though, and he was wrapped up in Hollywood's holiday season and I was rehearsing daily for the Go-Go's first show since Jane had left the band. We were debuting the refurbished version of the band at the Rock in Rio festival, a nine-day blowout in Rio de Janeiro that would draw 1.5 million people over a ten-day span.

A month and a half earlier, as we dealt with Jane's departure, Kathy, Gina, Charlotte, and I decided that Kathy would switch from bass to guitar, her original instrument, and we would look for a new bassist.

Word went out, and more than two hundred hopefuls applied for the job, including high school girls and moms. They sent in demo tapes, photos, letters, and videos telling us why they would make a perfect Go-Go.

We had a blast going through the material and watching the tapes. Some of the demos were downright awful, and others were hysterically funny; thinking back, they remind me of *American Idol*'s early audition rounds. After rehearsing with the ten best, we brought back three or four finalists. One girl was patently wrong; with big, puffy lips and long legs, we joked she looked too much like a supermodel. Then there was Paula Jean Brown, who not only played well enough, she matched in every other way.

"She looks like she could be one of us," I said.

"She doesn't act like it," Kathy said, meaning Paula seemed like a straight arrow.

"Give her a couple months," Gina added.

"Yeah, we'll corrupt her," Kathy said.

By the end of December, we hadn't corrupted her as much as worked her to death. After celebrating her induction into the band with a lavish dinner at Spago, we had rehearsed almost daily in preparation for our performance in Rio. We were literally getting our act together—or trying to. We were acutely aware that the band wasn't the same without Jane.

At one point, I would not have focused on anything except the band. But there was now more to life than the Go-Go's. My feelings for Morgan were deeper, stronger, and more mysterious and fulfilling than any I had ever felt in my life. He was unlike anybody I had ever met. He was attractive, elegant, smart and sophisticated, and very funny. I couldn't understand why he had been so aloof when we met. He was totally opposite from that arrogant guy.

Morgan said it was because he was shy and didn't know what to say. I believed him, of course, but have since wondered if he didn't have a special talent for reading into people that he applied to me.

Morgan drove a Ferrari. Although I had always thought guys who drove those sleek sports cars were creepy, Morgan looked appropriate in his car, just like he did in his finely tailored suits. It fit without pretension or attitude. He enjoyed himself and lived with a sense of fun, panache, and style.

And why not? He was Hollywood royalty, which I thought was funny but also something far beyond my sense of self-worth. When I told my mother about Morgan, she nearly gasped and made his world seem even more fantastic and out of my league by recalling how years earlier she and her mother had stood outside movie premieres and gaped at Morgan's parents as they walked the red carpet. She had read about the birth of Morgan and his sister, Portland, in celebrity gossip magazines.

In fact, my mother knew more than I did about Morgan's family. Married at sixteen, Pamela fell in love with James Mason when they worked together on a film, leading her to divorce her first husband and remarry in 1940. They moved to Los Angeles, with their dozen cats, in the mid-forties. In 1964, roughly twenty years later, the Masons divorced and pursued separate careers. In addition to raising her two children, Pamela hosted several daytime TV talk shows and wrote advice books, including *Marriage Is the First Step Toward Divorce,* a title that was perfectly Pamela.

Within a few days of our meeting, Morgan introduced me to her. I was intimidated just driving up to her home, a mansion that was on the grounds of the old Buster Keaton estate. It was on Pamela Drive, no less. Because he had told her that he was serious about me, I was more nervous meeting her than I was about singing to fifty thousand people. I was, in fact, petrified as we walked into the house.

I desperately wanted her to approve of me, which I thought was unlikely. On top of all my insecurities, I had been warned that she hadn't liked most of the girls Morgan had brought to the house. I thought she would see right through me, take Morgan aside, and tell him to send me back in a taxi.

But I was wrong. For whatever reason she liked me. I wasn't comfortable around her for years, but I think she saw in me a kindred spirit—or at least a spirit, something even I couldn't always see.

Of course, Pamela had plenty of spirit, sass, class—everything and then some.

She liked to say that she had dropped out of school at age nine and thus avoided the confusion an education produces. Her 1996 obituary in the *New York Times* said she began "her day by telephoning Hollywood friends for the latest news." The latter half was correct. Pamela didn't begin her day as much as she woke up in time for the night. She came downstairs around five P.M., perfectly coiffed, in her wig and diamonds and dressed to kill. She was just in time for cocktail hour and a party.

More often than not, she was the one throwing the party. By the time I met her, she was more famous as a hostess than anything else. She had parties almost every night, which was how Morgan had grown up. I came in toward the tail end of that run and met scads of amazing people. Over the years, I met George Burns (he was charming), Stewart Granger (boisterous and handsome), Dick Van Dyke (I talked to him about *Mary Poppins,* whose songs I sang as a little girl), Glenn Ford (a lovely man), Gregory Peck (wonderful), Milton Berle, Robert Wagner, Anthony Perkins, Berry Berenson, and Walter Matthau, who was always seated next to me at dinners. Every time I saw that I was next to him, I thought, Oh God, not him again. He was so cranky that making conversation was a chore. But I was young, naïve, and limited in what I had to say, and now I realize how lucky I was to have known him.

I used to stare at Esther Williams, whose beauty was luminous, and Anne Francis, who starred in *Forbidden Planet,* was one of the most gorgeous women I had ever seen. These women were wonderfully fun companions on these weird, boozy, and loud nights. Best of all, at the end of the evening, I got to slip my arm through Morgan's and go home confident that he was *the one*.

In early January 1985, Paula finally got an eyeful of what it meant to be a Go-Go when we traveled to Rio for the largest modern-day rock festival ever. It was a ten-day event that included Queen, AC/DC, Ozzy Osbourne, Rod Stewart, the B-52's, Iron Maiden, Yes, the Scorpions, and more than a dozen other acts. After checking into the hotel, I noticed that all the action was at the pool area. It overflowed with rock stars, wives, girlfriends, and groupies.

For a moment I got the sense I was looking at the parking lot outside the Rainbow, except these really were rock stars, not wannabe rockers. We joined the crowd, though I wished we hadn't when I saw someone from our management team blow his nose in the pool and then wash his hands in the water. I was mortified.

Another person from our management made it known that he had brought his son to Rio and planned to buy him a hooker for his sixteenth birthday in case anyone had some recommendations. I'm sure he received plenty of them. Rod Stewart organized a fancy, expensive dinner party one night and invited all of the Go-Go's because, as we were told, he wanted to meet us.

It was almost too fabulous for all of us to comprehend that this rock icon wanted to fete us. There was just one small problem. I told the girls not to be mad at me, but I was going to be a little late to the party because I wanted to venture out in the city to find cheap coke. They didn't think it was a wise move. On checking in, we had been warned that it wasn't safe to go beyond the hotel grounds, but I had heard cocaine was only $5 per gram compared to the $100-a-gram cost in L.A., and that was too much of a lure.

So as the other girls got ready for Rod's dinner, I hopped in a taxi and gave the Portuguese-speaking driver simple instructions: "Cocaine, *por favor.*"

He gave me a puzzled look in the rearview mirror.

"Coca," I said. "I want coca."

He sped away from the hotel and through the city until we were far away from the nice hotels and cruising through the underbelly of the city's dangerous and impoverished ghettos. I didn't know whether I should press my face to the window and stare or hide myself in the back, a young, white American traveling where she had no business.

I had no idea where we were or where my driver was headed, but enough time passed without us making any progress that I told the driver to turn around and take me back to the hotel. I didn't want to miss Rod's party. I wasn't too late when I finally walked into his party. I mingled for a while, getting introduced to members of Rod's band and various music industry people when I started talking with the daughter of a prominent local politician.

I told her that I had explored the city a bit in a taxi, which amused her for a moment—until she heard my description of the city, realized I had been in the slums, and asked where I had been going. I paused to consider whether to tell her the truth, which I decided to do after something about her made me think she already knew. Indeed, she gave me a funny look, then leaned close and told me she was tight with some major dealers. A moment later, she escorted me downstairs, put me in a cab, and said something to the driver—the address, I presumed—and I was off.

The driver stopped in front of a modern condominium building near Ipanema Beach and communicated that he would wait while I went inside. I have no idea if he knew what I was doing there, but I hoped and prayed he would wait while I went inside and, as instructed, up to the penthouse. I gave a hesitant knock on the door, and waited. No one answered. I knocked again. This time the door opened a bit, and a dark-haired man looked at me. It was not a friendly, welcoming look.

I mentioned the name of the girl I had met at the party and explained she said it was okay for me to come. Before I finished, he opened the door and I stepped in. I assumed he already knew why I was there, and he did. From what I saw as I glanced around, I realized there was only one reason anyone would be there. There was coke everywhere. It was stacked in bricks, and there were several tables where some guys sat in front of scales, dividing piles of coke into smaller amounts.

I couldn't tell who was in charge and didn't want to look around because I immediately saw a couple of guys holding guns and knew better than to see more than I had to. In fact, I had a very strong feeling that I shouldn't have ever gone into that place, and I would have excused myself and left if a guy hadn't stepped forward and in broken English asked what I wanted.

What I wanted was not to get shot. But I didn't say that. Actually, I didn't say anything. I was too scared.

"How much do you want?" the guy asked again.

"A gram," I said.

He glared at me with disdain and disbelief.

"We don't sell grams," he said.

I decided it was best not to explain that I had heard you could get grams for five dollars, and that's why I was there. I thought about how much I should buy. I didn't feel like asking what the minimum amount was they did sell. Apparently he didn't feel like waiting for me to figure out something to say. He asked if I wanted half an ounce.

I said okay and paid whatever he said it cost, which wasn't much given the amount I was taking away with me.

I wanted to hug the cabdriver for waiting when I saw his car still out front. I was thrilled when we pulled in front of the hotel, and I gave the driver a generous tip. I stood in the lobby for a moment and took several deep breaths. If only Morgan knew, I thought.

Thank God he didn't.

I went up to my room and took the coke out of my purse. I couldn't wait to look at this package that could have cost me my life. I opened it and saw more coke than I had ever seen. I set it on the coffee table. It was like a little white mountain. I couldn't believe it.

I did several lines and thought it was the purest, smoothest coke I'd ever put up my nose. Seconds later, I felt a strong, familiar jolt that erased the scare of men with guns and put me in a better frame of mind. I packed up the coke, put it in a dresser drawer, and went back up to Rod's soiree, which went on for a little while longer. Then I brought the girls back to my room, where we put on some music and continued the party.

My room had a wraparound balcony; half faced the ocean and the other half looked back into the hotel's other rooms and pool area. As we partied, we darted in and out onto the balcony, where we smoked cigarettes, danced, and waved to other people, including Rod and some of his band, who were on his balcony. We gestured for them to come over to our room. They said no, but communicated for us to bring our festive selves to their room.

We did, and we proceeded to stay up all night. As the sun came up, Rod was irritated that he had not gotten any sleep because he had a show that night. He said he had never stayed up all night, *never,* which I found hard to believe, considering his reputation. But that's what he said as he cleared everyone from his penthouse, explaining like an old fussbudget that he still wanted to try to catch a few hours of shut-eye.

We took the party down to the pool, where we ordered cocktails and smoked cigarettes. We weren't the only rockers who had stayed up all night; the place was buzzing, and buzzed, even as the morning sun bathed the hotel in new light. We saw people open their drapes, others head off to the gym, and every so often we looked up toward Rod's penthouse suite and saw him pacing back and forth on his balcony.

"I can't sleep," he yelled down at me.

I couldn't tell if he was really upset or playing up his annoyance. He seemed upset to me.

"I have a show," he continued. "I need my rest. What am I going to do?"

That night, the thirteenth, we played the first of our two shows. We went on after Nina Hagen and before Rod. Thanks to the live TV broadcast, we played in front of an audience estimated at ninety million. Afterward, we were sweaty and spent, and intending to go back to the hotel and clean up—that is until Rod sent for me, along with Kathy, and insisted we sit on the side of the stage as he performed. He wanted to, he said, be able to look over at me and see that I felt as tired and miserable as him.

I said it would be my pleasure—and it was. I wasn't so jaded that I didn't appreciate that I was having this time with a guy whose music I had sung when I was growing up.

In the meantime, Charlotte was partying so hard that she got kicked out of Ozzy Osbourne's dressing room. It was a story that became legendary among rockers, and years later Charlotte, who got sober, famously remarked, "How bad do you have to be to get kicked out of Ozzy's dressing room?"

Personal problems aside, we had another problem that was bigger than all of us. The Go-Go's just wasn't fun anymore. I had felt it when we had rehearsed in November and December for Rio, and I knew it when we finally went onstage that first night. I didn't feel any more spirit either on the eighteenth when we played our second show, which found us between two incredibly enthusiastic, inspired bands—the B-52's, whose set included guests Tina Weymouth and Chris Frantz from the Talking Heads, and the closing act, Queen, who, with Freddie Mercury out front, dazzled the worldwide audience.

By comparison, I felt like the Go-Go's played without a heartbeat. One thing about rock and roll—you can have the best songs in the world, but if you don't bring passion to the stage you might as well not show up. We came to that realization. It just took a little time.

fifteen

MAD ABOUT YOU

CHARLOTTE STAYED behind in Rio to fool around with a nice young Brazilian boy she had met. She wanted one last fling before she checked into rehab, which she did promptly upon returning to L.A. Around that same time, I saw photos in a magazine of myself from Rio; in them, my eyes were listless, dull, and elsewhere. I wish that I had noticed. I visited Charlotte a few times in rehab and thought I was getting away with something she had taken too far. I might have been farther gone than she.

Sometime toward the end of February, Morgan figured out the truth about me. I had been going back and forth at night between his condo and my dealer while he slept. I would buy the coke, come back, sit in the living room and get high, and then smoke cigarettes on the balcony.

I don't know what I was thinking.

Clearly, I wasn't thinking.

I was gone. Subconsciously, I was begging to be found out.

One morning Morgan woke up and came into the living room. He saw me seated on the couch, bending over something. As soon as I heard him, I shoved it under the couch. He saw me, though, and asked, "What are you doing?"

Instead of waiting for me to answer, he reached down and pulled out a mound of coke that I had piled up on a magazine. He took it out on the balcony and with a look of utter disgust dumped it over the side. I was busted, so completely busted. I hadn't moved. It was like I was waiting for him to do something.

"I'm sorry," I said, dissolving into tears. "I'm sorry."

He was upset and didn't know what to do. Neither did I. As his initial burst of anger and my shock dissipated, we shared a look of helplessness and desperation. He loved me, and I loved him, and it was just such a pathetic, disappointing, awful moment. The way Morgan looked at me, I don't know if anyone in my whole life had ever seen me as nakedly honest, vulnerable, and in pain as he was seeing me right then.

I needed him to hold me as I regrouped and we regained our equilibrium not just that day but going forward. He never gave me an ultimatum; I simply knew that I had to get sober. And that's what I did—sort of.

As any recovering addict knows, you can't be "sort of" sober. It's all or nothing. But I devised my own plan. I didn't want to check into rehab; I couldn't stand the thought of seeing my dirty laundry unfurled in the press. In retrospect, it shouldn't have been a big deal. If I was going to admit I had a problem, it shouldn't have mattered if I admitted it to one person or a million. What did matter, though, was admitting the whole and honest truth to myself, and I couldn't do that.

I thought I was taking the right steps when I confessed to Morgan and then sought out Charlotte, who was recently out of rehab and attending meetings. She was extremely understanding and helpful. With her help and encouragement, I stopped doing coke right away. She took me to twelve-step meetings and I began attending Cocaine Anonymous meetings on my own, too. But I concocted or rationalized my own version of the program, one where I could drink, pop pills, and do hallucinogens— anything except cocaine. That was my one rule: no coke.

I was proud of my progress. Once I told someone who had a number of years of sobriety under his belt that I was in "the program," a euphemism for being sober and attending twelve-step meetings. He asked if I attended meetings. I said, "Sometimes." Skeptical, he asked who my sponsor was. I said that I was sponsoring myself. Seeing that I was serious, he shook his head slightly, an almost imperceptible acknowledgment that I didn't get it, and said, "Okay, good luck."

Though I was deluded about my self-styled sobriety, I did straighten up considerably by giving up cocaine. In March and April, I went back to work with the Go-Go's. The five of us rehearsed with the intention of making a new album. We tried to come up with our own songs and we worked through songs outside writers had submitted. The record company wanted more creative control over the band's next steps. We didn't like it, but we didn't have any better ideas.

Frustrated at every turn and no good at communicating with one another, the band devolved into factions, with Charlotte and me pitted against Kathy and Gina, and Paula left uncomfortably alone on the periphery as we fought during rehearsals. The demos we recorded sounded terrible. I went home to Morgan at night and said what I didn't dare say in front of the other girls: The band had lost its creative center. It no longer felt like the Go-Go's.

I talked about it endlessly with Morgan, who advised me to think it through carefully and listen to my instincts. He also told me not to procrastinate and let a bad situation grow worse, because I would miss other opportunities.

And that was the thing. I wasn't able to retreat to a golden castle and do nothing for the rest of my life. I had less than $20,000 to my name when I moved in with Morgan slightly less than six months earlier. I had blown God only knew how much money on drugs, travel, clothes, and even a racehorse I purchased on a whim for some ghastly sum. I needed to work.

I finally met secretly with Charlotte, who agreed with me that after two months of work the only decent, Go-Go's-sounding song we had was "Mad About You," which Paula had brought in. Otherwise the band wasn't working anymore. It was early May 1985. We had an album to record and a tour to set up. But both struck us as unlikely. The lack of material aside, the dynamics were way off and no one was getting along. Charlotte and I decided it was time to call it a day.

We talked it through until we assured ourselves that the band had stopped moving forward artistically and that we as individuals were stifled. We could do other things. I had already been approached about doing a solo album. Though that hadn't been an option when the band was my top and only priority, it sounded viable now, and Charlotte was amenable to working with me.

The two of us called a meeting with the other girls on the second

Friday of the month and broke the news that we wanted to end the band. Kathy and Gina were not just shocked, they were blindsided and fought back with anger and bitterness at the way we handled the situation. Kathy insisted we were overreacting and had overcome worse, but I kept to the basic premise: the band wasn't working, the songs were terrible, and the chemistry wasn't there.

They also blamed the breakup on Morgan, as if he was the Yoko Ono of the band, maintaining I had changed since meeting him. I had changed, but only because I wasn't off my trolley on coke anymore and began to have some opinions. But they were mine, not Morgan's. It wasn't fair to blame him—or true.

For the next eight months, I worked on *Belinda,* my first solo album. I dove in without thinking about any of the pressure-packed issues I would face later on when I actually stepped out publicly and faced critics, Go-Go's fans, and the new reality that I was on my own. I moved quickly, sticking to the relatively safe and familiar pop territory for which I was known. Should I have tried to develop an edgier sound or gone back to my punk roots? In retrospect, I wish I had pushed it to a harder place. But I wasn't in that headspace. Nor did I have that kind of creative freedom as a new artist.

I was working with veteran producer Michael Lloyd, and we chose Paula's infectious pop song "Mad About You" as a starting point. I loved the song, as did Miles and the rest of his IRS team. I also relied heavily on Charlotte, who had five songwriting credits on the album. Plus Michael and I chose songs from such proven hitmakers as Fleetwood Mac's Lindsey Buckingham, Split Enz's Tim Finn, Tom Kelly, Billy Steinberg, and the Bangles' Susanna Hoffs.

The album was rounded out by musical contributions from Duran Duran's Andy Taylor and session legends David Lindley and Nicky Hopkins, among others. The danger of employing so many disparate talents, of course, was ending up with an album that didn't have a personality of its own. But after hearing an early compilation, I thought the album was good. I was proud of it.

Critics would say it wasn't much of a step forward (it's "the antithesis of the Go-Go's intelligent girl-group gestalt," said *Rolling Stone*), but it began a transformation for me whether it was evident or not. When it was time to take pictures for the album's cover, I realized that I photographed well and was considered pretty even though I didn't feel that way about myself.

No, when I looked at myself in the mirror, I saw me at ten years old, wearing the polka-dot dress my mom had gotten on special at Sears, the one the kids at school knew was my only outfit. Or I saw myself a year or two later in a sleeveless hand-me-down that was lime green with flowers and let me believe when I put it on and did my hair in pigtails that I was pretty like Marcia Brady. Yet then I ran outside just as a car carrying some kids from school drove past and one of them yelled, "Hey, fatso!"

Despite being almost twenty-eight years old, inside my head I was still that girl, scared, awkward, and full of shame and insecurity. I definitely didn't see the beauty other people kept saying I had turned into.

On the other hand, after cleaning up my act, I saw a profound physical change. I lost the bloat I had from doing coke and drinking every night, especially from my face. I also lived a healthier lifestyle, eating better and working out. I started my day in the morning, a positive change in itself, as opposed to ending my day at that time, and I hit the gym with a trainer, lifting weights and running. All in all, I shed about twenty pounds and received lots of compliments about the way I looked.

There was nothing like being in a boutique and hearing women whisper, "Isn't that Belinda Carlisle? I didn't know she was so pretty." (Hey, I didn't know it either.) I also heard people say I looked like a young Ann-Margret, whose starring roles in *Viva Las Vegas* and *Bye Bye Birdie* had made her one of my favorite actresses.

But I had mixed feelings about such compliments. All through the Go-Go's I never lacked for boyfriends, but the press constantly referred to me as pretty and plump or cute and chubby, which bugged me. Then, as I started to do some early interviews before my album was close to being released, I began to hear the flipside, that I was slim, svelte, and sexy, like a new, hot Belinda Carlisle.

I knew it was all well intentioned. But why did my size even have to be an issue? I was confused enough. Couldn't I just be liked for being myself?

Good question.

No easy answers.

When it came time to shoot the album cover, I knew I had the opportunity to do something special. I let the music inspire the image. I came up with the idea of modeling it after Ann-Margret's great look from *Viva Las Vegas,* in black tights and a sweater. Since people were making that comparison, why not? Matthew Ralston, the photographer, liked the idea, and so we went with it.

The resulting photo was stark and classy yet still pop. It sure didn't look like old pictures of me in which I always seemed as if I had just hit the deli tray, that's for sure. I thought it conveyed a slightly more grown-up vibe. I liked it.

The "Mad About You" video, directed by Leslie Lieberman, was a fun, romantic postcard that fit with the song. We shot it in Santa Monica's Ocean Park, overlooking the beach and on the sand itself. I wore a black cocktail dress, swept my hair back, and put on a pair of sunglasses. It was simple and classy and felt to me like it fit the song.

My favorite part was that Morgan played my dreamy love interest. He didn't want me kissing anybody else.

Fine with me. I didn't want to kiss anybody else.

I was in a good place, the best in years. I was most accurately described by my new catchphrase: 100 percent. I used it all the time. I was giving my career 100 percent. My attitude was 100 percent positive. I couldn't say I was 100 percent sober, since I allowed myself an occasional glass of wine. But I was 100 percent in love.

Morgan was, too. One night, as we ate dinner, he said we should get married. Both of us had always felt like we got engaged the first night we had dinner together. We never doubted we were going to get married; it was merely a question of when. As Morgan pointed out, with my album set for release at the start of summer, and a tour, our lives were going to get very busy. He thought we should make our relationship legal before we were swept up in events we couldn't control. I agreed.

After dinner, we got out the calendar and set a date. The rest was easy. I had always known that I didn't want to walk down the aisle in a white dress in front of tons of people. I knew better than to fantasize about a family get-together. Morgan, who'd grown up with parties every night, didn't want a big, fancy wedding either.

We set a date and without telling anyone, I went out the next week and bought a white suit and a pair of Prada pumps. (Back then I had to ask, "What's Prada?" Now I know.) We picked Lake Tahoe as a fun place to elope. The day before we left, Morgan broke the news to his mother and I filled my parents in on the plan. If any of them were disappointed we weren't going to have a large wedding, they didn't tell us. We heard only encouragement and congratulations.

For all of Morgan's planning, though, I forgot my makeup and had to wear cover stick on my face and blue eyeliner instead of mascara. Even though I looked like a Kabuki dancer in our wedding photos, he still held my hand, as I did his, when, on the evening of April 12, 1986, the minister from the local Elvis Wedding Chapel joined us in our hotel suite and pronounced us husband and wife.

We exchanged simple gold bands and a long, romantic kiss. Then we changed into our sweats and went down to the casino. I won $4,000 playing baccarat.

I had never considered myself unlucky. But now that I was married to this most wonderful man, I felt even luckier.

sixteen

I FEEL THE MAGIC

THREE AND a half weeks later, I was onstage in a small San Diego club, and I wouldn't have blamed anyone watching my performance if they closed their eyes for a moment and thought they had stumbled into a surprise Go-Go's show. It happened to me. After all, my voice still had the trademark let's-get-this-party-going timber of the group's three previous gold albums, and as I pranced around barefoot in a simple print dress, I radiated the same sun-kissed, surfer-girl looks under the spotlight. But some key elements were different or missing, starting with three out of the other four Go-Go's.

When I looked to my right, I still saw Charlotte on guitar and keyboards. Otherwise I was out there by myself. I was also singing brand-new material from my eponymous album, *Belinda*. I didn't have any proven hits to fall back on and get the crowd going. The only song people might have heard before was the first single, "Mad About You," which had been released days earlier.

No wonder before the show I was a bundle of raw nerves, knowing that I could no longer divide the responsibility up four other ways. The whole thing was on my shoulders. Once that spotlight hit me, there was no denying this next phase of my career. I was starting over.

Morgan supplied the confidence I lacked. He sent roses to that warm-up gig and channeled positive energy to me a few nights later when I headlined three sold-out dates at the Roxy. I had played there with the Go-Go's. It represented a lot of good times. But seeing my name centered by itself on the marquee felt more frightening. It was one thing to affect a different image in a photo session and quite another to step out onstage and embody it.

I was also open about the challenges I faced offstage. I told *Los Angeles Times* critic Robert Hilburn, as well as other reporters, that I had been on the road to physical ruin and needed serious help getting my act together. Though I stopped short of admitting my cocaine addiction, I did say that I attended twelve-step meetings. It was a good story, and I wasn't lying when I said that I probably would have been "broke, alone and desperate" if I didn't change my ways.

However, deep down I knew that I wasn't being entirely truthful with them or, more important, with myself. Prior to the Roxy shows, I had a glass of wine in my dressing room. What was one glass of wine? Most of the time I didn't even finish a whole glass. I drank only enough to take the edge off the jitters I always had before going onstage.

It was like there were two versions of me. There was the insecure Belinda who couldn't believe people would pay money to see her. Then there was the Belinda who drank a glass of wine and turned into a singer. At that point, anything was possible. The Roxy's audience was full of industry types and characters from the old scene, including Exene and some of her cohorts, who, I was told, came just to cackle. She was in the minority. The hometown crowd roared their approval.

I hung on Morgan afterward, grateful he was there and more grateful that he had stuck with me through some very tough times. I almost believed him when he said that I had given a performance that surpassed everyone's expectations but his. More than twenty years later, as I was redoing my website, I came across a video on YouTube of me from one of those shows, singing "Since You've Gone," a great song that featured Charlotte playing keyboards. Unsure if I wanted to watch it, I took a deep breath and clicked Play. I was surprised. I thought it was really good.

In June, I went on tour with Robert Palmer, who was having monster success with the chart-topping single "Addicted to Love." I was his opening act, and he was not very nice to me. He was aloof, condescending, and dismissive. He spoke to me only once during the entire month we traveled together and that was to ask if I had any drugs. I didn't. It was the first time I could ever say no. He shrugged, walked away, and never had anything to do with me again.

I struggled with jealousy when Madonna released her great song "Papa Don't Preach." From her *True Blue* album, it was an instant hit that took radio by storm and soared to number one. But my problem was with Madonna herself, not the music. I looked at her body and thought, Oh my God, she looks phenomenal and it's because she's skinnier than me. I have to get that skinny.

Poor Morgan. When we talked on the phone at night, he would ask me about the show and then have to listen to me go on about the food I ate that day, how much I weighed, and whether I thought I looked fat. Despite Morgan's reassurances, I never felt thin enough, pretty enough, or good enough.

My fans disagreed, too, but there was one admirer whom I could have done without. A few dates into the tour, my birth father contacted me again. It was the first time since I had seen him two years earlier. Going through my management company, he congratulated me on the new album and asked if he and his family could come to the show when we stopped in New Orleans. I put them on the list, but as the date drew near I complained to Charlotte that I didn't feel good about seeing him.

"What don't you feel good about?" she asked.

"Everything," I said. "It's a feeling I have."

"Why?" she asked, pressing me.

"I just don't want to see him," I said.

That was exactly it. I didn't want to deal with the emotions that would surface when I let him back into my life. I was much happier when I avoided him and other unpleasant realities in my life. As I knew, my father was one chapter. I had been telling journalists that I was helped by Alcoholics Anonymous, implying I was sober, when I knew the real story was different. Instead of confronting the truth, as well as why I still drank, I ran from it. Deep down I knew it, too. But... well, there was always a but.

Before the New Orleans show, I was tense and upset and not anything like myself on the previous dates. I thought about him throughout my performance and couldn't wait to get off the stage. But then that only hurried and exacerbated the confrontation that I wanted to avoid.

Large trailers served as dressing rooms, and I was peeking out the window of mine as he came backstage. He and his daughters got as far as the wooden barricade that had been set up to keep people from entering the artists' area unless their names were on the list. I watched as a large security guard stopped them and checked my father's name against the names attached to his clipboard. I took a deep breath; I knew what was going to happen. Indeed, a moment later, I saw the security guard shake his head and my dad turn around and walk away, dejected. His family followed.

I had tears streaming down my face. I felt cruel and sad. But I couldn't handle seeing him.

I know everyone—record executives, critics, my former bandmates, fans, and myself—all wondered if I would be able to pull off a solo album and tour. Given where I had started from a year earlier, the odds were stacked against me. But my single "Mad About You" reached number three on the charts and the album itself sold more than five hundred thousand copies in the United States, making it gold. It surpassed everyone's expectations, including my own.

Success also made comparisons to the Go-Go's, and resulting criticism, easier to take. I was happy with the album. It was like the romantic pop that I had listened to when I was growing up and lying in front of the stereo speakers. Like all my solo albums since, it reflected where I was at the time.

My life felt inexplicably charmed. Morgan and I sold our respective condos—his was where we'd been living, and mine was left over from my Dodger days—and rented a cute house in Benedict Canyon. He went to work at the William Morris Agency, and I felt like I was getting to start my life over again. I couldn't begin to explain the turnaround.

Then it got even better. We had barely settled into our rental when my business manager informed me that I had some significant royalties coming in from *Belinda* and should think about investing in a house. I had never thought about spending such money, but I dutifully looked around without seeing anything I liked except for one weird house up the street. It was covered in vines and looked like an English cottage that had fallen into a bit of disrepair.

I didn't let the fact that it wasn't for sale stop me from obsessing about it. I regularly stopped my car and stared at it. One day I left a note on the gate with my name and number, explaining to the owner that I loved the house and wondered if they might be interested in selling it.

The owner, an entertainment attorney, got in touch with me and invited me to see the house. He wasn't sure he wanted to sell it, but he was happy to show me around. The place was in terrible condition. He had let it get run-down. But I saw only magic. It had once belonged to Carole Lombard, who used it as a hideaway for her trysts with Clark Gable. The kitchen floor included a concrete square with her footprints and signature dated 1936. I wanted it more than ever, but as I left, the owner said he wasn't interested in selling.

However, a short time later, the house went on the market. It was more than I could possibly afford. Plus we had gone ahead and put a down payment on another house nearby. My heart sank. Then out of nowhere another chunk of money came in that allowed Morgan and me to afford our dream house. We lost the other down payment, but c'est la vie.

Morgan and I hired noted architect Brian Murphy to make our dreams real. I told Brian that I wanted the style to be "*Alice in Wonderland* on acid"—and that's exactly how it turned out. The kitchen had a lavender slate floor. A mural in the dining room was an homage to Maxfield Parrish. Outside, the French gardens overflowed with flowers and vines that bloomed year-round.

But I was sidetracked somewhat from that very personal project when I returned to work sooner than expected. Miles, who wished that *Belinda,* despite its impressive sales, had been edgier and more in the style of IRS acts, forgot to pick up the option on my contract with IRS and I found myself a free agent. My management and I decided to shop around for a new deal. Miles was furious. But we thought, Why not test the market?

It turned out to be a shrewd move. After a bidding war between several major labels, I signed with MCA in the U.S., kept my foreign rights till after the next record was finished, and eventually made seven figures on both sides of the Atlantic.

In a way it was like a reunion. MCA president Irving Azoff had managed the Go-Go's after Ginger, and he was very supportive and enthusiastic about adding me to his roster of artists. Irving was also an astute businessman. After spending a significant sum of money to get me, he wanted to recoup it. He put me to work, scheduling the release of my next album for the following fall, barely a year away.

Michael Lloyd expected to work with me again, but Irving had another producer in mind. I was given the difficult, if not heartbreaking, task of telling Michael, who was understandably upset. I felt awful, but it was one of those things. The silver lining was my new executive producer Rick Nowels, who had scored major triumphs working with Stevie Nicks, another MCA artist. In fact, Stevie had suggested he try to work with me. In a way, we may have been destined to partner. It sure felt like it when we met. We had instant chemistry.

Rick was tall and blond, a Californian from head to toe, very passionate and a little eccentric. He wrote songs with Ellen Shipley, an amazing artist in her own right. They created songs specifically for my voice. For me, it was a brand-new and exciting way of working. I had never been anyone's muse.

When Rick and I talked about the album and how we envisioned it— what we wanted it to feel like and how we wanted the listener to feel—I had the sense he was reaching into my soul, removing tiny pieces, and magically turning them into songs. I was at his house when I first heard "Circle in the Sand," and I thought, Oh my God, this is so good. He and Ellen topped themselves with "Heaven Is a Place on Earth." I heard the song the day after it was written. Rick sat at the piano, and Ellen sang. It was like they were showing me a newborn baby.

I've had few reactions like the one I had after hearing them. I knew the song, even better than a hit, was a classic. Then the great songwriter

Dianne Warren came into the studio one day and played me "I Get Weak." Few people know the quality of Dianne's voice; it's gravelly and soulful and always moves me. "I Get Weak" was a perfect example. As she sang the final chorus, I literally felt weak myself. Again, I wondered how I got so lucky.

At the same time, I had never worked as hard. Rick made me sing parts forty or fifty times. I could never figure out what specifically he was listening for. Thank God he eventually heard it, though, or I might still be there.

Everything fell into place. Through Morgan's best friend, John Burnham, I was fortunate enough to get Academy Award–winning actress Diane Keaton to direct the videos for "Heaven Is a Place on Earth" and "I Get Weak." I was almost intimidated to meet her, but she was utterly charming and thoroughly inspirational in her approach to work. I only had to look at her body of work or the way she dressed (beautifully and with style) to know she had great taste, so I said, "Just do what you want."

She came back a week later with concepts and a storyboard. I said great, and we got started. On September 18, "Heaven" was released as the first single. Within two months, the song hit number one in the U.S. It also topped the charts in the UK, Germany, and a handful of other countries. It's rare that lightning strikes twice. I knew the odds against it happening to me a second time. I had to pinch myself when my album, released in October to mixed reviews, turned into a worldwide hit: a top 20 platinum seller in the U.S. and multiplatinum around the world.

As I kicked off the "Good Heavens" tour, I asked Morgan if it was real or if I was dreaming. It seemed like a mistake. I figured it had to be. He didn't know how to deal with that kind of mind-set other than to tell me to realize that these things were *not* accidents; I had worked hard for years.

His comment caused me to flash back to a time when I was on tour in the early days of the Go-Go's, just as the band was first taking off. It all seemed too fantastic; I had a moment right before we went onstage when I wondered where I was going to be ten years later. Now I knew. A couple days into the tour, I had another similar sort of moment. I was standing behind the curtain, atop a small platform, getting set to descend the three stairs as the spotlight hit me, and yet instead of breathing, focusing, and doing all the things I normally did in the seconds before the show started, I was thinking about how weird it was that I was doing this.

Me? Belinda Kurczeski from the Valley? What was I doing here?

I felt an odd and slightly unnerving disconnect between what I was doing and...and me...whoever that was.

seventeen

R U N A W A Y   H O R S E S

WHO WAS I?

It was a good question, and one I was trying to figure out. For the *Heaven* album and tour I grew my hair long and dyed it red. I was wondering if being punk's Ann-Margret suited me when I was walking down the street one day in Beverly Hills and ran into the Sparks brothers, Russel and Ron Mael, whom I hadn't seen in a while, and Russell blurted out, "Oh my God! You're a redhead! It looks great!"

He had great taste, so I figured it must be true. My friend Jeannine, who had been my roommate after I split with Mike Marshall, also reassured me it was a good color, and she had excellent taste, too. She came on the road with me, along with Jack and Charlotte, all of whom knew to one degree or another that I needed their friendship and support. They didn't know how badly I needed it, though.

On my previous tour I had seen Madonna's "Papa Don't Preach" video and got it in my head that I had to be as thin as her. For this tour, I wanted to be even thinner. The irony was I knew I photographed well no matter what I weighed, and beyond that, in discussions with friends, I always took the position that you didn't need to diet or reshape yourself to look a certain way in order to be beautiful.

I could even hear myself telling girlfriends, "You can diet all you want, but beauty comes from the inside. You have to like yourself before you can ever feel beautiful." But I wasn't listening to my own advice. I had become my mother, a gorgeous woman who had, when I was growing up, always been on a diet even though she didn't need to lose weight. I never understood that until I had done the same thing and later came to realize the diet wasn't at all about weight; it was about feeling inadequate and wanting to be in control.

Once the tour started, I fell into a bad state of mind. Publicly, I told people that either it was impossible to eat healthy on the road or I told them that I was on a health kick and exercising regularly. In reality, I was obsessed with eating and exercising, to the point where I weighed myself ten to fifteen times a day. And my day was ruined if I gained a pound. If I got dressed in the morning and the waistband to my trousers felt a little tight, I got hysterical.

All the self-doubt and insecurity I never dealt with during my so-called recovery bubbled up to the surface, making it so nothing I did made me feel good enough. I should have been ecstatic as "I Get Weak" rocketed up the charts in early 1988 to number two and was then followed into the top 10 by the next single, "Circle in the Sand." My tour sold out, too. However, I wasn't able to celebrate or enjoy the achievements. Instead I stood in front of the mirror when I was on the road or in front of Morgan after I returned home and asked, "Do I look fat? Am I fatter today than yesterday? Okay, forget that. Do I look fatter than I did this morning?"

It was all about holding on, and holding myself together, when inside, without such insane resolve, I could have easily fallen to pieces. Morgan wanted no part of such craziness and was somehow able to detach himself from it. He turned his attention to producing and spent most of 1988 working on *Sex, Lies, and Videotape,* a low-budget independent movie that his young discovery, Steven Soderbergh, had written and was set to direct about the effect a voyeuristic guy has on his former college roommate and the roommate's wife.

Morgan had given me the script and asked for my opinion. After reading the opening dozen pages, I told him it was fantastic. After I finished reading it, I was unsettled by Steven's take on sexuality and fidelity, but, as I told Steven at some of the dinners we had together, getting a strong reaction from me was a good thing.

I liked the freshness of his work, and I liked Steven even more. He was a brilliant nerd. He reminded me of a lot of artists I had met in the punk world—guys with talent, vision, a strong, unique voice, and a need to work in their own unconventional way.

Morgan was wrapped up in production when I went into the studio to make my next album, *Runaway Horses*. Though a number of major producers inquired about working with me, I teamed up with Rick Nowels again. For a second time I was in the studio trying not to think about the pressure and high expectations. Yet the industry's reigning A&R guru John Kalodner laid it right out there by saying, "If Belinda gets this album right, she's going to be the biggest star in the world." I tried not to think about it, but I knew the opportunity was there.

Rick, who immediately brought in some amazing songs, like "La Luna" and "Summer Rain," wanted to record part of the album in the South of France, and after the label gave permission, we set up camp outside Aix-en-Provence in the massive Château Miraval, the same thirty-five-bedroom estate Brad Pitt and Angelina Jolie lived in twenty years later.

Although the château was beautiful and on first getting there I imagined myself a princess arriving at her castle, I found it to be a depressing place in the middle of nowhere. I got a boost when Charlotte and Jeannine arrived. At first, they thought they'd gone to rock-and-roll heaven. We went on long morning hikes across the countryside, ate rich lunches prepared by a private chef, recorded, took naps, and then ate dinner in the nearby village.

It was ideal—for a week. Then they were as bored as me and the three of us took off to watch a Formula One race.

For me, the highlight came during work on "Leave a Light On," another gorgeous Rick and Ellen Shipley song. Rick said we should try to get someone cool and with a distinctive style to play the lead guitar part. I thought for a moment and said, "What about George Harrison?" I had met George briefly a few years earlier in San Remo, Italy, and Morgan, through his work on *Sex, Lies, and Videotape*, knew someone who was close to the former Beatle and able to get word to him. George responded right away, saying he'd love to help out.

He had worked with very few artists, so I was honored. I absolutely loved the work he eventually did. After he passed away, his widow, Olivia, told a mutual friend that she had found an old *Runaway Horses* cassette as she went through some of his stuff. She said, "Please tell Belinda that George really loved her voice."

Overall, we worked on the album as if money didn't matter. We took a year and spent close to $1 million. That may have sounded great in the press, but now when I hear something like that I know, because it was the case with my album, that it signals trouble. We second-guessed ourselves right and left and lost touch with the basics and ended up with an expensive album, not the *great* one we had hoped to make.

In January I was with Morgan at the Sundance Film Festival in Utah when *Sex, Lies, and Videotape* debuted and captured the Audience Award. Four months later, we went with the film to the Cannes Film Festival. We stayed at the Hotel du Cap and partied on yachts, and I bought a pink Chanel suit for the premiere. The film was awarded the festival's top prize, the Palme d'Or. It was an unbelievable time.

Morgan was pegged as Hollywood's hottest, most imaginative young producer. There was no doubt he had a Midas touch. I stared at him admiringly as he chatted with stars on the red carpet and spoke with reporters after the awards. He handled the attention with graceful appreciation. I could not have been prouder.

But my smile was pretend. As I did press in preparation for my upcoming album, I knew I wasn't telling the truth when reporters focused even more on my looks. Each time they asked about my transformation from the cute, chubby Go-Go to the glamorous pop siren with the chic, skinny body and long, red hair, I felt my skin crawl. I gave them the answer they wanted, but the truth was different.

Privately, my eating disorder had a stranglehold on me. I was either a good girl or a bad girl. I would go five days in a row where I was a "good girl," eating lettuce leaves with vinegar, a couple vegetables, and not allowing myself anything else. I was always on a severe diet. It was like holding a ball underwater, because I'm not built to be skinny. Then I would wake up starving, "allow" myself a bite of chocolate chip cookie, and immediately spiral into a depression.

As far as I was concerned, at that point my day was ruined. I used it as an excuse to go on a disgusting, all-day binge. All I could think about was food and putting something in my mouth. I would eat until I went

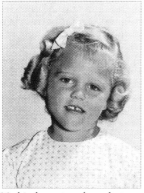
My kindergarten class photo

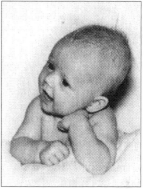
A performer from an early age

After my first big weight loss at age thirteen. I made those shorts!

Matching outfits for Christmas 1968—my very talented mother made them.

Early photo of my mom and Walter "Duke" Kurczeski

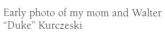

Newbury Park High School fox

My mom made this very chic mini.
(© *Jenny Lens/Cache Agency*)

The big party at Agincourt Road
—I have no idea who the guy is.
(© *Jenny Lens/Cache Agency*)

Passed out—God knows where! (© *Jenny Lens/Cache Agency*)

My infamous trash bag dress
(© *Jenny Lens/Cache Agency*)

Early photo of Lorna Doom (Teresa) and myself.
Note the Dior bag . . . I starved to buy that.
(© *Jenny Lens/Cache Agency*)

The Go-Go's live on stage, possibly at the Starwood (© *Jenny Lens/Cache Agency*)

Early Go-Go's shot with Margot (© *Jenny Lens/Cache Agency*)

An early photo of Morgan and me on a date

The girls and me with Paul Shaffer after appearing on *Letterman*

My mug shot after cutting off my locks. I was in the midst of an identity crisis.

A classic photo of three broads—
Debbie Reynolds, Phyllis Diller, and myself

The incredible Brian
Wilson and myself

Wedding day at Lake Tahoe

Baby shower invitation for the "girl" I was supposedly having

VANITY FAIR

BELINDA'S BABY SHOWER at ·TRUMPS· 1784 melrose ave. 310 855 1480

saturday MARCH 28, 1992 12:15 PM .

GIVEN BY: Andrea and Jeannine

IT'S A GIRL!

F.Y.I. registered at auntie barbara's 310 855 0872 AND nationwide baby 310 204 4104

PLEASE R.S.V.P. BY MARCH 20 th 213 852 0627

see ya there!!!!!!

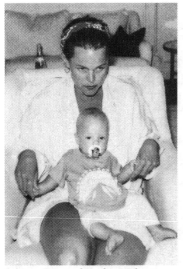

A very suntanned mother and son— photo was taken at Hôtel du Cap, France

The amazing Pamela Mason with Duke and me

Sweet family photo on the beach at Hôtel Belles Rives, Juan les Pins, France

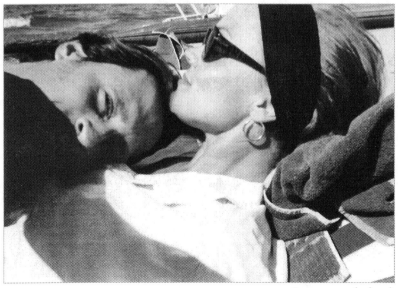

Romance on the beach

Giving offerings at the River Ganges
in Varanasi, India

After all the years of turmoil, we are still a happy family.

to bed, obsessively counting the calories I consumed. Sometimes I got up to five or six thousand in one day.

If I didn't punish myself, I picked fights with Morgan. I wasn't any good at feeling happy. I attended Overeaters Anonymous meetings and called my sponsor every day to tell her what I planned to eat the next day. But those calls made me feel like my food obsession got worse, not better. All I thought about was what I was going to eat.

I found reasons OA wasn't for me. First I didn't like the people, and then I said I couldn't connect with my sponsor. Obviously I wasn't ready to make it work. As with any twelve-step program, you have to invest in the system and work the steps, and I didn't. I wasn't willing to acknowledge the first step: admitting I was powerless over my problem and my life was unmanageable.

I thought I was managing.

In September, "Leave a Light On" came out and was a hit everywhere in the world except the U.S., where it failed to crack the top 10, an indication that times and the music-buying public's taste had changed. When *Runaway Horses* hit the stores a month later, it opened well overseas but struggled here at home, needing six months to creep its way to a very disappointing peak of 37.

Although I put on a positive face for the press, I was deeply hurt by the album's failure to live up to expectations. In many ways, it was my favorite collection of songs. Morgan counseled me to work at the things I could influence and let go of everything else. I tried. Some days I managed. Other days I was filled with anxiety and struggled with all of my issues.

On the bright side, I crossed paths with Gina one day. After a fun catch-up, the two of us on a whim arranged for a reunion with the other Go-Go's. Without telling anyone, we met for dinner at an Italian restaurant in West Hollywood. It was the first time the five of us had been together since Jane left and our subsequent breakup. All of us were nervous. Jane held up her palms and said, "They're sweaty!"

We agreed to one ground rule: none of us would say anything that would piss off someone else. Then we had a great time. We reminisced about the crazy times we'd had in the early days, offered apologies for things said in the latter days, worked through some hard feelings, and, as we told a local reporter who got wind of the reunion, we realized "even the bad times we've gone through didn't seem so bad."

I left dinner appreciating the special camaraderie the five of us shared—and that it had survived. But all was not rosy. As I later confessed to Morgan, I felt uncomfortable about having a successful solo career when some of the other girls were struggling in their endeavors. While Jane and Charlotte were both working on albums, Gina's label had dropped her and Kathy didn't have a deal.

I realized everyone might benefit from a Go-Go's reunion. I mentioned it to my manager, Danny Goldberg, who had a lengthy background as a political activist. A former *Village Voice* journalist, he had coproduced and codirected the 1980 documentary *No Nukes* and was involved with the ACLU, all in addition to managing Bonnie Raitt, Rickie Lee Jones, and other artists.

He loved the idea of a Go-Go's reunion. But it sat a few months until Danny found the right event, a fund-raiser Jane Fonda was spearheading for California's environmental ballot initiative. It sounded good to me. I called the girls. Everyone was game.

In January 1990, we announced our reunion show at a press conference with Jane Fonda. Two and a half months later, we got together for rehearsals at SIR, where I was also in rehearsals for my *Runaway Horses* tour. I felt self-conscious running back and forth between rehearsals and maybe some resentment from the other girls, who I sensed—and it could have been me being overly sensitive—looked at me as Miss High and Mighty with her rock band, getting ready for her world tour. At the end of the day, I was left feeling like I should apologize.

But I was able to set that aside and enjoy stepping back into the Go-Go's. It wasn't hard for me to switch gears. The band was part of my DNA. On March 27, we played a surprise warm-up show as the KLAMMS at the Whisky, a stage that was like a second home in our punk days. We still looked like an odd collection: Jane wore short-shorts, Kathy was in a polka-dot negligee, Charlotte radiated laid-back L.A. rock chic in a long, embroidered shirt, Gina had on her trademark jeans and T-shirt, and I was in a fancy black gown that a girlfriend of mine laughingly said made me look like I had dressed to go to Harry's Bar in London.

The fun we had carried over into the next night at the Universal Amphitheater when we performed a set of the band's hits to a crowd of L.A. politicos and celebrities that included Jodie Foster, Rob Lowe, John McEnroe and Tatum O'Neal, and Sandra Bernhard. Afterward, all of us were agreeable to doing more shows and maybe even a tour later in the year when IRS released a greatest-hits package.

There was one downside. Obviously I didn't tell anyone about my eating issues, but I felt a clutch of anxiety when I read the reviews of our one-off and saw that all of them talked about my weight. The *Los Angeles Times,* while noting my "untouchable supermodel look," said I had formerly been "the most roly-poly and tomboyish-looking member," and the *Orange County Register* called me "the Oprah Winfrey of pop," a reference to my up-and-down weight.

If I wasn't obsessing about my weight, others were.

I should've known I was going to get in trouble. Shortly after the May kickoff of my world tour in the UK, I was in my hotel reading through the latest press clippings. I came across a recent review that described me as looking like a singing secretary onstage. He had taken exception to the Chanel-inspired suits I'd had custom-made for the tour. I took offense, but in retrospect he was right.

I looked like shit. I was way too skinny, wore too much makeup, my bobbed hair was wrong, and the suits—well, they were a different issue. They reflected the trouble I'd had at the outset deciding on a look for the tour. If you have to think too much about those things, it's a sign of confusion and uncertainty—and that was me.

One thing I wasn't confused about was my birth father. He had started writing me letters again before I left home and continued sending entreaties through my management after I started my tour. I had spoken to him a few times on the phone out of the guilt I still felt from having not seen him on my *Heaven* tour, but I had no intention of letting him back in my life at the level he wanted.

I also found something slightly creepy about the way he professed such strong affection for me in his letters. How can you love someone you don't know?

Finally, I came straight out and told him that I didn't want to have a relationship with him. Considering how much I had adored him as a little girl, I agonized about sending him that message. He responded by sending me letters saying that I was going to burn in hell unless I found forgiveness in my heart. I ignored him, hoping and praying he would go away—and he did for a while.

Morgan was such a rock. So were my friends Jeannine and Jack and my makeup artist Pearlie Whirly, who kept me company on the tour. But I struggled to keep my emotions in check. Although still coke-free, I was drinking more. I also started keeping a secret stash of pills, including Valium, Halcion, and Rohypnol. I never thought I might be traveling back down the road to addiction. As long as I wasn't doing coke, I thought I was fine, no big deal.

And it wasn't, I suppose, until I had to perform a promotional show on the same bill as Beach Boys' genius Brian Wilson in Ibiza, an island off Spain. I had never been to this Mediterranean playground, but I knew of its reputation as a decadent, party-hearty getaway for the rich, something that was confirmed when I spotted director Roman Polanski with a pretty young girl at the baggage claim. I thought, Perfect, this is my kind of place.

On the way to the hotel, I got my friends Jeannine and Pearlie to promise we were going to be healthy, jog and hike, lay out in the sun, eat right, and get plenty of sleep. By night, though, I was whooping it up at the giant nightclub Amnesia and enjoying my first time doing ecstasy. It seemed like everyone was on it.

We hit all the big ecstasy clubs, including a party in the middle of nowhere—it seemed like a desert—where I watched columns of drag queens go-go dancing. It was a magnificent spectacle. I was both stunned and drawn straight into the unfolding circus. I had never experienced such a night. The whole place was like a Fellini movie. Suddenly, I was drinking tumblers of vodka, smoking cigarettes, dancing, not just listening to but absorbing the music, and having the time of my life. On E, I loved everyone I met.

At one of the clubs, someone offered me a hit of coke. I did it without thinking; my response was automatic. Right after, though, I knew I shouldn't have done it. I thought, Uh-oh.

I hadn't done coke in four years. But that one hit triggered a reaction straight out of the drug addict's textbook. I went on a binge and came out of the last club in the morning. Awash in hot sunlight, I said to myself, "I'm a disaster. This is fucked."

I had yet to call home to check in with Morgan. I sat in the back of a cab and rehearsed what I was going to say to Morgan. *Hi, honey, it's me. How are you?* I tried different inflections. I was panicked about how I was going to sound. At the hotel, I got out of the cab and walked straight into Brian Wilson and his twenty-four-hour therapist, Dr. Eugene Landy. I tried to act normal as I said hello, but I wasn't fooling anyone. My hair was twisted and gross, my lipstick was blue, and I was covered in filth. Dr. Landy knew what was going on. He also knew Morgan, which made me fear he might call him. I was fucked.

I went up to my room and paced back and forth with my cigarette, trying to come down from the coke and rehearsing what I was going to say. Finally, I called Morgan and said I had woken up early and was going to the beach for a jog. He believed me.

On hanging up, though, I was hit with a one-two of shame and guilt for lying to him and for what I had done. Ibiza wasn't good for me. The place was full of temptation. I wanted to get out of there. I performed that night and let some local friends take me out to a club. But this time I didn't drink or do anything, including enjoy myself. In the morning, I caught the first available plane out of there.

I felt like I would've died in Ibiza if I had stayed any longer. I didn't want to do coke ever again.

But soon it was like I had never stopped.

eighteen

EMOTIONAL HIGHWAY

SINCE THE TALES of drug abuse and acrimony had already been told at least in part in the press, the Go-Go's two-month reunion tour in November and December 1990 gave us a chance to focus on the thing that mattered most: the impressive collection of music we had put together before calling it quits six years earlier. With a new greatest-hits package that included a snappy remix of "Cool Jerk," plus a video featuring the five of us looking like a million bucks, everyone agreed we could make a point about our contributions to the eighties. If we also made a profit, no one would complain.

More important, having already come to terms on past disagreements, we felt like we could get along, and for the most part we did. We preceded a kickoff appearance on David Letterman's late-night talk show with a heavy-duty shopping spree in New York City that reminded me of the fun we used to have together. Onstage, I had a blast singing the old songs and looking to either side and seeing Gina and Kathy in sync and watching Jane and Charlotte trade riffs.

Occasionally the old jealousies reared their head. The girls didn't like it when we pulled up to one venue and the marquee read "Belinda Carlisle and the Go-Go's." Several hotels also gave me a larger room than the others even after we made sure to tell them everyone in the band was equal. I even forced a couple of the girls to see my room before they checked into theirs so they knew I wasn't creating the problem. After a few more times, though, I got fed up with the carping and complaining and had a Neely O'Hara–type moment when I snapped, "I can't help it if I'm a bigger star than you!"

Needless to say, my outburst didn't go over well. But everyone had moments when they cracked, and we got over them.

Barbs from the press directed at me were harder to ignore. I knew it was part of being the lead singer, that when you stand out front you put yourself in line for the most attention and criticism. But reviewers seemed to use me for target practice, like the *Chicago Tribune*'s guy, who worked up an excuse to call me the group's only nonwriter and intimated that I had reunited with the band because my "hits finally dried up." Never mind that he had his facts wrong. What was the point of being hurtful?

Ironically, I kept myself on the road as much as possible. Without consciously realizing it, I was running from my life. In mid-December, though, the Go-Go's tour ended and I returned home, which meant either facing hard truths about my behavior or lying to Morgan.

I chose the latter. I didn't want him to know that drugs had crept back into my life—a life where the stakes had risen and I had much to lose. Morgan and I had a beautiful home, a glamorous social life, and a genuine friendship. Morgan also wanted to start a family. He looked forward to being a father. But having helped raise my brothers and sisters, I didn't share his enthusiasm about dealing with a baby. I'd been there and done that. I liked my freedom.

Our talks on the subject resulted in an agreement that we wouldn't purposely try to have a child but we wouldn't try to prevent it from happening either. I was grateful to reach a compromise. The last thing I wanted was to confess the real reason I wasn't as enthusiastic as Morgan about starting a family—that I was back on drugs. How could I take care of a baby when I wasn't able to take care of myself?

After New Year's, I began working with Rick again on my fourth solo album, *Live Your Life Be Free*. Unlike with my earlier solo albums, I wasn't able to focus. I was distracted by my secret coke binges.

As hard as I tried to keep Morgan from finding out, he eventually caught on. He busted me a couple times. Not in the act, but I was high. Angry and upset, he pleaded with me to stop. He wanted to know why I was back on coke. With all I had going for me, why? I didn't have an answer. Crying, I promised to stop. I swore "never again," and I meant it from the bottom of my heart. But deep down I knew I couldn't keep that promise. I wasn't ready to admit I was an addict, but I knew I was powerless.

After many tear-filled confrontations, I chose a different tack. I decided I wasn't going to keep it a secret from him. The lies were tearing me apart, and I feared it was having the same effect on us. So I told Morgan almost everything. If I was at the studio all day or night, I adopted a "don't ask, don't tell" policy. But if we went out and I had the opportunity or inclination to buy, I would tell him that I was getting half a gram. Sometimes he objected. Other times he looked the other way. And still other times he couldn't contain his disgust or fear.

He was frightened that I was getting back into the habit again. But I insisted that I had things under control.

"No, no, no," I said. "I'm fine."

After the problems with *Runaway Horses,* I went into the making of *Live Your Life Be Free* feeling like it wouldn't receive much support from the record company in the U.S. Rick was more optimistic. He was always more positive and forward-looking, a trait that infuses his songwriting. However, between changing times and tastes, the public's fascination with newer artists, record company politics, and my own personal issues, I sensed that my career was on the downslide.

Good songs failed to excite me. I felt like the songs "Live Your Life Be Free" and "Half the World" were as good as any I had put on a solo album, but I didn't think they would be enough this time around. It brought up my fears of being an imposter and undeserving of my life. I was terrified the clock would strike midnight, my designer clothes would turn into rags, and I'd end up a bag lady on the streets.

Morgan's reassurances helped. But periodically I found myself thinking about other career moves or saying to myself, "You can always go back to hairdressing or stenography."

The one option that didn't cross my mind was motherhood. I should have thought harder. In early September, while in London at a photo session for the *Daily Mail,* I found out that I was pregnant. Thinking there might be a reason I was waking up nauseous, I bought a home pregnancy test the night before the shoot and took the test in my hotel room. It came back positive. What was a joyous occasion for most women, learning they had a new life growing inside them, caused my world to come crashing down.

I had known for a while there was a possibility I could get pregnant. But the reality was different. Part of me was excited for what it would mean to Morgan, and part of me was horrified. I had a lot of mother issues that needed to be addressed. I feared that my life as I knew it, at almost thirty-three years old, was about to end. I also had a terrible concern, one that I knew I eventually had to tell my doctor.

After a long cry, I pulled myself together and called Morgan at home with the good news. He was ecstatic. I sounded like everything was wonderful, too. It was easy for me to put on a smiley face. I was genuinely happy for Morgan and thought I would grow to feel the same way. At the moment, though, all I felt was nauseous. I had a rough bout of morning sickness—which went on through my promotional tour of Europe and Scandinavia, as well as the next four months. I vomited every morning. I was either sick or hungry all day long. There were no in-betweens.

As soon as I got back home, I went to the doctor to address another, deeper concern. Prior to learning I was pregnant, I had binged on coke and done ecstasy. Unable to hold back the tears, I confessed everything to the doctor, explaining that I had drank and done drugs during the earliest weeks of my pregnancy and I was terribly frightened about possible damage I might have inflicted on the baby.

He told me not to worry because the placenta wasn't developed yet and the baby would be fine if I quit immediately. I told him that I already had. He gave me a stern, sober look.

"Tell me the truth. You aren't still using cocaine or other drugs, are you?" he asked.

"No."

"When did you stop?"

"I haven't done anything since right before I took the pregnancy test," I said.

As he got my file off the counter, he saw a pack of cigarettes in my purse.

"You're smoking cigarettes?" he asked.

"Yes," I said.

"Stop."

I nodded. "I will."

And I did.

At the end of September, MCA released "Live Your Life Be Free" as the first single off my fourth album of the same title, which came out a month later. Both stiffed in the U.S., as I had anticipated. I blamed a lack of support from my record company, conveniently ignoring my own contributions. Yet others noticed. *The Boston Globe* called the album "emotionally vapid" and said that I merely "went through the motions," and a January 1992 *Rolling Stone* review said my "biggest shortcoming" was "my failure to impart any real feeling to the words" I sang.

Such criticism pissed me off, but deep down I knew they had a point, and in fact, years later, when I was able to take an honest and uncompromising look back at my efforts, I not only agreed but understood why. I had numbed myself with drugs until I found out I was pregnant. But even then, I found ways to stay disconnected. It took me sixteen years to admit this, but I had a glass of wine every day throughout my pregnancy. I knew it was unhealthy, but that's the degree to which my addiction affected my judgment.

I was open about my drinking, too. But it didn't win me any fans. At a party, actress Marilu Henner, a well-known health fanatic who wrote several bestselling books on the subject, came up to me and rather bluntly let me know that I shouldn't have been drinking while I was pregnant. I knew she was right, but I didn't want to be told what I should and shouldn't do.

I needed my relief. I gave up my workouts, let my trainer go, and allowed myself freedom to eat and gain weight guilt-free. To satisfy my craving for sour things, I carried a bottle of vinegar with me and poured it over everything. I gained weight steadily, like twelve pounds every three weeks. And I continued to feel sick. The nausea I thought was morning sickness never passed. I was due at the end of June, and I would stare at the calendar, counting the days.

On days when I wasn't bemoaning the imminent change to my life, I indulged my curiosity about the miracle occurring inside me, what sort of person fate would have me create. If the baby was a boy, Morgan and I decided to name him James Duke, after his father and my stepdad, Walt, whose nickname was Duke. We couldn't settle on a girl's name, but given a choice I saw myself with a daughter. I wouldn't have wanted an independent troublemaker like me, but I saw myself being able to relate better to a girl. I could take her shopping and dress her up.

I was thrilled when my doctor read my latest ultrasound and informed me that I was having a girl. I had a thematically appropriate baby shower at Morton's restaurant, at which Morgan's mother, Pamela, and his sister, Portland, represented old Hollywood, and Roseanne Barr made sure everyone knew the new, brash show-business crowd was also present. A smartly dressed black guy crashed the party, but he passed himself off as a friend with such charm and aplomb that Pamela and Porty began inviting him to their own parties at the big house on Pamela Drive.

They were shocked when we informed them that he wasn't a friend. All of us had a good laugh. We had an even bigger laugh a few weeks later when another ultrasound showed that the baby was actually a boy, not the girl for whom I now had a stockpile of pink baby clothes.

But my smile was short-lived. Soon after the shower, my mom expressed concern at the way I looked. I was about six and a half months along, and she had come to visit. I'll never forget the expression on her face as she stared at me. It was as if she was looking at something no one else could see.

"Is something wrong?" I asked.

"I don't think you have a good doctor," she said.

"What?"

It was such an odd thing to say out of the blue. I didn't understand. She stepped closer and put the back of her hand against my skin.

"Something about you doesn't look right," she said. "Have you been to see your doctor?"

"Yes," I said. "I go regularly."

"Then I think you need a new doctor," she said. "You look like you're sick."

"What do you mean?" I asked.

She took hold of my hands and looked at them as if she was a palm reader. Like the rest of me, my fingers were fat. I hadn't noticed anything unusual up to that point. But now that I looked along with her, they did have an abnormal, sausage-like tumescence. My face was the same way: large, but without definition. As she said, I didn't look right.

I saw my OB, who confirmed my mom's intuition. I was diagnosed with severe toxemia, a serious disorder that my doctor referred to as preeclampsia, a condition defined by high blood pressure and elevated levels of protein in the urine. I also suffered from other symptoms, including headaches, abdominal pains, and nausea. He sent me to bed with strict orders to stay there.

I stayed in bed, ordered in Italian food, and watched *The People's Court* and *Sally Jessy Raphael*. I never had a day when I felt pretty or like I glowed, as some women do when they're pregnant. I had a big pumpkin face and looked distorted and grotesque.

After slightly more than three weeks in bed I came down with what I thought was the flu, except it felt stranger than the flu. It was a Sunday and I had a doctor's appointment the next day, but I told Morgan that I was going to cancel until the bug passed and then go in. He advised against it, and thankfully I listened to him. My doctor discovered that I didn't have any more amniotic fluid and sent me directly to Cedars Sinai Medical Center for an emergency C-section.

I was hungry, and on the way to the hospital I stopped for a burrito, figuring it would be my last fattening meal. The nurse checking me in saw me holding the half-eaten burrito and, with a look of disbelief, asked, "What are you doing?"

"Eating," I said.

"Don't you know you aren't supposed to be eating before surgery?"

"No," I said.

By the time I was ushered into a private room, Morgan arrived from his William Morris office. I was given an epidural and taken to surgery.

A short time later, my son, James Duke Mason, announced his arrival in this world with a slight cry. Little Dukey, as we called him, was immediately whisked off into the arms of specialists while I was taken into the recovery room. Doped up on morphine from the surgery, I sailed off into la-la land. As I came out of it, I sat in bed and read the *National Enquirer,* the *Star,* and the *Globe* as if everything was fine.

But it was definitely not fine. Unlike the other babies delivered at Cedars on April 27, 1992, Duke was three weeks early and weighed a mere three pounds, thirteen ounces. He was jaundiced and suffering from a virus, probably the same one that I'd had a few days earlier. Morgan had the unpleasant job of calling all the relatives with the good news but tempering it with an asterisk. It was a scary time.

Late that day, a doctor appeared at my bedside and confronted me about my drug use. Cold, unsympathetic, and aggressive, he ran through a list of drugs from coke and pot to pills and heroin, asking me if I took them during my pregnancy. Each time I answered no, he looked at me and asked, "Are you sure?"

I insisted I was sure, absolutely sure, until it was painful. I felt like I was getting beaten up even though I knew I didn't have anything more than a daily glass of wine throughout my pregnancy. I didn't know if I was going to get arrested, have my baby taken away, or what. I answered his questions; he didn't respond to mine. Once he left, though, I never saw him again.

But I couldn't relax. I had the TV on as I recovered in bed, and it was full of nonstop news reports about the four police officers on trial in Simi Valley for the beating of Rodney King a year earlier. It wasn't like I wanted to hear the same story over and over, but I was hooked by reports that made it seem like the city was a powder keg ready to explode if the verdict came back in favor of the police. It was like a weather report predicting sunny today, Armageddon tomorrow.

Sure enough, the next day, April 29, I was watching TV when the local news broke in with a special live report that the four LAPD officers had been acquitted. Within minutes, or so it seemed, riots erupted across the city. Like millions of people across L.A., I watched coverage of four black men pull white truck driver Reginald Denny out of his cab and beat him senseless. I was glued to the set as stores were looted, cars were overturned, and fires broke out.

I told Morgan to look out my hospital room window. From our perch, we could see black smoke less than a mile away from the hospital. As time went on, we were able to smell the smoke. It went on for days. The National Guard was finally called in to stop the violence and restore order. Seeing tanks and armed soldiers patrolling in front of hamburger stands and shopping malls I'd been to was surreal—and terrifying.

On May 1, Rodney King went in front of the media and made his now famous request, "Can we all get along?" By then there had been 53 deaths, more than 2,500 injuries, and more than 7,000 fires. People were aghast, outraged, and frightened by what they saw happening to the city.

Morgan and I were profoundly affected. We had the same reaction: we had to get out of L.A.

In the meantime, I was out of la-la land and worried about my baby. No one gave me a straight story, at least not one that I could understand. I didn't like the look on Morgan's mother's face when she came into my room after seeing Duke. I saw the fright in her eyes. I saw the same thing in his sister's, too. It was only after three or four days that my doctor finally met my repeated questions with more optimistic responses. Even then, I felt he was being vague.

When I got clearance to go back home, I didn't want to leave unless I could take Duke. But he wasn't ready. The doctor wanted to keep him until he had gained another two pounds—which ended up taking three weeks. I went back and forth between home and Cedars numerous times a day, taking him freshly pumped breast milk and holding him in my arms so he could feel the warmth of his mother.

I was diligent until I was able to bring him home, and then I relied on a trained baby nurse. Soon I began to have trouble pumping my milk and eventually I gave it up in favor of formula and a wonderful nanny.

Was it a coincidence? No. Just as I never felt pretty while pregnant, I didn't have the bonding experience that most mothers have with their newborns. It wasn't postpartum depression; no, at the very beginning, his fragile state frightened me. I wasn't as confident in myself as I needed to be in that situation. Beyond that, I was, I think, in a prolonged state of shock and denial about being a mother as well as an addict and had a host of other issues that kept me on the run from myself.

So while I was loving and nurturing when I was around Duke, I wasn't as available as I should have been—or as I wish I had been. In other words, I could have done better.

On the other hand, Duke thrived. With the help of our nanny, he gained weight and progressed quickly. Morgan was also a sensational dad. Despite my shortcomings and fears, things worked out. I got tips from other mothers and read the basic new-mom books to fill in the gaps. I was a vegetarian then, so when it came time to add solid foods to Duke's diet, I asked my more experienced friends for advice and found out it was okay to raise him as a vegetarian, too.

My pediatrician disagreed. But then he generally didn't offer the support I needed. Neither did his staff. In fact, they were all so horrible that I hated going there. When I told him that I wanted to raise Duke as a vegetarian, he took a step back as if I had absolutely no sense and in a scolding tone of voice said, "No, Belinda, you can't do that. Did you see how small he was? He's playing catch-up. If you raise him as a vegetarian, he'll never be a football player."

I immediately thought of my experience with Mike Marshall and said to myself, "Good. I don't want to raise a jock." Truth be told, I didn't want my pediatrician any longer either. After double-checking with my friends who were raising healthy children on a vegetarian diet, I took Duke to a new doctor. At the beginning of that first appointment, he asked why I was in his office when I already had a highly regarded doctor. I explained the situation. By the end, I was in tears.

He then took me into his confidence and said, "I could get in a lot of trouble for telling you this, but your pediatrician called when I requested your file, and warned me that you had been doing cocaine throughout your pregnancy."

I turned white as a sheet with both outrage and humiliation. I looked down at Duke, who was cradled in my arms. Yes, he had been born early, sick, and small. But you wouldn't have known that from looking at him then. The doctor let Duke squeeze his finger and looked at me.

"I can see he's not a cocaine baby," he said.

I wanted to explain.

"I haven't done—" I stopped, unsure what to say. I decided on the truth. "I had a cocaine problem," I said. "But I didn't—"

"You don't have to say anything," he interrupted.

"Ask me," I said. "I may not have always told the truth in the past, but I will tell you anything where my son is concerned."

I switched doctors, and a short time later a story appeared in one of the English tabloids that I had done cocaine throughout my pregnancy. The newspaper cited unnamed sources at the hospital. I suspected my old pediatrician as the source. Who else could it have been? Almost four months had passed since I had given birth. I was livid. I wanted to sue. Morgan urged me to ignore it and calm down.

"Let it go," he said. "We know the truth. We have to move on."

nineteen

BIG SCARY ANIMAL

WHEN MORGAN'S MOTHER, Pamela, threw Duke his first birthday party, I was already in the process of trying to go back to work. It was a juggling act familiar to other mothers. My days were full. I played with Duke, helped organize his day with the nanny, planned most meals, and made sure our six dogs felt like they received attention, too. We may have lived in a multimillion-dollar home, but inside it was filled with toys and the chaos of busy lives. Outside, there was dog poop that needed to be cleaned.

"Where's the glamorous life?" I laughed one day when I was talking on the phone to Charlotte, who was a few months away from her marriage to Redd Kross guitarist Steven McDonald and mulling whether her future would include children. "I have to watch where I step or I'll ruin another pair of shoes."

I could have said the same about my career. It was in an even more perilous state than a walk through my backyard at night. After *Live Your Life Be Free* flopped, my label dropped me. Most people thought I was cut after I had a run-in with MCA president Al Teller. Not true. I had already been tossed in the trash before I spotted him one night before an Arc Angels show at the Roxy, holding court at a table of executives.

He had no idea a storm was about to blow in. But I knew. Emboldened by a couple of margaritas, I strutted across the club until I was looking down at the thinning hair atop his round pate.

"If it isn't Al Teller," I said. "Well, fuck you."

Then I unloaded all my frustrations at the duplicitous way I thought the label had treated me on my previous effort, assuring me that they were behind my record in the U.S. but leaving me out to dry as the singles failed to chart. I understood the business—just don't tell me one thing and do another.

"You're a fucking liar!"

Left to shop for a new deal, I signed with Virgin America. Cochairmen Jeff Ayeroff and Jordan Harris were excited to have me on the label. They were veteran music guys, ages forty-six and thirty-eight respectively, and they had three albums at or heading toward the top of the charts when I began work on my album. Buoyed by their enthusiasm, I felt like I had another chance at resuscitating my career.

Drug-free and present, I focused on making the album. I rolled up my sleeves and went to work on every aspect of the project. I worked closely on the songs with Charlotte, her brother Tom Caffey, and Ralph Shuckett, who was married to Ellen Shipley and had as a keyboardist played with a long list of music luminaries, including Carole King, Lou Reed, and Todd Rundgren. I had credits on half the songs. I felt like an artist as opposed to the puppet I'd felt like so many times in the past.

It was my first time being in the studio as a producer, and I found that I enjoyed showing up every day, working with the musicians as they laid tracks, and making the important creative decisions. I had always known I had more to offer; I had always been lazy or irresponsible. Not this time. I put in long hours. Sometimes I brought Duke into the studio. I found the hard work very satisfying and was quite open about feeling like I needed to prove myself.

For the first time since the earliest days with the Go-Go's, I wasn't abdicating responsibility. Good or bad, my signature was going on this piece of work. Sometimes I wondered if it was motherhood that was causing me to mature. I fell into a good, productive rhythm—and a creative one.

Real became a metaphor or mantra as well as a title. Musically, I wanted a sound that was stripped down and organic, a change from the previous effort especially. It was also one of the first albums to use a loop, predating Alanis Morissette's phenomenal 1995 megaselling album *Jagged Little Pill*. Charlotte, Ralph, and I were listening to a loop of music one day, trying to come up with a concept for it. One of us asked, "What is love?" Another answered, "A big scary animal." The first single, "Big Scary Animal," was thus born. One of my favorite songs on the album, "Too Much Water," was written at Charlotte's house, where we sat around in the afternoon and worked on melodies.

She's an amazing writer, and I appreciated that ability even more this time around since I was more involved in the writing process. I brought in a few melodies. I wished it had been more. I frequently heard amazing tunes in my head, but unless I immediately sang them into a tape recorder, which I rarely had with me, I wouldn't be able to capture the magic. It made me wish I played an instrument.

I was pleased with the record. I remember having a good listen to "Big Scary Animal," "Too Much Water," "Tell Me," and "Lay Down Your Arms" and feeling very satisfied with that collection of songs, like I had accomplished something good. As on other recent solo albums, I wanted the cover photo to reflect my mood at that point in time. I wore a white, long-sleeve T-shirt and jeans, and looked natural.

Real was released at the end of September 1993. I told reporters it was a frank look inside relationships, particularly the dark side. Reviews were mixed, with some refusing to acknowledge any artistic growth beyond the Go-Go's while others understood what I was going for, including one reviewer who wrote, "Will somebody please tell me who her shrink is?"

Not only did I find that funny, I appreciated that someone took the time to think about what I was trying to say.

Commercially, *Real* followed the same pattern as my other solo albums. It charted in the top 10 in the UK and a handful of other European countries, and then lost steam. Here in the U.S. it was a disappointment out of the box after, unfortunately, getting caught up in label politics. A month before *Real*'s release, Jeff and Jordan, the two executives who had signed me, resigned amid rumors of conflict in the boardroom. Industry veteran Phil Quartararo replaced them as chief executive, but insiders said the real power at the label was wielded by Nancy Berry, the wife of Virgin's global chairman, Ken Berry, and I heard she didn't like me or my album.

True or not, I didn't get the support the guys who signed me would have provided and my record died. And so did my deal.

Maybe it was for the best—even fated. Although severely disappointed and frustrated, I felt like I had my eyes open. Of course, it occurred as the result of a shock. And Morgan played his usual calm, clear, and wise role in getting me to see that life wasn't determined or defined by hit singles, radio play, and chart position. When I focused, I saw that he was absolutely right.

It didn't mean that I wasn't wounded, but I saw how fortunate I was. I only had to look at my family. My parents worked extremely hard, my dad in construction and my mom as a waitress at Café California in the Broadway department store. My brother Butch, two years younger than me, worked in construction. My sister Hope became an RN and aspired to get a master's and teach—which she went on to do. The others were still growing up.

I can't say my notoriety helped any of them. For some of them, in fact, it may have created unnecessary pressure as they developed their own identities.

My mom didn't feel more pressure, per se, not the way my younger brothers and sisters often did, but she was frequently introduced as "Belinda Carlisle's mother." People didn't realize that negated her own individuality—or they didn't care. One day a woman came up to her, complimented her on giving birth to such a talented daughter, and said it wasn't a surprise since she'd heard that my mother had worked on Broadway. My mom good-naturedly corrected the mistake, explaining she had worked *at* the Broadway *department store*. At that, the other woman turned and walked away.

"I guess she was disappointed that I'm a waitress," my mom later told me. "I wasn't good enough for her to talk to anymore."

I helped my parents out when possible and gave them gifts and vacations, but the reality was—and remains—that no matter what anyone's advantages or obstacles in life, each of us must make our own way and come to our own peace. I was constantly at war with myself over such matters, sometimes consciously, other times not.

Morgan and I frequently spoke about our lives, whether we were headed in the right direction, how we wanted to live, and where we wanted to live—which was a major theme with us following the riots. We had many discussions about this with our friend Deepak Chopra, the bestselling author, physician, and truly wise man. Morgan was working with him on projects, and we had dinner with Deepak and his lovely wife, Rita. You can't find better counsel.

In the beginning, though, I was intimidated around Deepak. I was also skeptical. I didn't trust people who talked about meditation, spirituality, and the mind-body connection. Basically I was ignorant and insecure. I didn't know any better.

At the same time, Deepak was utterly fascinating and obviously a man with great insight and wisdom. Morgan knew how to access that gift. As a result, we had intimate and probing dialogues about finding your gifts and experiencing joy—the joy in the meaning of your life. I was inherently negative, albeit with an adventurous side, but Deepak was a very optimistic man. He thought we should move and change our lives if that was what we felt was right when we looked deep inside ourselves.

"And if it doesn't work out? What's the worst that can happen?" he asked. "You move back. It's not that big of a deal. You just start over."

In early January 1994, Morgan, Duke, and I traveled to Cabo San Lucas for a brief post-holiday vacation. On the beach and away from home, we were able to assess our lives with a new perspective. We talked about Deepak, and I underscored how both of us were feeling when I quoted Helen Keller: "Life is an adventure or it's nothing."

Morgan agreed. We were still young, both of us in our mid-thirties, and yet it felt like we had been through so much separately and together. We kept asking each other, "What next?"

I knew what I didn't want. Earlier that summer, Morgan and I had attended a dinner celebrating William Morris chairman Norman Brokaw's fiftieth anniversary at the agency (he had started in 1943 as the very first mailroom employee). On the beach at Cabo, I flashed back on that night and thought, Oh my God, is that my future? I told Morgan that I didn't want that life. I didn't care about status in Hollywood, a big house in Brentwood, membership at the right country club, or driving a Mercedes or a Range Rover.

"That's not what life is about," I said. "That's not my adventure."

"I feel the same way," he said.

So we sat on the beach and talked, and we agreed that it would be such a shame not to have an adventure, not to take a risk if we could afford it. We were young and healthy. We were hooked on the movies *To Catch a Thief* and *Breathless*, director Jean-Luc Godard's influential French new wave film about a crook on the run in France. We kept watching them over and over, each time feeling the ache for our own adventure. More relevant, I read Calvin Tomkins's enchanting book *Living Well Is the Best Revenge,* the almost unbelievable story of Gerald and Sara Murphy, an American couple who moved to the South of France in the 1920s and befriended Picasso, Ernest Hemingway, and other great artists and writers. F. Scott Fitzgerald patterned Dick and Nicole Diver of *Tender Is the Night* after them.

I had Morgan read the book and he adopted my South of France fantasy, too. The two of us, though bourgeois on the outside, thought like bohemians. I could see us chucking everything familiar like the Murphys. How exciting! Much more so than the predictable life I saw unfolding if we stayed where we were.

"Wouldn't it be amazing to have a life like that?" I said.

"Let's do it," Morgan replied.

My jaw nearly hit the ground. What? Morgan was serious. For the next few days, we sat on the beach with Duke and tried to figure out where to move. Australia was too far, we decided, and Mexico was too close. We mentioned a dozen spots, but none sounded right. The last place we brought up was the one that both of us knew was the only place we could possibly move—the South of France.

It was obvious. We had spent a week talking, reading, watching movies, and fantasizing about it. Maybe we had purposely avoided it out of fear that the other one would say "Yeah, let's do it," which was what happened. As soon as we mentioned France, I thought, Okay, that's it. I said something to that effect, too. And Morgan agreed.

He then did something that to this day remains one of the most romantic, risky, and amazing things I have ever seen in my life: He went downstairs—there were no phones in the room—to the phone booth off the lobby and motioned for me to step inside while he called William Morris and gave his notice.

I was in shock. So were our friends, who tracked us down at the hotel as word of Morgan's resignation spread through the agency and then across town. "What do you mean you're leaving?" they said, freaked out. "You can't do that!" But we *had* done it—well, Morgan had. But I was ready to go, too. It was a movie-type moment, an unexpected plot twist in our lives. Most people fantasize about packing up and moving into a new life, but they don't do it. We were taking the leap.

Or so we said. Other than Morgan quitting his job, obviously a huge step, we didn't make any specific plans or set a time line.

We flew back from Mexico on Sunday, January 16, 1994. On Monday morning, I woke up just before four thirty A.M. I heard our Jack Russell terrier barking under the window. Annoyed, I got out of bed and put on my robe to let him out and see what had caught his attention. Suddenly, everything began to shake—the floor, the roof, the walls. It was violent, loud, and completely disorienting. My first instinct was to think, Oh my God, the house is exploding; a second later, I realized that it was an earthquake. It felt like the proverbial *big one* that I, like every other Southern California resident, had been warned would one day hit. Here it was—or so I thought.

Morgan woke up and tried to pull me into bed. I shook him off and ran down the hallway to get Duke. My mother instinct took over. With adrenaline racing through me, I wanted to get my baby.

The shaking from this quake, which turned out to have a magnitude of 6.7 and was centered in Northridge near where I grew up, seemed to last for a minute or two. Actually, it felt interminable. It turned out to be only twenty seconds. But those twenty seconds changed life across the southland. Some seventy-two people died as a result of the powerful upheaval, more than nine thousand were injured, and damage was eventually estimated at $20 billion.

At first, we stood outside like everyone else, nervous, on edge, wondering about the state of our family, friends, and the city itself. It was still dark and eerily quiet. We saw occasional flashes of light in the distant sky where transformers were bursting with loud pops and blasts of white flame. After a little bit, we went back inside. Our power was out, but we listened to the news on the transistor radio we had in our emergency earthquake kit. We were shocked at reports of collapsed freeways and hospital patients being wheeled out of buildings and into the safety of outdoor parking lots.

Like many in L.A., I freaked out at aftershocks, which continued throughout the day and for days afterward. When your house shakes and the ground rumbles, you don't feel safe. Nothing does.

Later that night, after things began to calm down and we had checked in with our loved ones, all of whom were okay, Morgan and I looked at each other with a sense of having already prepared for this moment on the beach in Cabo. He had quit his job. My career was happening only in Europe. We had agreed to restart our lives in the South of France. Our only outstanding question had been when—when would we go?

The Northridge earthquake made that decision for us. It was like a push out the door. We said to each other, "Okay, we're out of here."

twenty

LAY DOWN YOUR ARMS

THE EARTHQUAKE HIT on a Monday. We left on Friday. We would have gone sooner except that we had to get a visa for our Filipina nanny.

Once in the South of France, we checked into the small La Colombe d'Or Hotel in Saint Paul de Vence, Provence. It was a dreamy place to stay as we set about looking for a house, like a French fantasy. Situated up in the hills with picture-book views, the hotel's stone walls dated back to the 1600s. There were only twenty-six guest rooms. The dining room boasted artwork by Picasso, Klee, Calder, and Dufy, all of whom had stopped at this chic outpost early in their careers when they had little or no money and traded paintings for room and board.

After a couple weeks, we found a house in Cap d'Antibes and returned to Los Angeles to pack our belongings, take care of loose ends, and put our house up for sale. Financially, we couldn't have picked a worse time for this dramatic change, especially selling our house. The real estate market had bottomed out, and we had poured a ton of money into renovations over the years. My business manager warned me we were never going to recoup our investment. His voice was among the loudest in the chorus of our friends and associates who said, "Just stay. Take your time. There's no need to rush."

Morgan and I didn't care. We wanted to get out of there. We were following our instincts. We weren't concerned about conventional wisdom. If the house didn't sell, we'd leave it empty and figure out what to do with it later, which was what happened.

In the meantime, before leaving, I made an appointment with my hairdresser Art Luna and asked him to cut off my long, red hair.

"Really?" he asked.

"Cut it," I said, thinking of everything else I was cutting, too. "I want it an inch long."

In March, we returned to France. With our nanny in tow, we piled into a black stretch limo with about eight duffel bags bursting at the seams and set out for the airport. Everything else we had was boxed up, shipped by boat, and expected to arrive six months later. We returned to Le Colombe d'Or, where Duke ran up and down the halls and Morgan and I found ourselves having afternoon cocktails and playing boules with actor Yves Montand.

A few weeks later, our house was ready. We had rented a beautiful pink villa in Cap d'Antibes. It had a guesthouse in back and a large, rolling lawn. The famous Hotel du Cap was down the street. It could not have been more gorgeous or glamorous. Every day I expected to see Noël Coward or Zelda Fitzgerald cross the lawn on their way into the house. I couldn't believe that we lived there.

A month later, my sister Hope brought our menagerie of dogs from Los Angeles. I had a good laugh seeing her with all those doggie crates at the Nice airport. It wasn't the way she had imagined arriving in the South of France. I loved seeing my pets again, though the reunion was frustratingly brief and then they were quarantined for a month. Since our furniture wasn't scheduled to arrive for four more months, we sat in lawn chairs and used boxes as tables. The humor of roughing it in a beautiful home wore thin pretty quickly.

The reality of life there was a trying adjustment. Everything closed for three hours each afternoon, including the local supermarket. The French lessons I had taken were no use, and no one in the area spoke English—or if they did, they didn't want to speak it around me. The French people can be nice and helpful, but back then I found them surly and difficult. Shopkeepers scoffed at my bad French. We had housekeepers who didn't want to work. Then four of our six dogs died suddenly from various causes—poisoning, old age, hit by a car, and a dog fight.

I finally had a meltdown one day when I couldn't figure out how to use the washing machine and couldn't find anyone to help. I pulled at my hair, then covered my eyes as if to wish myself away, and then slowly crumbled to the ground and cried.

Ugh. I figured we had made a terrible mistake. We were supposed to be living our fantasy. But this was crazy.

Homesick, we returned to Los Angeles and stayed with Morgan's mother for several weeks. We celebrated Duke's second birthday there. I saw friends and family, went to a few meetings, and came to my senses. I didn't need to sever all ties to life in L.A. I didn't need to go to such an extreme. I realized that life abroad could be more manageable if I knew I could return to L.A. every so often for business or a fix of friends.

I had reason to come back. In the fall, IRS was planning to release a special collection of old Go-Go's material. Though Miles had the right to put out a boxed set of our material, the idea of him gathering our B-sides, rarities, and outtakes, along with the hits, without our input, upset all of us girls. Miles may have owned the songs legally, but they were our lives. We couldn't just let him open the vaults without being there. Or could we?

We talked about our options. As we saw it, we had three—fight him and lose, ignore him, or get involved and try to add some new luster to the old gems. We chose the last, and the end result was that we decided to write and record some new songs and make our reunion permanent.

The idea of getting back together, as far-fetched as it might have sounded a couple years earlier, felt strangely right. Timing is everything. The five of us were having fun together. Why not?

Personally, I wanted to have a reason to return to Los Angeles. When I was there, as became my routine starting that summer, I slipped back into party mode without Morgan knowing, and without the day-to-day responsibility or guilt of being a mom. I thought of it as a vacation from my life. Without hurting the two people I loved, I could be naughty—and I was.

Work was good. To prepare for *Return to the Valley of the Go-Go's,* I listened to tons of old tapes and soaked up the memories of an era that bright, fun, and full of youthful enthusiasm. I knew not everything had been golden, but there was a spark and spirit on those tapes that was magic and couldn't ever be duplicated. In the studio, Jane and Charlotte were in reflective moods; Charlotte was pregnant and looked wonderful, Jane was mellow and mature.

I was the only one who didn't appear to have grown up and learned the requisite lessons from past mistakes. Instead I was still making the same old mistakes. Charlotte may have had my behavior in mind one day in the studio when she and Jane sat back and reflected on the disappointments of our second and third albums, saying each of us had been responsible in some way for various problems.

I knew that I hadn't been much of a presence on those albums because I was partying too much, and in retrospect I wished I had been there to help write and offer my opinions. I said as much to Jane and Charlotte without admitting that I had slipped into the same pattern of behavior a decade later. I couldn't face the truth. It would have been too painful.

I had a hard enough time leaving home. I flew to Los Angeles so often that Duke said, "Mama lives at the airport." I cried when I heard him say that. I felt incredible guilt for the way I treated my family, and even more shame for the secrets I kept from them. And yet it didn't stop me.

In November, I blocked out the sadness in lieu of celebrating the release of the 36-song, two-CD boxed set and a new Go-Go's tour, albeit a relatively short one. Since Charlotte was close to her due date, we enlisted Vicki Peterson from the Bangles to substitute on lead guitar, and she did a fantastic job. She fit right in, starting with gigs at the Coach House and the Troubadour.

Music was very different in the mid-nineties, with flannel-shirt-wearing rockers popularizing a grungy rock that spoke to kids the way punk had once been our salvation. However, the *Los Angeles Times* still found merit in our live shows and said the Go-Go's "made a persuasive, celebratory case for their curious mix of punky drive and bittersweet pop confection."

By the time we finished a six-night stint at Las Vegas's MGM Grand hotel and played New York's Academy Theater, I'm sure my partying left Vicki surprised and shocked. I was pretty messed up when we did two weeks of Christmas-themed acoustic dates, and I slipped even further when we traveled to the UK for dates in February. In London, I went on an all-night coke binge prior to our appearance on the iconic morning show *The Big Breakfast,* and I showed up at the studio sweating and unable to string together two sentences.

Embarrassed and frightened, I broke down afterward to Kathy and Charlotte and for the first time confessed that I had a problem. They were sympathetic and consoling, but they were also honest. They said they couldn't do anything to help me until I was ready to help myself.

"Are you ready to help yourself?" Kathy asked.

"I don't know," I said.

"Then you aren't ready," she said.

What was it about being on the road that made the five of us have such trouble getting along? I didn't know. But we had once again broken down into bitter factions by the time we played the O2 Shepherd's Bush Empire in London at the end of February. We were barely able to get onstage together for the two nights. Drugs were usually the biggest problem, plus egos, and this time there were also squabbles about royalties. A critic noted that onstage I was "detached from the others, swearing and bitching." Lovely, right? It was a perfect storm of problems, and we left England saying the Go-Go's were done forever.

Jane was furious with everyone—and rightfully so. She felt we were a great band, with new songs that were excellent and not being given their due because of problems that were a decade old, and thus boring and pathetic. She flat out said we were blowing a big opportunity.

She put us on notice, saying that this time she wasn't the only one walking away from the band. The rest of us were screwing up. She may have looked directly at me when she said that. I didn't know for sure.

Nor did I care. The band's reunion had been an excuse for me to run away from home and indulge my addiction without sneaking around, but following the O2 Shepherd's Bush Empire debacle I gave up and went home, telling myself that I was going resume normal life, whatever that was. But how normal was life when I found myself at a party talking to Sarah Ferguson, the Duchess of York, who suggested we get together?

Deep down I was still a Valley girl. I had a hard time reconciling that anyone connected with the British royal family wanted to socialize with me, but Fergie and I got together. She was renting a house in the South of France. Her marriage to Prince Andrew was over in every way other than an official divorce, but that was coming. In the meantime, from what I could see, she was really struggling to make a life for herself. In a way, I understood.

We had lunch several times, and Fergie impressed me as a nice, funny woman who seemed lonely. We were a pair. She was lonely, and I was lost, and there we were, reaching out to each other, though she did much more reaching than me. I was surprised, in fact, by how much she opened up to me, a relative stranger in her life, but it revealed how desperate she was for someone to talk to about Andrew and the press, her life as a royal, and various other intimacies she shared about the Queen Mother, Prince Charles, and even Princess Diana. Basically, I was amazed by what and how much she told me.

As I said, she barely knew me. If she was telling me that stuff, she must not have had anyone else in whom she could safely confide. I knew what that was like, to keep secrets and not feel like you could talk to anyone.

One day I invited Fergie to go to the beach with Morgan and me, which she thought would be great fun. I remember her lighting up at the thought of a relaxing day on the water. I had the same thought. As she had to do, she sent her secret service to scout the area and somehow word leaked, as seemed to always happen around her. When we got to the beach the next day, the water was full of paparazzi in motorboats. We went water-skiing and had a blast. However, as we walked back to the beach from the boat, Fergie shook her head at the way we were grouped. She stopped and told Morgan to move into the front and me to stand closer to her.

"The tabloids," she explained. "They'll get the pictures, crop you out, and distort the photos to make it seem like I'm with Morgan."

We listened to her, though I didn't understand and even thought she was being a tad extreme if not paranoid or alarmist. But a few days later I was at the Nice airport, on my way to Los Angeles, when I stopped at the newsstand and saw the new *Voici* magazine. There was a small picture of Fergie on the cover and mention of her new love. I was both surprised and curious since she hadn't said anything to me. From what she had told me, the opposite was true.

I bought the magazine and opened it up on the plane. Luckily I was wearing my seat belt. Inside, there was a photo of Fergie and Morgan, who was identified as her new boyfriend, along with an accompanying story about how she had rubbed sunscreen on his back. The funny part was, even though I knew every word was false, I found myself getting jealous—and even asking myself, "Is he her new love?"

Morgan didn't have a new love. He was busy producing movies and working on projects. But I worried if only because for the first time in our married life we were seriously out of sync. After I returned from Los Angeles, we hit a new low point when he found my secret stash of pharmaceuticals and confronted me about them. Instead of admitting I had a problem, I blew up at him for invading my privacy and then went out and started another stash. I was an ass.

Morgan tried to get through to me. Perhaps he had no idea of my behavior on the road, though chances are he did and overlooked it because he didn't know what to do.

I wanted him to do *something*. I think I wanted to push to the point where he would leave, where he would have no choice but to walk out, just as my father had done when I was five years old. Then I would be able to say that all the men I loved in my life left me. And then I would be miserable—as miserable as I felt. Or else I wanted him to bring the hammer down on me. He didn't do either.

I was left to flounder. As expected, my record label dropped me. I was confused to say the least. I didn't know whether I wanted to continue in music or leave the business. If I had been happier living in France, I probably would have chosen to put my career on hold. I don't know what I would have done. I would have made a good gypsy, though no gypsies traveled the countryside in the comfort to which I was accustomed. Of course, if I had been happier in France, I wouldn't have felt the constant need to run away from my marriage and my child.

Actually, France wasn't the problem either. I saw the problem every day in the mirror. No matter how fast or far I ran, I couldn't get away from it.

twenty-one

HOW MUCH MORE

WITH WOMEN, hair can often reflect the way they feel about them-selves, and so it was with me in early summer 1995.

I was opening for Rod Stewart in Europe and playing festivals. It was a convenient way to keep my solo career alive without much effort and an even more convenient way to avoid problems at home. I had a solid set of songs, and my shows were well received, but every time I looked at myself in the mirror I hated my short cut. I wanted to go back to long, red hair. I tried extensions, but they looked awful.

I told people that I wanted *my* hair.

But that wasn't really the story. What I wanted but couldn't say was a better, happier me.

I had no idea what to do or how to even start when I returned home from touring exhausted, confused, and depressed. I figured I was done when Miles Copeland came to see me. The South of France was a long way to come for lunch, even from his home in England, but Miles wasn't just showing up to spend the afternoon catching up. Unbeknownst to me, he had a plan.

The funny thing was that I couldn't remember if Miles was furious with me and the Go-Go's or if I was on the outs with him. I realized it didn't matter. He was someone who was always going to be in my life as a mentor, a protector, an antagonist, maybe a plaintiff, and ultimately a friend. We sat down in the living room, and for a long while I stared out the window as he caught me up on various projects with which he was involved. My mind was elsewhere when he asked about me.

I snapped out of my reverie and told him that I wasn't sure I wanted to stay in music. My tour had gone well, I said, but I wasn't feeling it. I could've added that I wasn't feeling *anything,* but that would have been too much information—too much for me to have revealed.

Miles focused his glacier blue eyes on me as if I was missing something obvious.

"You aren't going to leave music," he said. "You're an artist. I want you to make another album."

"Then you're the only one," I said. "No labels want me."

I couldn't have felt any sorrier for myself. And Miles, as crazy and fierce as he can be, couldn't have been kinder.

"I want you to make an album," he said.

"I'm flattered," I said. "But I don't have any plans. I don't see any options for me."

"I'll figure it out," he said.

And he did. I signed with Chrysalis Records in the UK and Miles's own Ark21 label in the United States. Later that year, I began working with Rick Nowels in Los Angeles on what would become *A Woman and a Man*. For some reason I still didn't understand, Miles didn't like Rick. He had expressed that opinion when I made my second album, *Heaven on Earth*, and he hadn't changed his mind. It may have cost us a hit.

One day Rick played me "Falling into You," a song that he had written with Billy Steinberg and Argentinean singer-writer Marie Claire D'Ubaldo, who recorded it on her 1994 album. I loved it on my first listen. I had the same feeling I did when Rick and Ellen Shipley had played me "Heaven Is a Place on Earth." It was beautiful.

We recorded a demo and played it for Miles, who thought it was terrible. I'm pretty sure that he said, "This is shit." After a heated debate, I quit insisting it be put on the album. It was the first time I had ever gone against my instincts when they were speaking that loudly to me, and I was heartbroken. Many months later, I was filling up my car at a gas station in France and I heard a familiar song coming from the speaker near the pumps. I realized it was "Falling into You." Celine Dion was singing it, and my heart sank.

I looked into it and found out that Celine had heard the demo with my voice on it and said yes to the song. Of course, it ended up being the title track of her mega-smash 1996 album, *Falling into You,* which won two Grammys, sold more than thirty million copies, and spent more than a year in the top 10.

In the meantime, Miles installed David Tickle as my producer. David, who had worked with Split Enz and engineered for U2 and Prince, was also a very talented man. He had a studio in Malibu, which appealed to me for obvious reasons. But I relinquished too much control over the crucial elements that commit an artist to an album, starting with the songs. Basically, I checked my instincts at the door. I didn't fight when the record company insisted on using two songs from Roxette's Per Gessle that may not have been perfect for me. Nor did I point out that Rick, whom the executives didn't want to produce me, wrote or cowrote five of the album's eleven cuts, including "In Too Deep," "Love in the Key of C," and "California." Why not go all the way with his vision?

There were some magical moments, though. We asked Brian Wilson to provide background vocals on "California." As a lifelong Beach Boys fan, I was amazed, thrilled, and honored when he said yes. I greeted him at the studio when he and his assistant David Leaf arrived and introduced them to David, Rick, and everyone else who was there to meet the legend. You could feel the excitement in the studio. Everyone there was accomplished, but Brian was one of the extraordinary geniuses of pop music.

Our excitement, however, quickly turned to discomfort. A few weeks earlier, Brian had been given a cassette tape with my vocals. He had used that to come up with his part. As he stood in front of David, Rick, and me and half-explained and half-sang what he intended to do, we traded secret worried glances with one another. It sounded awful. We huddled afterward and talked about our problem. We were going to have to tell Brian that we weren't going to be able to use his part.

"How awful is that?" I said.

"How's he going to take it?" David asked.

I volunteered to tell him. But I didn't do a good job. I went back into the studio and hemmed and hawed, and then lost both my nerve and train of thought as Brian began to burp and fart up whatever he had eaten earlier in the day. Epitomizing the disheveled, scattered genius, he was oblivious to the noises coming out of him. Before I burst into laughter, I gave up and said we were almost ready for him.

Moments later, we watched and listened in complete and utter awe of this man's inexplicable gifts. He went in the booth, cued the track, and between burps and farts began to layer in his vocals. It was achingly beautiful, like a Santa Ana wind lifting my voice, and it made this plaintive, semiautobiographical song with a dark Mamas-and-Papas undertone come alive.

All of us sat at the soundboard and looked at one another incredulously as Brian sang. We didn't speak. What could we say?

I was crying when Brian finished. During the playback, my tears kept coming. I felt like we had watched Mozart at work. It was a privileged experience. To this day, I get chills when I hear that song and think about Brian in that booth.

If only the album itself had lived up to that same standard. I didn't have focus, and the album lacked the same. I think when all was said and sung, I was more into the idea of being in Malibu than making an album.

One morning at the end of June, days before the release of the new album's first single, "In Too Deep," I was at home and making breakfast for Morgan, Duke, and my friend and sometime assistant Jack when I heard a tap-tap-tap on a window. Our kitchen windows in Cap d'Antibes were extra large to let in big shafts of soft morning light. Except on this particular day the sky was gray and dull. I saw a little black bird with yellow eyes tapping on the thick glass.

It was strange. I wondered what it was trying to do. It wasn't a cute bird either. Its beady little eyes gave it a frantic look. It seemed like it was determined to get inside the house. Morgan was reading the paper at the table. He hadn't noticed the bird.

"Come take a look at this," I said.

He got up and saw the bird continuing to tap away. He put his face closer to the window; the bird didn't seem to notice or care.

"It's not a cute bird, is it?" he said.

"No."

"Don't let it in," he said.

My friend Jack hurried over and looked, too. He was horrified and freaked out, claiming it was an omen. It was as if I was twelve years old again and browsing through books on black magic. I was intrigued. I quickly got a handful of millet we had in the closet, put it on the shelf, and opened the window. Before Morgan or Jack could react, the bird flew in the house and fluttered in the kitchen, its yellow eyes pointed directly at my husband. A second later, the bird flew back out. Unnerved, Morgan begged to know why I had let the bird in.

"That was not a good sign," he said. "Now something bad is going to happen."

The very next day, June 29, we received a call informing us that Morgan's mother, Pamela, had died at home in Beverly Hills. She was eighty years old. The official cause of death was heart disease. As far as I was concerned, though, she had died from too many parties and too much fun. She was a remarkable, one-of-a-kind woman.

Eerily, Morgan's sister, Portland, said that in the hours before Pamela had passed away, a black bird had tried to fly into her bedroom window. Porty said she had made eye contact with the bird, which, according to her description, sounded exactly like the one we had seen at our window. She said it had looked creepy. She hadn't let it in.

"It finally just flew into the window and dropped dead right outside the glass," she said.

About a year later, Morgan and I were at a party with Rupert Sheldrake, a noted British biologist who did research on morphic resonance—or the mysterious way different organisms, including birds, communicate telepathically. We told him our story about the black bird. He brought out a large encyclopedia of birds and showed us a picture of a black bird.

"Was that the one you saw?" he asked.

We said yes.

"The jackdaw!" he said. "It's a favorite throughout folklore—and most commonly a bird of ill omen."

And so it was with us. I was unable to accompany Morgan when he went to Los Angeles to help his sister deal with Pamela's affairs. The first single off my album was about to come out and I had a full calendar of promotion lined up. With my career seeming to be on the line, and the record company, though sympathetic to our loss, letting me know they were counting on me, I couldn't cancel. I felt awful about not being able to be with Morgan during this difficult personal time, and yet, sadly, it was typical of the trouble we were having connecting with each other.

Just two days after Morgan left, I was running through the Nice airport, catching a plane for London, where I was launching my PR campaign with an in-studio radio interview. I was feeling pretty good and had even gone water-skiing with a friend the day before. But that afternoon, right before I did the interview, I began to feel odd. I described it to a friend as tingly. My right arm hurt and I felt like something was wrong.

During the interview, I got worse and took myself straight to the hospital as soon as I was finished. Tests came back negative and the doctor assumed I had slept on my arm wrong. I returned to the hotel and woke up the next morning with my arm swollen and purple. My fingers were also discolored and the size of small cigars. Alarmed, I hurried back to the hospital and this time was diagnosed with a double thrombosis, or blood clots, in my armpit and forearm.

I was immediately set up in a room, given blood thinners, and told not to move while doctors waited for the clots to dissolve. I was told the condition was extremely dangerous. If one of the clots were to break off, I could die instantly. The nurse said she had never seen a case this severe.

I spent twelve fretful, boring, frustrating days in the hospital before getting the okay to go home. By then I had canceled numerous promotional dates and missed an important window. Although "In Too Deep" cracked the top 10 in the UK, as did the second single, "Always Breaking My Heart," the album itself, after being released at the end of September, got as high as number 12 in England and then began a downward spiral that eventually made it the worst-selling record of my career.

In November and December, I opened for Tina Turner on her relatively brief trek across the UK. While she was a dynamo onstage, I was not at my best. A writer for *The Independent* was dead-on when he noted, "[Carlisle] seemed unsure of why she had accepted the job." Later in the piece, he described me as "stiff and disengaged." He was absolutely right.

I had always defined myself by what I did. Now I was completely and utterly lost.

I told Morgan that I was fed up with France and insisted on moving to London. He agreed, in part because he loved that city but mostly because he desperately wanted to appease me. He knew that I was floundering, but as a former agent and natural diplomat he was more about negotiating settlements than delivering ultimatums. In hindsight, he should have come down hard on me.

I had purposely never sought a drug dealer in the South of France. I knew it would be over for me if I had one there. I wouldn't have been able to control my addiction, and in that small, cloistered world, Morgan would have quickly found out about my secret life of getting high and behaving inappropriately. In London, all the temptations were right in front of me. It was a recipe for disaster.

twenty-two

A L W A Y S   B R E A K I N G   M Y   H E A R T

WE MOVED INTO a beautiful, three-story Victorian flat across from Hampstead Heath, better known as the Heath, a 790-acre respite from urban life featuring endless parkland with forests, ponds, and hills from which you could see across London. Boy George lived behind us, actors Jeremy Irons and Emma Thompson were nearby, Nick Mason of Pink Floyd was next door, and Tracey Thorn from Everything but the Girl was down the street.

I was obsessed with the talented female singer. I loved her voice, but I was equally if not more intrigued by her quirky personality. After finding out she was in the neighborhood, I became a borderline stalker. I found excuses to walk past her house and peek through the Venetian blinds. I saw Tracy's partner, but never her. I hope she never saw me.

London was party central. I hung out with the Pet Shop Boys and a group of gay friends with whom I hit the clubs. Different clubs were hot every night of the week, and I was at most of them. I would roll into bed late at night—actually, early in the morning—and pretend to be asleep, knowing that Morgan would wake up or at least open an eye to check on me. He would usually see through my charade and fume, "I can't believe this. I can't believe this is happening."

We seemed to hit a streak of bad luck all around. On Christmas Eve, we were in Los Angeles visiting family and friends when we got a call informing us that our flat had caught fire. It didn't burn down completely, but the damage was pretty severe (I lost most of my clothing, some furniture, and some photos)—and whatever didn't burn was tinged with soot and smoke. I heard that Boy George had watched the conflagration from his bathroom.

Whatever. I was glad we weren't there. The fire had started in the clothes dryer and spread to Duke's room. I shuddered at the thought of what could have been if we had been home. I didn't want to go back and deal with it. Neither did Morgan. We surrendered ourselves to the fact that it wasn't good and there was nothing we could do to fix it. So we kept our holiday plans and continued on to Mexico.

Why not? If the fire was another omen, we didn't want to face it.

When we returned to London after New Year's, we sifted through the damage. Strangely, in spite of the losses, I wasn't upset. Our dogs had been boarded; they were safe. My pet parrot gave me the biggest scare. Though he was in the fire, he had survived, somewhat miraculously, by imitating our winter coughs, as he was wont to do. The firefighters heard him, thought it was a human, and saved him.

We sublet a small mews house owned by Richard Burton's daughter Kate. It was somewhat coincidental since Burton had lived in Morgan's parents' Hollywood home before hitting it big.

A few months later, Miles finally released *A Woman and a Man* in the U.S. and I returned to the U.S. to do promotion. Nearly a year had passed since the album had come out in Europe and Asia. I didn't have much enthusiasm for its prospects—or for anything else. I turned thirty-nine years old and didn't like the feel of where I was in my life. And it came out. In interviews, I was lackluster at best and blatantly negative when I was being honest.

"I can't wait to get out of here," I told a Knight Ridder reporter who met me in Beverly Hills. "I don't like it here anymore." I mentioned that I had grown up less than forty-five minutes away. "There's a lost innocence here," I mused with a faraway look, "and I think it's sad."

Without realizing it, I was talking about myself. Radio host Howard Stern all but drooled on me as he said, "Goddamn, you held up well. Too many women just sour. You must be happy." I rolled my eyes and shrugged. "Happy? Yeah." A few weeks later, I sat with another reporter, a woman who seemed to see straight into my troubled soul. Before she asked the first question, I had the sense she knew too much about me without even knowing me. She had that look, X-ray eyes that saw every wound.

Indeed, she wrote a piece that described me as a lost and trouble-filled woman nearing forty years old and drifting like a boat that had come unmoored during a storm and was floating aimlessly on a gray sea. I was angry when I saw the story. I felt betrayed. I had been exposed—but not enough to stop my self-destruction.

Back in London, I was barely able to manage my addiction. The worst was when I took Duke, then five and a half years old, to school and snorted coke in the kids' bathroom. I knew I was in a nightmare as I towered above the fixtures meant for children and got high. But I couldn't stop. I had to do a line before I walked home; I couldn't deal otherwise.

I remember having to sit in the Heath and come down before I could pick my son up from school. What was I doing?

Morgan was afraid. I saw it in his eyes and wary approach to me. I don't know why—I certainly didn't understand it then—but he loved me. I've asked him numerous times why he didn't leave. He explained that he could always see the beautiful person underneath all the pain, and he couldn't let go of her.

I heard that and cried. It still makes me tear up.

I wish that I had been able to appreciate everything I had going for me. I wish that I had been able to see the things that Morgan saw in me. But I was too cut off. I was incapable of giving or receiving love. Sometimes I knew it. Other times I only knew that I was in pain. I had no idea how I had gotten to that point.

It wasn't where I had imagined myself. I was about to turn forty, a difficult passage in time for any woman and even harder when you feel like you're at a dead end. I spent a good amount of time reflecting on where I had been and where I was going and decided I didn't have a clue. It was sad.

Encouraged by Morgan, I began seeing a therapist. It was apparent that I needed professional help in dealing with my demons and sadness.

My therapist was a woman with a momlike demeanor. When she asked why I was there, I told her that I felt like my baggage was too heavy to carry around anymore. Then I burst into tears, crying, "I just can't do it. I'm cracking under the weight."

I saw her several times a week, but I didn't care enough to make it work. It was like when I had cried to Charlotte, Kathy, and Gina on the last Go-Go's tour, before we imploded, that I was in trouble and they responded that they couldn't do anything until I was ready to help myself. This was the same thing. I was still incapable of being honest with myself or anyone else around me.

In my sessions with her I would conveniently leave out information. I was afraid of what I would find if I opened up.

Nonetheless, it was a start. I inched forward a little more when I read *The Celestine Prophecy*, James Redfield's New Age adventure novel about a man's spiritual awakening as he searches for the secrets contained in an ancient book in Peru. It was filled with an easy-to-understand blend of Eastern and New Age thought that underscored my sense that there was something more to life—and I was missing it.

I took another step forward a few weeks before my fortieth birthday. I went with a group of friends for a three-day weekend to a secret place on the west coast of Ireland, where we hooked up with a promoter who did a lot of work in Dublin. Essentially, he was a rich hippie who lived in an old farmhouse on 160 acres of lush ground. He moved with the unhurried deliberateness of someone who was either stoned or into life's more spiritual and sacred side.

I thought it was the latter.

It may have been both.

He led special, exclusive mushroom walks across his property and the neighboring landscape. I'd heard they were like therapy sessions: medicinal, healing, and spiritual. That's why I had gone there with my friends.

Our walk began with all of us sitting in a circle as our guide led us in what he described as a sacred ceremony. He spoke to us about the profound insights and connections we would likely experience as we went into the world of mushrooms. We breathed deeply and meditated to calm and clear ourselves. I had the feeling of being in an outdoor temple. Then we drank some mushroom tea, stuffed our backpacks with fruit and nuts and water, and took off for the day.

I had no idea what to expect as we hiked up into the hills. Pretty soon, as I took in the scenery, I lost track of time. I felt a rumble in my stomach, a wave of nausea sweep over me, and then all of a sudden—or maybe it wasn't all of a sudden—I saw everything around me pulsate and breathe. It was as if the trees were alive. I sat down next to one, caressed its trunk, and purred, "I love you, tree."

I felt like it loved me back, even talked to me. I'm not exaggerating; that tree and all the others spoke.

All of nature came alive as we went deeper into the forest and came upon streams, climbed hills, stared at lakes, and slid down heather-covered slopes on our butts. Looking up through the canopy of branches and leaves, I saw the clouds as giant crystals in a velveteen blanket of blue.

A couple times we stopped to eat fruit and nuts and have some more tea when we needed to top off. I saw nature in an altered state, one I couldn't possibly have seen unless I was in this different dimension. At one point, I laid down next to a giant mushroom I found growing beside a log. As I reached out to feel it, the mushroom shouted, "Don't touch me."

Both of us recoiled.

"Okay, I won't touch you," I said.

Afterward, we went back to the house and discussed the trip. It was dark outside. We had been gone for more than twelve hours. The thoughts, insights, and reflections people shared about the day took a very intimate yet philosophical and almost holy tone. There was also a surreal element to many of the observations that people shared. I was comforted to know that I wasn't the only one who had seen trees breathe and flowers pulsate.

People had experienced a range of visions and revelations. But the takeaway was fairly uniform—namely there were many more dimensions to life than we allowed ourselves to see, and not seeing them caused us to squander so much potential. I could attest to that.

Such insights were easier said and thought than put into practice, but I spent the rest of the weekend thinking, and wondering, about these things and how to incorporate them in my life, and how to change. Indeed, change was a big, scary word to me. I thought about it often, but avoided it like the plague, and yet in the aftermath of that hike I wanted change more than ever.

But while change might start with an aha moment, like the Big Bang, it's a process that happens slowly, and incrementally, over time. It's about evolution, not revolution. The Go-Go's were a perfect example. It may have started with three girls sitting on a curb in Venice agreeing to start a band, but it took years of hard work before it happened.

And so it was with me. At some point I began picking up books about spirituality including the Dalai Lama's primer *The Art of Happiness: A Handbook for Living,* which had a profound effect on me after I read it. I don't remember how I actually ended up coming upon it, but I have a theory about books. I think they find you; you don't find them. In any event, *The Art of Happiness* made me realize that I'd ignored the spiritual side of my life, something I had been thinking about since my trip to Ireland.

It wasn't the only thing I'd been thinking about. The fact that I was turning forty hung over me like a dark cloud. The dark cloud metaphor is a terrible cliché, but so is getting depressed about turning forty. I hated that I was upset about something that was completely unavoidable and much better than the alternative, but I didn't like it one bit. And I liked it even less when, on the day before my actual birthday, an executive from my record label called and said they were dropping me. I felt bad for having let Miles down. I knew I hadn't committed myself to the work. But the timing sucked.

On my birthday, I felt exactly as I had feared—old and washed up. All I wanted to do was get through the day. I did allow myself a nice dinner with Morgan and Duke, who was six and a half and more concerned about me than I ever considered. Many years later, he confessed that he felt like he had an almost sixth sense that caused him to worry about me even though he didn't know what he was worrying about.

Hearing that cut to the quick, though I don't know what I would have said if my son had sat at my birthday dinner and asked me if I was all right or, God forbid, something more direct. I'm sure I would have lied. Why not? I lied to Morgan and myself.

As was often the case, instead of being forced to take constructive action, I was provided with an out through work. In this case, producers Ted and Amanda Demme approached Jane, Charlotte, and me about turning the Go-Go's story into a movie. The Go-Go's were still getting over some serious infighting stemming from Gina's 1997 lawsuit against Charlotte for unpaid royalties. The suit had settled out of court, but bad feelings had lingered until the movie forced us to patch up that and other problems.

Thank goodness for email, I quipped to *Rolling Stone*. We could "air all of our crap" without seeing one another. It was a joke, but was true.

The five us of got together to talk about the movie, and we enjoyed working on an outline with Ted and Amanda. As was usually the case, we laughed and cringed as we dredged up old stories, and in the process we revived bonds that were too strong to die. I envisioned Drew Barrymore or Christina Ricci playing me—girls with curves or, as I said back then, girls with "meat and potatoes." We were realistic about the odds of actually getting our movie made. In the end, it didn't happen.

Meanwhile, Miles heard that we were getting along and suggested the five of us once again reunite for a short tour the following summer. In a big surprise, everyone was game and marked their calendars. Our reunion inspired a writer to remark, "Not since the Who has a band had a harder time sticking to breakup vows."

He was right, but there was a lot of time—and several adventures— to get through before that tour. At home, my friend Amanda organized a holiday outing to Thailand for both of our families. Amanda was a free spirit and out of her mind in a great way. I realized she had an ulterior motive when she suggested the two of us go to Burma for a few days before meeting our families in Thailand.

"Burma?" I asked.

"It's supposed to be spectacular, darling," she said, and then, with a grin, she added, "and quite the dangerous place."

I don't know why, but I agreed to go. Fortunately we never made it there, but when we found ourselves in Thailand ahead of our families we hired a guide and driver to show us around. One day he took us way out into the jungle. Although we were in the middle of nowhere, I noticed we were traveling on roads that were paved and well tended. It was odd given the location. Our guide explained that the drug lords paid for them.

I heard the word "drugs" and perked up.

"Do you know where we can get something?" I asked.

He turned around and looked at me in the backseat.

"What do you want?"

I knew opium was farmed in the Golden Triangle of Burma, Thailand, and Laos and wondered if we could get some. He nodded, made a phone call, and said, "Tomorrow morning at nine." His English wasn't great, but we understood that he was going to take us into the mountains to meet the opium farmers. He advised us to bring candy and pencils for the local children.

We were waiting for him the next morning, though when I saw Amanda in the hotel lobby, I said, "You can't wear Vivienne Westwood high heels into the jungle."

"You don't think so?" she asked.

"Go back up and get some sensible shoes for the outdoors," I said.

A few minutes later, she returned wearing platform sneakers. From my expression, she knew I didn't approve of those either. But my feet were barely any better. I had on Prada sandals.

When we got up into the mountain village, we saw only old people. All the young men and women were working in the fields. After a friendly welcome, we were led into a large hut, an opium den. People were sitting or lying on the ground, puffing on pipes. We went to the center, where I noticed a grandmother nursing an infant. I was instructed to sit next to an ancient-looking woman who smiled at me, revealing a few brown teeth that were completely rotted from betel nut. They looked like dirty cars in a vacant lot. She herself looked like she had been there for years. She offered her pipe. Afraid to decline, I took a deep hit and tried to enjoy the mellow that followed.

Off to my side, Amanda, who had never done drugs, was going through a similar indoctrination. Both of us were trying to decipher lots of chatter we didn't understand. A situation like that can make you paranoid; after a couple hits of opium in a mountain jungle in Thailand, you go into a whole other level of paranoia. I did.

After I bought a small ball-sized chunk of opium, some of the regulars with whom we had been trading pipes, plus our guide and various other people who moved in on us, made it clear they wanted to sample some of our purchase. I was happy to share. But when I turned around to get Amanda's consent, I saw she was lying flat on the ground while some guy rubbed her back. From her dazed eyes, I could tell she had no idea what was going on.

We made it back to our hotel and put the two balls of opium in the hotel safe. That night, we wanted to go out. We accepted our guide's offer to show us around and ended up at a karaoke bar where he met up with a friend. Our guide became too friendly for our comfort. We had no idea where we were in the city's maze of neighborhoods. As our fear grew, Amanda took out her cell phone and called her husband in London. He hung up on her, thinking it was another crazy tale of hers that would turn into a funny story the next day.

We feared there might not be a next day. The guide was behaving inappropriately with us and my survivor instincts went on red alert. Without our guide and his friend hearing, I let Amanda know that we had to get out of there. A few moments later, I screamed, "Run!" and we tore out of the bar. We ran across the parking lot and saw our car and driver. We jumped in just as our guide was racing to grab us. I slammed the car door on his arm and yelled at our driver to go, which he did, leaving our guide and his friend in a cloud of exhaust smoke. It was a scene straight from a movie—except it was real.

Once back at the hotel, I feared our guide, angry, maybe injured, and aware we had opium, was going to show up and perhaps bring friends to rob us and get even for what I did to him at the club. He never did, but we locked ourselves in the room and tried to smoke the opium. I attempted to fashion pipes out of various objects and pieces of fruit, all tricks I'd learned in my early days on the road with the Go-Go's. To my frustration, none of them worked. Then I remembered another bit of useless information I had picked up with the Go-Go's. You could stick opium up your butt and get high as it was absorbed.

Indeed, a while later, I was very high. Poor Amanda, though. She got high *and* suffered terrible diarrhea all night.

A month later, I began 1999 with a three-month acoustic tour across the UK, with stops in Glasgow, Aberdeen, London, Birmingham, Leeds, Cambridge, and Dublin. My fourteen-song set was filled with hits and audience favorites, from the opening number, "In Too Deep," through the encore, "Heaven Is a Place on Earth." But I still found myself peeking out at the crowd beforehand in disbelief that they had come to see me. I was like, Why?

Even on this intimate little tour I went back to my dressing room and did what I had done for so many years before going onstage, and would continue to do for more years to come: I opened up a bottle of wine and drank a glass, sometimes more, and transformed myself into that person who could go onstage and have people looking at her. At this point in my life, I didn't only wonder if I was good enough. I also wondered what they could see.

You'd think that after all these years I would have come to some kind of an understanding with myself. But no, instead of coming to terms with myself, as I had hoped would happen after my mushroom-inspired epiphanies, I was still as insecure and troubled as ever—maybe more so since deep down I was more aware than ever of my failure to get myself together.

I knew a better, happier, saner, and even sober me was out there and available. I just couldn't get to her.

twenty-three

BEHIND THE MUSIC

BY THE END of that tour, Morgan was disgusted with the state of our relationship—and me. As he pointed out, London had too many temptations for me to handle. He hated going to sleep knowing that I was sitting up in the living room, doing coke and blowing cigarette smoke out the window. He was frightened knowing that I often got in my Citroën that was parked in front of the house and drove off in the middle of the night to get more drugs or cigarettes.

"We can't live like this," he said. "It's like we're back to when we first started out."

"I don't know what to say," I said, sobbing, ashamed, and praying silently that the next words out of his mouth weren't going to be about a divorce.

They weren't. We decided to move back to France, where our adventure had begun, and out of the blue we ran into Dave Stewart from the Eurythmics, an old friend of mine, who suggested we use his house in Provence. We weren't sure. He had a rambling villa in the hills between Cannes and St. Tropez. It was very rock star–like, on six gorgeous acres overlooking the Mediterranean with a guesthouse, chicken coops, and even a track for quad racing.

We looked at it and loved it. After making sure we could get our son into the international school there, we accepted Dave's offer. Without us realizing it then, the house may have saved our marriage. It was so large and rambling that it afforded Morgan and me the ability to live in our own wings. If not for that space, we might have split up. But he moved into his half of the house and I moved into mine, and we lived distinctly separate lives.

It was an odd arrangement, but we had never been a conventional couple. He spent a large amount of time in Amsterdam, where he was helping to launch Europe's first New Age cable TV network, the Innergy channel, and I had my occasional meetings in London and Los Angeles, and we went through a period where we rarely knew what the other was doing. However, when we were home at the same time, we had dinner together with Duke and made sure he knew that despite our problems, he had two parents who loved him and were always there for him.

I liked this part of the South of France much better than Cap d'Antibes. But it wasn't without its drawbacks and quirks. For starters, we were half an hour from the nearest grocery store, so I tended to stockpile food and perhaps went a little overboard in that area when I got swept up in some Y2K conspiracy madness. We were also in the middle of nowhere, and old, traditional, ways still applied.

One time, soon after we had moved in, Morgan and I were on our way into town to get supplies, and as we headed out, he had to suddenly jam on the brakes. A band of Gypsies had set up their camp in front of our driveway. They were real Gypsies with wagons full of supplies, horses, chickens, and tents they had pitched at the edge of our property. Several women were doing laundry at the end of our driveway.

"What do I do?" Morgan asked. "Honk? Turn around?"

We turned around and waited a couple of days until they moved. There wasn't much we could do. There were local laws allowing Gypsies to camp wherever they wanted. Our house was off an old Roman road and there were certain ancient ways that were left in place and simply understood as they way things had always been.

It was a small price to pay for living in such an impossibly beautiful place. I knew I could never go back to living in a city full-time.

My friend Amanda was also going through a hard time with her husband, and one day she called full of excitement. She had just returned from Marrakech, where she had a villa, and where, she said, she had met a man who was like a guide to various shamans and practitioners of magic and voodoo. She said he had helped members of Led Zeppelin find the right sorts of mystics in Morocco. He could provide anything, she said.

"I don't know," I said.

"Our husbands," she said. "He can help us find someone who can fix our marriages."

"Amanda, you're nuts."

"Come with me to my villa," she said. "We'll go for a few days. Both of us are going through some things. We'll find someone who can help."

I sighed. "All right."

I met Amanda at her home in Medina. We went out on the town, which was like a nonstop party, with streets filled with vendors and snake charmers and people dancing and singing. I heard music coming from every direction. At night, it was surreal. I had the feeling anything could happen. It was like living on the edge of a matchstick.

While out on the town, we met up with the man who had offered to introduce Amanda to shamans and sorcerers. He took us to a small house and led us inside. There an old man who I guessed was in his eighties came out and the two of them spoke in Arabic. I noticed the walls were filled with photographs of the old man with royal families from all over the Middle East. I had no idea what the two men said to each other, but our guide finally turned to me with a satisfied smile on his face.

"I told him that you are having love problems," he said. "He's going to fix you."

As the old man led me into another room, Amanda went outside again to walk around until it was her turn. Before the creaky front door slammed shut, I heard the old man call out to me to pay attention. He laid me down on a table and started to burn things around me. I tried to look around the room to see what he was doing, but I couldn't move. A fly buzzed right over my face, and I was unable to shoo it away. He had put me in a trance.

When he saw I was frozen, he stood over me, touching different points on my body, checking to see if I was really powerless. Suddenly, as I was looking into his dark eyes, wondering what he was doing to me, he reached up under my skirt and took my underwear off. I thought he was going to rape me. I saw he was aroused. Just then, I heard Amanda at the door, asking, "Darling, are you in there?"

Startled, the old man immediately stepped back from the table. I was able to call out, "Yes, I'm here. Come back here—into the room!" All of a sudden I was able to move. As I sat up, the guy handed me my underwear. Neither of us said anything. The sickest part was that before Amanda and I left, he asked for my phone number, and even though part of my brain said "No, don't do it," I still gave it to him. As I told Amanda outside, I couldn't help myself. He had put some sort of spell on me and I felt like I was in love with him.

At any rate, Amanda and I left with a bunch of potions and instructions on how to use them, which we took back home and tried to put into practice. The whole thing was ridiculous.

However, I did end up with an idea for a new solo album, a pop opera that I called *Once Upon a Time*. It was a girl-meets-boy story modeled after my relationship with Morgan. In it, the main character fell in love and got married, believing that life was a fairy tale. Then she discovered there was no such thing as a fairy tale.

Charlotte helped write the songs and we worked up some excellent ideas until we hit a roadblock at the point where the main character was desperately trying to figure out a way to spare her husband from her own misery. As in real life, I didn't know where to go with the story beyond the fact that I knew the main character wasn't going to leave her marriage. She needed to fix herself.

In both cases, the question was, how?

The work on both the opera and myself was put on hold when the Go-Go's finally set out on the mini summer tour that Miles had organized. We kicked off the road show July 1 with a surprise warm-up at the Viper Room, the Sunset Strip club infamous as Johnny Depp's L.A. hangout and the site where actor River Phoenix had died of a drug overdose in 1993. Though it was the band's first time together in years, our show was a party-hearty frolic that showcased a reborn attitude alongside old hits.

"Why are we back together?" I asked the crowd, which included Sonic Youth's Kim Gordon and Thurston Moore, Exene Cervenka, and L7's Donita Sparks, as we segued into "Cool Jerk." "We're still foxy, but we might need a few nips and tucks before we get too old."

We had decided to have fun this time 'round—and we did. At one point, Jane even lifted her white T-shirt and flashed her boobs. The crowd went wild, and quite a few flashed her back. We were a bunch of forty-year-olds having a girlfest. "Who says women don't age as gracefully as men?" said one reviewer, who added we were foxier and sounded better than in our heyday.

Our tour took us to Seattle, San Francisco, and through a handful of other Western states. I appreciated the girls more than at any other time since the band's earliest days. Gina was no-bullshit and one of the funniest people I had ever known. Jane was a wonderful eccentric whose creativity bubbled out nonstop and made life infinitely more fun and interesting. Charlotte, aside from being a great writer, was a true Libra. She was able to see both sides of an issue and supply the calm, mature, levelheaded voice the rest of us often lacked. Kathy, a superior musician, was the band's most honest-to-goodness rock and roller.

As for me, I could see why I gave the others fits. In true lead singer form, I just wanted to have a good time. At home or on the road, I didn't want to be accountable to anything and the girls let me be, as they always had. While they had busted their butts, I had flitted from party to party, traveled the world, rented stupid cars, bought a racehorse, and done all sorts of dumb things—and still did.

At each stop on the tour, we were asked if we intended to make this reunion permanent. Early on, we didn't know the answer. If we felt good about the shows and ourselves, we didn't see any reason why we wouldn't continue. By the end of the tour, we were already planning a longer, more extensive tour for the following summer and a new album, as well as several projects with VH1, including our own *Behind the Music* episode.

"We'll tell everything," Jane said to reporters. "It'll be sassy and sordid. I don't care if they know everything."

All of us shared that attitude as we were questioned in front of cameras separately and together. During my interview, I admitted to having had a $300-a-day coke habit. But I explained that was in the past. I was now married and a mother and living a serene if not downright dreamy life in the South of France, and being in my forties made me more content with myself and into searching for a more spiritual connection. If only such BS had been true.

On-screen, you could see the real story. I looked like shit in that *Behind the Music* episode. Everything I was doing to myself in private, all the things I didn't admit—the drinking, the pills, the coke, and the late nights—showed up on camera. When we regrouped in October for QVC's breast cancer benefit, I was out of control. I got extremely drunk before the show, which was broadcast live. After the second song, I turned to Gina and asked, "How much more do we have?"

As she told me later, her parents watched in disbelief at home in Baltimore. They were mortified for her when I picked up the set list and said, "I hate this fucking song." Like Gina's parents, viewers heard everything. Apparently I was bleeped constantly. Our manager, Ged Malone—Jane's husband at the time—wouldn't speak to me afterward. I didn't blame him.

I wouldn't have spoken to me either.

I dismissed well-intentioned suggestions that I take time off to rest and recover from the road—in other words, dry out. I spent November and December opening for Cher in the UK. At the end of January 2000, I performed at a gay-rights festival in London. Over the next few months, I kept in touch with the girls as they wrote new material. I also worked with Charlotte intermittently on our pop opera.

At home, I went through periods where I tried to be a better person than I was when I was in Los Angeles or on the road. I went through a stint where I enjoyed getting up and walking in my lavender slip like a 1950s movie star out to the chicken coop and getting fresh eggs for breakfast. I took Duke on mini-vacations, just the two of us. As the weather warmed, I also spent a lot of time lying beside the pool, drinking wine, and floating through the day with a mild buzz.

Frequently, I thought about Morgan and Duke with considerable guilt about my inattentiveness. If there was any light in my life, as I well know, it came from them. I was fortunate to have them. When the record deals ended and the crowds went home, they were still there, loving me. Why?

That's what I wanted to know.

Why did they put up with me when I could barely stand myself?

I didn't know how to do any better for them. The Go-Go's weren't your typical girl rockers for a reason. Similarly, I was not your typical stay-at-home wife or mother. When I thought about it, I had been running away from home since I was a teenager. At eighteen, I left permanently, and I had been on the move ever since. Those Gypsies at the end of our driveway had nothing on me.

I sometimes thought of the Gypsies with an envious fascination. They hitched their trailers to horses, threw their belongings in a wagon, and moved. I saw in them a sense of freedom from the type of responsibility that I feared. They had wild eyes and untamed spirits. They were mystical and taboo, part of a world I was drawn to. I had created my own complex, taboo world, too. One day I would be driving to a doctor's appointment on the ancient Roman road that ran down our mountain and thinking about the people who had followed this same path through the centuries. I'd have this weird sense like the one I'd experienced on my mushroom trip of being part of the unfolding of an immense story, like I was where I was supposed to be, on an adventure. Then I would zip back to Los Angeles, get caught up in the Hollywood scene, and end up feeling lost and disconnected, like a grain of sand on the beach.

At nearly forty-two, I should have been more together. Sadly, I wasn't.

In July 2000, we supported the release of the new *Behind the Music: Go-Go's Collection* with a monthlong tour. We coheadlined with the B-52's, who were as sensational offstage as they were on. We had fun with them every night. It was that kind of tour: special. Everything clicked for us, and it showed. "The Go-Go's played with the vigor of a hungry young band," said the review after our show in New Jersey. "Adept as ever," said the *Boston Herald*.

I liked that one reviewer along the way noted how we fell perfectly into sync when we played "How Much More" and chanted, "How much more can I take before I go crazy, oh yeah!" That line could have been a mantra for the band as well as all of us individually, especially me. Apparently we could take a lot. Even the three new songs ("Apology," "Kissing Asphalt," and "Superslide") we debuted from those Jane, Charlotte, and Kathy had finished for the next album also went over well.

Gina was emphatic when she declared ours wasn't "a reunion. We're back." Given the hot acts were Christina Aguilera and *NSYNC, I wondered. But I found myself rooting for us as we went into the studio that fall and recorded our first studio album in seventeen years, *God Bless the Go-Go's*. The good vibes from the tour carried over into the creative process and we actually had a fun time.

If all was good on that front, Morgan and I had reached a crossroads. A few months earlier we had moved from Dave Stewart's rock star–sized villa into a more normal home of our own on the other side of the mountain. We knew our marriage still wasn't firing on all cylinders, but we took the place anyway and promised to spend more time together. The house wasn't my taste, but it was filled with light and felt cheerful and cozy, perfect for a fresh start.

For Valentine's Day, we went to a favorite little hotel of ours in Florence. It was only a five-hour drive from our house. Morgan had booked a tee time at the nearby golf course, and I was content to be pampered at the spa. On an intimate note, we had never lost interest in the things that attracted us to each other. Our problems related to the inescapable fact that a relationship requires two people making an effort to be together, and I wasn't always present.

But this getaway started out nicely until Morgan came back from the golf course looking concerned. He said he had been looking out the window in the clubhouse when a black bird had tapped on the glass right in front of him. He had tried to shoo it off, but it wouldn't go away.

"It freaked me out," he said with a look in his eyes that telegraphed the reasons he felt that way.

"I understand," I said. "But you can't freak out every time you see a black bird. It could just be a coincidence. Don't even think about it."

Early the next morning we received a call from Los Angeles. Morgan's sister, Porty, had suffered a stroke during a medical procedure and gone into a coma. She had recently struggled with health issues. But only a few months earlier, she had visited us in France. It was something of a triumphant visit, too. Earlier, she and Morgan had learned that their father's second wife had kept his ashes in a safety deposit box, never having buried him. After their stepmother died in 1994, Morgan and Porty entered into a legal battle with her estate. Finally, they obtained the ashes and Porty had come over to help bury them next to Charlie Chaplin's grave in Vevey. It was all true to the family's unorthodoxy.

Porty's husband told Morgan that he needed to get to Beverly Hills right away. Morgan was justifiably shaken. His sister was all the family he had left. As we drove back to France, Morgan opened his heart to me and talked about how we needed to get our act together. Along with Duke, I was his family, and as he made so very clear to me on that drive, his family was the most precious thing in the world to him.

He asked me if I understood.

With tears streaming down my face, I nodded yes.

"I want to keep it together," he said. "I love you."

"I love you, too," I said. "And I want to always be together, too."

Whether I could get myself together . . . well, that was another matter. As much as I wanted to, as much as I promised to try, I didn't know if I could.

twenty-four

MISS AUGUST

WHEN THE GO-GO'S hit Las Vegas for a couple of corporate dates in mid-January 2001, I made a vow to stay healthy for the tour. I wasn't telling many people why I had cut back on my drinking and made a point of hitting the gym. As they would see soon enough, I had posed for a *Playboy* magazine pictorial scheduled for later in the year. In the process, I had gotten into pretty good shape. I couldn't remember starting a tour feeling this good. It was better than being hungover.

Like the other girls, I had high hopes for our new album, *God Bless the Go-Go's*. We heard positive comments from those who got early listens. We felt like it would be welcomed by fans without giving critics a reason to ask why a couple of forty-plus-year-old moms and their gal pals had gone into the studio to play rock star. Whether it could compete commercially with younger acts was another question. All of us were hopeful. We crossed as many fingers as possible.

My expectations were dashed when our management team gave us a frank talk about the latest rules of radio. You had to buy your way into the top 10 these days, they explained, and the cost was several million dollars. Since that sum was beyond the means of our tiny label, we were told they had obligated us to do a million dollars' worth of personal appearances for Clear Channel. To hype the album, we were told. Groans filled the room. We knew better.

But we believed in the album, so we grudgingly agreed to go forward with the grueling promotional schedule. We began in March with a ton of radio and press and a performance on *The Late Show with David Letterman*. We also participated in a tribute concert to Brian Wilson at

Radio City Music Hall. We were the only act whose dressing room was in a completely different building. We figured they must have heard about our reputation. You couldn't have found us if you wanted. We joked about having to take a cab to the show. But we had a good old time.

I was obsessed with meeting Elton John, who was among the other participants. I had met his boyfriend, David Furnish, at soirees in Nice, where they had a house. But I had never had the honor of meeting Sir Elton, one of my heroes. I kept a lookout when we were onstage, but they herded us on and off so quickly I didn't see anybody until we were led back onstage for the finale, which included all the participants joining voices on "Good Vibrations." Then I saw Elton across the stage.

As soon as the song ended, the producers tried to usher everyone off to different sides of the stage. I saw Elton being directed to the opposite side. It was as if someone knew what I had in mind. I said to myself, "No fucking way." I tore across the stage as if I was back on the high school track team and introduced myself to Elton, who was warm, gracious, and friendly.

"My boyfriend is always going on about you," he said. "You live right near us in Nice, don't you?"

"Yes," I said.

"Why don't you just call us when we're there and pop over?" he said.

A moment later, I was writing down Elton's phone number and promising to call. Inside, I was thinking, Yeah, right, like I'm going to just pop in on Elton John. It was too bad that real life wasn't as accommodating; I bet Elton and David were a hoot. But I didn't have time to socialize.

In May, *God Bless the Go-Go's* was finally released to the kind of warm critical reception we hoped for: a B+ from *Entertainment Weekly,* four stars from *Blender,* and a three-and-a-half-star high five from *Rolling Stone,* which said, "Leave a bottle of champagne out for twenty years, and you'd expect its essential bubbly brightness to be ravaged by . . . let's not fool ourselves: drugs, infighting, egotism and what have you. To the credit of the Go-Go's, they don't forfeit any California sparkle with this slick and listenable reunion effort."

With the album's release, we set off on a month of nonstop promotion the label had arranged without considering the effect of such a grueling schedule. Or maybe they had but didn't care if we were run ragged. We did a show in Irvine, California, then a USO show in Turkey, then television in New York, in-stores, radio shows, and more. We ran from morning till night. I thought it was bullshit. I broke down at a golf tournament in Chicago. We were only two weeks into the schedule and we had an arts fair and a chili cook-off ahead of us. I just started to sob hysterically.

It wasn't a good vibe with the record company either. As veterans, we knew how the business operated. We also had ambitious expectations for the album. But we heard the label was having financial problems. It wasn't a good scene.

As a way of coping with the stress and exhaustion, I slipped back into party gear. It was good-bye gym, hello late nights, booze, and coke. I got on a roll where after shows I invited people up to my room without any idea of who they were. If they wanted to party, my door was open. In one Midwestern city, I had about thirty people in my suite. As I walked through, I realized that I didn't know a single person. It was like that night after night. I continued the party wherever we went. It was the same circus in each city, just with different clowns.

When I think about it, I was courting danger. I could have been letting all sorts of crazies into my room. I probably did, in fact—and who knows, I may have wanted something bad to happen as a way of getting me out of that situation. I remember that I panicked every day when it was time for me to call home and check in with Morgan and say good morning to Duke. Sometimes I was still off my trolley. I always felt like shit, both physically and about my ability as a mother.

How I got to there from the place I was when I shot my *Playboy* layout was a sad commentary on the sneaky hold of addiction. The August issue of the magazine came out at the end of July, during a short break prior to the last leg of the tour. I had been at home in France when my manager had called with an offer from *Playboy*. I reacted by going, *Me?* My parents happened to be visiting, and my mom immediately said, "It sounds great. You have to do it!"

I thought, If my mom says it's okay, I might as well consider it. So I went to New York and met with a team from *Playboy*. I explained that I would pose if I could do it in the guise of a 1950s pinup. I didn't have a problem with nudity, but I wasn't an exhibitionist either, so for my own comfort I needed to feel like I was playing a character. I also insisted they keep the airbrushing to a minimum so I could show the real me. I was intent on making the point that you don't have to be skinny, blond, wafer thin, have fake boobs, or be twenty years old to be sexually viable.

Morgan enjoyed the idea. He had dated Playmates before we met—but never, as I pointed out, a Miss August.

I did take the magazine up on its offer to work out with a trainer. I thought, Why not? This was an opportunity to get in incredible shape, something I would never do on my own. I also *needed* to clean up for my sake and Morgan's. So I flew back and forth to work out with veteran trainer Dion Jackson. I worked my ass off for a month, lost twenty pounds, and could see and feel the difference in my body when it came time to drop my robe in front of the camera.

I did the shoot in Thailand. Duke came along for the adventure, though I made sure that no one told him what I was doing there. A few years later, when he was twelve years old, he found a stack of the *Playboy*s at home and freaked out. But until then he was blissfully unaware. I had a blast taking the photos. They put body makeup all over me, lit me perfectly, and made me confident that I was going to look my best.

When I saw the test photos, I flipped. They were gorgeous, and I got even more into the session. It was only when I was back home and heard that the same person who airbrushed Elle Macpherson and Pamela Anderson was also working on my pictures that red flags went up and I said, "Uh-oh, how is this going to look?"

Then I saw the photos and they were beautiful—but it wasn't me. The girls in the band thought they were great. My gay friends didn't look—or they didn't tell me—and my straight guy friends didn't bring it up and I didn't ask. I didn't ask my family for their opinion either. I thought I'd leave that alone. However, a girlfriend of mine was looking through the magazine one day and let out an envious sigh that spun me around. *What?* She pointed to a picture of me holding a parasol and looking over my shoulder and said, "I wish I had a butt like that."

"I do, too," I said. "Because the one you're looking at isn't mine."

A month later, I was in Italy, finishing a late lunch with an Italian friend at my favorite little restaurant, when Morgan called my cell phone and informed me that America had been attacked. My voice resonated through the small restaurant as I shouted, "What?" He told me about the planes crashing into the World Trade Center, the people fleeing through the streets of New York City, and the chaos, concern, and uncertainty he was seeing and hearing on news reports.

I hung up and looked off in the distance, dazed. I filled my friend in on the details, at least what I knew, and paid the bill. I wanted to go home. On the way to the car, we stopped in a delicatessen for cheese and sausages. Then I was walking back to my parking space when an older Italian man approached me and asked, "Are you an American?"

"Yes," I said.

He reached out, wrapped his arms around me, and squeezed. It was such a warm embrace I could almost feel his heartbeat. He let me go and looked in my eyes.

"I'm so sorry," he said. "I'm so sorry for what happened to your great country today."

Throughout that day and week, my European friends called and expressed their sorrow and condolences as if I knew the victims. What I realized when I woke up from the shock was that it didn't matter that I wasn't personally acquainted with the people who lost their lives in the terrorist attacks. In one way or another, we were all connected—and affected. I watched news reports nonstop that first day and night, but then turned the TV off after I realized it was making me sick.

In the months following that profoundly tragic and sorrow-filled time, I came down hard on myself. Why, I asked myself, was I such a mess when I had so much going for me? Why was I unable to get it together? Why were things such a struggle? Why did I feel full of gloom and despair?

Obviously I was an addict. But I wasn't facing that reality, not when I relied on drugs and alcohol to take me away from my guilt, shame, and depression.

More conveniently, I assumed my problems stemmed from an inability to connect with the world and with life, not myself. I was so happy one day when I picked up the book *The Buddha in Your Mirror: Practical Buddhism and the Search for Self*. I had been reading various related books, but this one practically screamed at me to pick it up. It was about Nichiren Buddhism, the practice of chanting "Nam-myoho-renge-kyo" as a way of recharging physically, mentally, and spiritually, and also getting to enlightenment, or Buddhahood.

The book was clearly and simply written, the sentences acting like translators to make a complex idea accessible. I thought the idea of finding peace through this chant, which means "I devote myself to the mystic law of cause and effect through sound," was a beautiful idea. The author recommended chanting with other people and finding them through local sects of Soka Gakkai International, Nichiren's global organization. I learned there was a headquarters in Santa Monica and another in New York City. I contacted both, and a woman from the Santa Monica group called me back. Vera and I had an excellent, thoughtful talk, and the next time I was in Los Angeles, I met her at a morning meeting, *gongyo*, at her home in West Hollywood.

*Gongyo*s were twice-daily services where people recited the Lotus Sutra, the highest teaching of Buddha. There were twenty of us at this first one I attended. We sat in front of a *gohonzon*, a large mandala, beside which were placed displays of water, plants, fruit, and incense. Once the group began to chant, the room took off. It filled with an energy that sent me flying through a different dimension. I had no idea what to expect; it turned out better than I could have imagined.

Back in France, I started chanting on my own to a *gongyo* tape, but it wasn't the same. Through a French chapter of Soka Gakkai, I was referred to a woman in Valbonne who organized Soka Gakkai meetings at her house. She turned out to be from San Francisco. We bonded over the difficulty of practicing in French. Little by little, though, I proved myself adept enough to receive my own *gohonzon*.

Despite my twice-a-day chants, I ended up more torn apart than enlightened. All that time sitting still and thinking seemed to cause the shit in my head to line up like soldiers in front of a review panel. During chants, I asked to be freed from my obsession to use. I pleaded for guidance. I wanted answers. Most of all I wanted release and relief from the dark alleys and self-destructive corridors I walked day in and day out as if I was held captive in a maze.

At the end of the day, chanting forced me to sit with myself and face my feelings, my sense of failure and regrets, my guilt and shame, my fears and insecurity. None of the stuff that other people saw—the rock star, the lucky marriage, the exotic life in a foreign country—none of that mattered. None of it was even relevant when I sat face-to-face with myself. Never mind posing for *Playboy*. People talk about the naked truth. The person I saw when chanting was the real me, the naked truth. I was fucked-up, unhappy, and seriously depressed.

Maybe that *was* enlightenment.

If it was, I was in trouble.

twenty-five

I PLEAD INSANITY

DESPITE MY best efforts, the inside of my head was not a pretty place. Even while touring with the Go-Go's in February and March, and then on my own after the group went on a yearlong hiatus as Kathy waited to give birth to her first child in October, I chanted twice a day and said my recitations, always with the same hope that such religious devotion to the mystic sound would free me of my addictions and deliver me into a normal life. It didn't.

I was spiraling deeper into negativity when I met a drug dealer in a Belgian restaurant, a meeting that put my life in danger, though I didn't know it at the time. I had made a brief trip to Belgium, and while lunching with a friend I asked if she knew where I could get drugs. She nodded toward a waiter, then got up from the table, walked across the room, and gave him a tap on the arm as she walked past. They met in the back by the bathrooms, spoke briefly, and she told me everything was taken care of.

After dinner, my friend and I walked to a nearby bar and a few minutes later the waiter came in and sat at our table. A few minutes after that, I had some coke and a new contact. I used him a number of times over the next few months. Then he started to blackmail me.

It was early summer 2003, and I was in Los Angeles, rehearsing for Go-Go's dates in August, when I received a message from him. What drug dealers call their clients? It doesn't work that way. I listened to the message and turned ice cold. He wanted money from me, a pretty good sum, and he threatened to go public with my drug use if I didn't give him what he wanted.

Obviously something was going on with him. I didn't want to know. I just wanted to be able to get rid of this problem. But I didn't know how. I had no idea what to do.

I thought about telling Morgan, but I chickened out after considering all of the confessions I would have to make and the repercussions. Instead I did nothing. I appeared on *Who Wants to Be a Millionaire* and the British version of *Hell's Kitchen* (the show's star, chef Gordon Ramsay, made me mop the floor), and then I returned to France until I had to go on the road with the Go-Go's.

Once the monthlong tour began at the end of July in Redding, California, I immediately slipped into that place I got to only on the road, when I could drink and use and isolate myself from the responsibilities and concerns of real life, including the drug dealer trying to extort money from me, which I thought about from time to time. It always upset me. It was one more secret I kept that weighed me down.

In mid-August, the Go-Go's played the Summer Sonic Festival in Tokyo, and I was boozing and using heavily. We opened for Green Day, and thanks to our friendship with Billie Joe Armstrong, who had cowritten "Unforgiven" on *God Bless the Go-Go's,* they rolled out the red carpet for us. Literally. They had a red carpet to the side of the stage, with our own little tent stocked with coolers of booze and beer. A sign said GO-GO'S ONLY. And I took full advantage of it.

The Green Day guys had us over to their hotel several times for champagne and caviar. We ended our nights drinking at two or three in the morning. One night they took us to the hippest rock-and-roll bar in Osaka and I ended up dancing on top of the bar to "Immigrant Song." The next night, Green Day performed the Led Zeppelin classic onstage and dedicated it to me.

I went out drinking afterward with the guys and followed Tré Cool, Mike Dirnt, and a couple of Green Day roadies back to Tré's hotel room for more of the same. From what I heard through the grapevine later on, they told people they were amazed the Go-Go's could outdrink them.

I saw them a couple years later, after I had been sober for a while, and they said, "You look really good. And different."

"I got some sleep," I said.

They thought I was a badass, hard-partying rocker, which they said was even cooler since I was a chick. They had no idea I was an addict whose life was out of control.

I had left home in bad shape, and I returned in worse. Worn-out and drugged out, I was in a depression that had me feeling empty, worthless, hopeless, and like I had nothing: no energy, no thoughts, no anything. I thought about taking my life. It seemed like a solution, even a resolution to many problems. I had hurt too many people. I thought things might be better for me and everyone else if I wasn't around.

I considered various ways, some painless, some inexplicably grue-some, like taking a handful of pills or veering my car off one of the steep mountain roads. I figured Morgan might be able to deal with it, but each time I was stopped when I thought of the pain I would cause my son. Even in the depths of my sickness, I couldn't be *that* selfish and heartless.

I was stuck in that state of mind until September, when Morgan had enough of the depression and drama. One day after Duke, now twelve and old enough to know what was what, went to school, Morgan confronted me, insisting I tell him what was going on. He was angry and scared—angry at whatever I was doing and the life I was wasting, and scared that he and Duke might lose me.

That was the trigger. I couldn't pretend or hide any longer. Nor did I want to. Crying, I told him everything. I was mortified, ashamed, and sorry. I wished that I had told him sooner. I wished that none of it had ever happened.

I asked Morgan to hold me. I needed to feel safe and protected. If he had said no, I don't know what I would have done next. But Morgan took me in his arms and held me for a long, long time. Only God knows why, but he had an amazing ability to love me.

"This is all drugs and alcohol," he said. "It's not the real you. You have a problem. You need treatment. And if you don't deal with it, I'm going to tell you this right now, our marriage isn't going to survive."

I understood the next move was up to me. And I understood I had to get help or Morgan was going to let go of me for the sake of his sanity. But once again I refused to admit the truth to myself, even when I saw it clearly. Instead of saying yes, I have a drug problem and need help, I told myself that my problems stemmed from my depression and that if I checked into a hospital for a while, I would come out better. It was a perfect example of the way addicts will lie—even, or especially, to themselves.

I went to London and met with a doctor from the Priory, the city's leading private mental-health hospital. I told him everything—from my drug and alcohol addiction to the lies I had told Morgan for years to my struggle with depression.

At the conclusion, I expected him to check me into the fifty-six-bed facility for a much-needed cooling-off period. Instead, he said, "You're not depressed. You're a drug addict and an alcoholic, and you need to check into rehab for at least thirty-six days."

What?

That's not what I had wanted to hear, and I was furious. I wanted my depression treated, not my drug addiction. I tried to change his mind, but he refused to budge and I found the truth too much to handle. I returned to my hotel thinking, The hell with him, and that night I bought coke and partied myself into oblivion at Stringfellows, a high-end lap-dancing club.

It was the start of a two-day binge, as well as more lies and more problems.

twenty-six

FADING FAST

A FEW WEEKS later, aware that I needed to do *something* to convince Morgan I was making an effort, I made an appointment with a therapist in France whose name I had gotten from a friend. The therapist was a Dutch-Indonesian woman. She spoke perfect English with an accent that made each sentence seem like a song. If she hadn't been my shrink, I would have wanted her to be my friend. I was telling her a story one day and she put her hand up.

"Stop," she said.

"What?"

"Are you serious? Is what you're telling me real?"

It was some story about craziness on the road with the Go-Go's.

I nodded, and she burst out laughing.

"Are you supposed to laugh?" I asked.

"Why not?" she said. "The story you just told me is funny—almost unbelievable."

When I told her more of my antics with the Go-Go's, she reacted as any sane person would, by asking, "Are you nuts?" I laughingly said, "Isn't that why I'm here?" After hearing about my frustration with the doctor in London who wouldn't admit me to the psychiatric hospital, she stared at me until I felt uncomfortable.

"What?" I said.

"You tell me," she replied.

"He wanted me to check in for being a drug addict," I said. "I wanted to go in for depression."

"What do you think?" she asked.

"I think that I'm not going to rehab for thirty-six days," I said.

"Ah, that's a different issue." She paused. "Why don't you check out AA? You might see something you like there."

"Do you think I'm an addict?" I asked.

"It's not about what I think," she said. "What do you think?"

I knew the answer. At home, I went online and found the schedule for an AA meeting in Cannes. Morgan and Duke drove me. We pulled up in front of a small church. Only a couple cars were in the parking lot. Nervous and wary, I saw an open door on the side of the building. I turned to Morgan and Duke, both of whom were looking at me with eyes full of hope. If they could have given me their strength and courage, they would have done it. But I had to go myself.

I got out of the car, walked slowly up to the church, and poked my head in the small room. Inside there was a table with a dozen or so folding chairs around it. Even though no one was there yet, I already felt exposed and claustrophobic. I turned around and went back to the car.

"No way," I told Morgan. "No f-ing way am I going into that room."

"What's the problem?" he asked.

"It's not like AA meetings in L.A. where the room is big and you can disappear in the back."

"Can I go with you, Mom?" Duke asked.

"No, honey," I said. "I wish you could. It's something I have to do myself. And I just can't."

"Then what next?" Morgan asked.

"I'll just deal with the shrink," I said.

For a while, it worked. In December, though, I slipped while on a two-week solo tour. Then in February, during a short stint through the South with the Go-Go's, I lost it, setting off a downward spiral that I knew would be bad. It started with the show at the Capri Casino in Bossier City. I followed that two days later with an all-nighter in New Orleans. I was in such bad shape when I called home from the airport that I couldn't hide it. Morgan busted me immediately.

"Oh my God, I can't believe you," he said.

"What?" I said defensively.

"What?! You're high!" he said.

"No, I'm not," I said.

At that, he freaked out. It was like years of frustration erupted. "Don't lie," he said. "I'm so sick of this. I can't take it anymore."

I hurried to a quiet area in the airport and tried to hide myself against the wall.

"I promise I'll check into rehab when I get back," I said.

"I don't care what you do," he said. "I'm just sick of this. I don't believe you anymore."

I didn't blame Morgan. I had made countless promises over the years and, as I cried into the phone at the airport, I knew I had meant every one. I just couldn't keep them. I swore this time would be different. Sobbing, I called my manager and asked her to find me a rehab facility to check into after the tour. She was as relieved as anyone. Gina then gave me a couple tranquilizers to get me through the flight. But after recovering in Atlanta, I went out and partied through the last two stops in St. Petersburg and Orlando. I was pathetic—and powerless.

At home, Morgan barely looked at me. Neither of us mentioned rehab. As a way of avoiding that discussion, I traveled back and forth to London as often as possible for meetings about a new album of French songs and a tour. I also taped *Hit Me Baby One More Time,* a reality TV singing competition for charity. I used it as an excuse for another binge. I rolled into my hotel around two A.M., all coked up, and spotted the hotel manager, a young girl, with a drunken businessman. Wanting company, I invited both of them up to my room to hang out.

By six A.M., we had emptied the minibar and I was kicking them out so I could call home and tell Morgan that I was fine. A few hours later, I checked out of the hotel, still buzzed and disgusted with myself yet again.

The late-morning flight back to Nice was a rough one. The sky was a thick gray blanket full of nasty bumps and gullies. About three-quarters of the way to our destination, lightning struck the airplane. At the moment of impact, there was a loud *boom,* then a sickening lurch, followed by the sensation of the pilot accelerating as he struggled to regain control of the plane. While others screamed and panicked, I sat serene, unaffected, and relieved.

Yes, relieved.

I thought, Thank God, I'm finally going to die. I won't have to face my husband and son being this high when I get off the plane.

They weren't the problem. Two weeks later, I was back in London for more meetings with the producer for my French album, plus rehearsals for a brief tour starting on the fifteenth of March. After checking into a suite at the Metropolitan Hotel, I went out to dinner with friends. Before the night ended, I scored two or three grams of coke, and needless to say I didn't show up to my rehearsals the next morning. Instead I got more stuff, and then more after that, and by five in the afternoon I was standing in my pajamas on Park Lane, waiting for my drug dealer.

The ATM around the corner was broken and I was too high to go anywhere else, so I went back into the lobby. I had gotten cash from the concierge all night. The manager came out instead and confronted me. In front of everybody in the lobby, he gave me a knowing, stern look and said, "Mrs. Mason, we gave you cash all night. We cannot give you any more."

His attempt to embarrass me worked. I walked hurriedly away before I panicked or broke down, and managed to find a working ATM. My dealer came with more stuff, a lot more this time. I didn't want to go through that humiliation downstairs again. I sat in my room and did it all evening. Between lines, I smoked cigarettes, played games on my laptop, and paced the room. I must have smoked ten packs of cigarettes those two days.

Later that evening, I was still in full binge mode when I had a vision of myself being found dead in that hotel room of a cocaine overdose. It came to me accompanied by a loud, clear voice that said, "You are going to die here if you carry on like this." I saw the scene unfold: the coke, the messy hotel room, and me slumped over, eyes shut and chest no longer moving, dead. The Who's bassist John Entwistle had gone the same route a few years earlier in a Las Vegas hotel room, suffering a heart attack in his sleep brought on by cocaine. He was in my thoughts because only a week before I checked into the Metropolitan, I had read that his longtime girlfriend, Lisa Pritchett-Johnson, had been found dead while visiting a family member in Memphis. About a gram and a half of coke had been found nearby. At forty-three, she had been around my age. As I did another line, I heard a voice again. This time it said, "You're next."

How embarrassing to be found dead in a hotel room at my age of a cocaine overdose. I shuddered at the thought, knowing it was true. Such an end would humiliate my husband and especially my bright, loving, and concerned son.

"Okay, I quit," I said out loud.

I looked at the coke left on the table. Then I glanced upward.

"Please let me finish what I have," I said. "Then I'll quit."

And that's what happened. I finished the last of my coke and then I was done. I knew if I did even one more line after that I was going to die. I knew the choice was mine, as with everything in life, and I chose to live.

The date was March 14, 2005.

I had a show the next day. I couldn't believe I had to get onstage for nearly two hours. I looked like I felt, like someone who'd nearly died. My skin was gray and my eyes were almost black, as if the light inside me had gone out. It was a shocking reality, a sad sight that finally registered with me. After thirty years of using drugs of one kind or another to boost my mood or spirit me away from hard times, I vowed never to use again—only this time, having made the choice to live, I meant it.

I was horrified and embarrassed at the shape in which I returned home. I could barely breathe from having smoked so many packs of cigarettes the week before. I didn't want to look at myself in the mirror. I told Morgan and Duke that I was sick with the flu and stayed in bed for about a week as my body went through a sort of detox. I could literally smell the chemicals coming out of my skin.

For the first few days I was too out of it to worry about whether Morgan believed that I had picked up the flu on the road. Then I figured he had to know that I had lied. I had no idea what he knew or didn't know about my using, what I had told him, and what I was keeping a secret. All I knew was I had too many secrets. As they say in AA, you're only as sick as your secrets, and they're right. I was one very sick girl.

Toward the end of March, we went on a family holiday to Austria. I wanted to talk to Morgan and relax with my family, but I didn't know how to do either. Here was Morgan, the person I loved most in the world, who was my soul mate, and here was my son, a human being whose life I had created, and I couldn't talk to either. It was pathetic. I asked myself, "If this is the case, why did I choose to live? What was the point if this is my life?"

I thought if I could tell Morgan everything, he would understand. When I woke up the next morning, he was on the golf course. I called his cell and started to apologize. He said that he had heard this too many times before. He wanted to play golf.

"I'm finished," he said.

"What do you mean?" I asked.

"I'm mean I'm finished," he said. "It's up to you."

I replayed his words in my head. He had said he was finished, not *it's* finished or *we're* finished. If he'd said either of the latter, I would have thought he was through with our marriage. If he was simply finished, I took that to mean the door was still open. But it was now up to me. I got it.

If this was one more chance, I knew it was my last one.

twenty-seven

(WE WANT) THE SAME THING

IT WAS the end of March, and I knew that I was at a crossroads. This was the moment of truth. I could either fold or fight. I decided to beat this addiction. I wanted my life with my family, with Morgan and Duke. I called a woman whose name had been given to me as someone from AA who could help. Sobbing, I told her that my life was terrible and I couldn't take any more.

"Meet me in Cannes at four o'clock and we'll talk before the meeting," she said.

We met at a café and I told her everything that was going on. She was a cross between Pamela Mason and my mom, a perfect combination for me: both earthy and outrageous. She digested all the information I dumped on her, stories about my last coke binge, Morgan, and the Belgian guy. I noticed her eyebrow go up when I mentioned that I still drank.

"It's okay," I said. "My problems were with drugs, not alcohol."

"I'm not going to debate you," she said. "I want you to just concentrate more on the similarities than the differences in your stories. Listen to yourself. See how you're feeling about things."

"I know what you're getting at," I said. "But I think I can still drink. As I said, I had a drug problem. I'm fine with a glass of wine or two."

She smiled. A wise Auntie Mame.

"Just pay attention," she said. "Listen to yourself. Then come to your own conclusion."

I followed her into the AA meeting, my first one. She became my sponsor. From then on, I attended at least one meeting a day and spent the rest of the day working out and chanting. Morgan still wasn't speaking to me. He wasn't the only one. Most people close to me at the time were either pissed off or disgusted with my irresponsible behavior. I understood. I had to prove myself.

I kept to a routine. In the morning, I chanted and worked out for several hours with my friend Lorenza. I did the same thing later in the day. I believe the chanting I did, often up to four hours a day, gave me the strength and optimism to get through this difficult period of my life. I felt my energy return and my thoughts focus on rebuilding my life. I was like, Okay, what needs to be done?

But I was still fooling myself. I got in the habit of buying a bottle of wine before my AA meetings, tucking it in my car, and then cracking it open afterward at Lorenza's house when we got together to chant and work out. I fixated on alcohol. As I chanted, I thought about what I was going to drink later that night. I also made notes on my calendar about what I was going to drink when I traveled.

I remember on a flight to Los Angeles making a note to drink a nice Pomerol. Once in L.A., though, I didn't have anything since I knew that if I drank and worked, I would want to do coke. But then I obsessively marked off dates when I could resume drinking. Eventually I realized this kind of obsession wasn't healthy or normal.

I called my sponsor and told her what I had been doing. She responded with an almost gleeful "Aha!"

"You heard yourself," she said.

"It's another addiction," I said.

She was quiet for a moment. I'm sure it was by design.

"We don't drink," she finally said. "We don't say one thing is okay, but another is not. None of it is okay."

"Uh-huh," I said.

"If you're going to stop, you stop everything," she said. "Why don't you just try it? Do what we tell you works. And see how it feels."

"I don't want to," I said. "But all right. I will."

By now, Morgan and Duke knew what was going on and I had their support and encouragement. However, before giving up alcohol, I let it be known I wanted to have one last bottle. My sponsor, people I had met in AA, and Morgan and Duke were telling me not to do it. I reassured everyone it was okay. I was going to stop after that bottle. I had no doubt. It was over for me.

"Just let me have this last one," I said to my sponsor. "I'll see you at Monday's meeting."

It was the weekend. On Sunday, I went out and bought a bottle of my favorite Corbières, as well as groceries for the week. At home, Duke was helping me unload the bags when I dropped something and went into freak-out mode. The accident triggered a flood of regret and remorse for the way I had neglected my son over the years. I don't know why, but I pulled a carton of eggs out of a shopping bag and began throwing them one after the other on the ground.

"Mommy!" Duke said. "Stop! Please stop it!"

It was like a scene from a Lifetime movie where the mother's addiction comes to a head through an act that's absolutely insane. It was a detox, in a way—the emotions I had refused to deal with for years came out of me whether I was ready or not. I hoped and prayed this was the last of my episodes Duke had to witness.

He had seen way too much as it was. About a year earlier, I had returned home from London, grateful to walk into an empty house because I was still too high to face Morgan and Duke. Morgan was not yet back from picking Duke up from his after-school activity. After taking a few pills to bring me down, I began to prepare dinner. When they came in, Morgan took one look at me and said, "What did you take?"

"Something," I slurred.

"You're disgusting," he said before sending me to bed.

Duke took my hand and said, "Come on, Mommy. I'll help you."

As I got set to drink my last bottle of wine, I vowed never to repeat one of those scenes ever again. Then I sat in front of the TV, drank the wine, and passed out. I woke up the next morning, April 3, and went on a hike around a lake near our house, and was like, Okay, I'm ready for my new life now.

Indeed, I haven't had a drink or used any drugs since.

*   *   *

My new sobriety was tested less than a week after giving up alcohol when I went to Paris for a birthday party a very wealthy friend of mine was having for her child. I took Duke, who was nervous about me attending a celebration *and* being there with me, when my sobriety was so new. I assured him that I was fine—and I was. I got through dinner at La Tour d'Argent, one of Paris's best restaurants. I declined numerous temptations, including a $2,000 bottle of Château Pétrus.

My next test came when I guested on a TV show in London. For me, the city was full of temptations and bad memories. There were few hotels I could stay in that didn't bring back memories of a binge. Before leaving for London, I talked to my sponsor daily for nearly two weeks. Once there, I was okay—that is, until I went into the Harrods department store to do some shopping and suddenly, inexplicably broke down. I was hit from out of nowhere with a wave of guilt and shame.

I went to a dressing room and called my sponsor. She reassured me that things like this happened.

"Don't worry," she said. "It's okay to cry and feel bad about past mistakes. Soon enough you'll be able to see the divine person you really are."

I had almost forgotten about my problem with that Belgian drug dealer when he left another message, demanding money and reiterating his threat. I didn't know whether or not to take him seriously since he had never made good on his initial threats. To be safe, I contacted an expert in such matters who told me not to respond. He predicted the creep would go away.

I thought about what this guy was doing and got angry at him—and at myself, for creating this situation. But I didn't react to the anxiety as I had in the past by using, and I also realized I wasn't helpless. I could talk about it therapeutically, and I did. I discussed it with my sponsor, who was very helpful.

"If he tries anything, you go to the police," she said. "And if he talks to the press, what are the headlines? 'Rock Star Has Coke Habit'? Hasn't the public already heard that story?"

"Yeah, I guess," I said. "I've already talked about that on my *True Holly-wood Story.*"

"Right," she said. "So don't fret."

She was right. Until something happened, if it ever did, I chose to ignore him. Again, my sponsor helped me see I had some measure of control here. I could put him out of my mind. I also changed my number and then helped myself by continuing to talk about it with Morgan, my sponsor, and my AA group.

With their advice and support, I dealt with this and other problems from a place of strength and understanding, rather than fear and emotion and booze and drugs. This was no small matter. I actually *dealt with my problems.* And thankfully, the dealer disappeared.

Now my slate really was clean. But life wasn't all of a sudden easy or carefree. I still had to work hard every day at being myself, and hoped I could work up to being my best self. Despite my chanting and workouts, I was fragile, like a baby deer trying walk on new, wobbly legs. I wasn't sure what was going to happen with my marriage. I wanted to stay married. Morgan wasn't sure. Actually, he just wanted proof I was serious about sobriety. I had to walk the walk—and that took time.

Gradually, I became a different woman inside and out. The obsessive, unhealthy, drug-addicted, alcoholic liar and cheat faded into the background, and a kinder, more open and loving, more honest and healthy woman stepped into view. I worked my steps. I made amends to the many people I had hurt over the years—the hardest and saddest of which were to Morgan and Duke. I made an honest inventory. One day my sponsor had me write twenty ways I had been protected through my use. I had no problem doing that many, and more.

"My God," I said to her as we reread the list. "It's all divine intervention. I mean, the same thing that protected me from OD'ing that night in London has always been watching over me."

"It watches over all of us," she said. "That's why a while ago I told you to be patient, that you will see the divine person you are."

*   *   *

One thing I never doubted was my French album, *Voila*. It was waiting for me when I was ready to dive back into work, making the project seem as if it had been manifested for a reason. Two and a half years earlier, I had met David James, the head of a small label in Cannes. Over coffee, he asked if there was anything I wanted to do, and I said, "Well, I'd love to do a French album."

Until I heard myself say those words, I had never had such a thought. The idea just came out of my mouth.

"I think that's a great idea," he said.

He tried to start the project in fall 2004, but I missed various appointments with David and his producer, John Reynolds. I was too messed up. In January 2005, I managed to record three demos with John. I don't know how I got it together since that month was sandwiched between two of the worst months of my life. In March, the record company was set to make the album, musicians were lined up, and I was supposed to rehearse a batch of songs with John. Unfortunately I was in the midst of my last coke binge and never made it to the studio.

Once I got sober, though, I was thrilled to find the opportunity to make *Voila* was still there. I threw myself into the project in a way I hadn't done with any album through my entire career, including with the Go-Go's. We spent about eight months recording it in London (yes, it's ironic—and we used mostly Irish musicians), so I spent quite a bit of the early days of my recovery traveling back and forth from France. I wasn't tempted to drink or use, not once.

Somehow a wish list of artists agreed to lend their talents, including Brian Eno, who heard tracks and played for free, and the Egyptian singer Natasha Atlas, who specialized in Egyptian and North African music. I picked my favorite French songs as well as those standards I thought I could sing well. Over the years, a few people had said they heard bits of Edith Piaf in my voice, and I thought, Well, after all the years of booze and cigarettes, I could probably pull it off.

I went into serious work mode. I studied with a vocal coach, took lessons with a French teacher, and taped the lyrics to each song all over the interior of my car. I sang them wherever I went.

The results showed up on the album. By the time I went into the studio, I felt like I owned the songs, like I had made them my own. Critics agreed. "Carlisle has never sounded as comfortable within a persona as she does here," said the *Boston Phoenix* shortly after Rykodisc released the album in February 2007. The paper also noted that I was "about as French as a bag of 'freedom fries,'" but for this first studio album in a decade I'd gone "all ou-la-la."

The review was right on all counts. It was, like all my previous albums, a measure of where I was in my life. I was ready to sing these songs from Serge Gainsbourg, Jacques Brel, and Charles Aznavour. I didn't listen to much pop music anymore. I'd heard the best, and although good stuff still came through, it sounded like the originals regurgitated. Instead I was listening to world music, French music, and Indian music.

It made sense. I was no longer a California girl. At almost forty-nine years old, I was a product of the world.

As I was making *Voila,* the Go-Go's reunited briefly to celebrate the twenty-fifth anniversary of our first album, *Beauty and the Beat.* We weren't ones to look back, but we enjoyed reminiscing about the 1981 album. We knew it was special. As I said at the time, "It encapsulated a moment and captured a lot of people's imagination." Fans constantly told us how much those songs meant to them. I was always flattered and appreciative since I could still recall the songs I listened to over and over again when I was growing up. Music was—and remains—that important.

A quarter of a century later, we were aware of the album's place in rock history. We knew it had captured a moment in time and opened doors for other women with the same dream we had. It was even more personal for us. Those songs were snapshots of our lives, who we were at the time and what we were doing. It was pretty wild.

I took the opportunity to sit down for the first time with Kathy and

Charlotte, both of whom were also sober, and tell them about the last days of my boozing and using. Despite the time we had spent together on the road, they had no idea. They were stunned and horrified. Kathy said she thought I was on my way out. Charlotte confessed that she had expected to get a call saying I was dead.

By the time I hit my second year of sobriety in April 2007, I was on a very different journey. You could see it from looking at me. I had reacquired a healthy skin color and life in my eyes. My body was fit and I woke up with an enthusiasm for facing the day. Not as apparent was the way I had reconnected at home with Morgan. He watched with relief as I slowly but steadily emerged from the gruesome shell of addiction to become the person he always said I was, the person he saw even when I couldn't. It took about eight months for me to regain his trust. Then we entered a period of rediscovering the reason both of us felt we were meant to be together.

The biggest problems we continued to have were mine: I regretted the pain I had caused this wonderful, almost saintly man—and the time I had wasted not being with him.

The other role I worked to reclaim was that of mom to Duke, who was suddenly so grown-up and mature. I was thrilled when we started going on weekend trips together and even more delighted and impressed when I saw he was a fine, thoughtful, and intelligent young man. At his age, now almost fifteen, I was cutting school, running away from home, and experimenting with pot and alcohol. His biggest vice was C-SPAN. He loved politics and worshipped Nancy Pelosi.

Duke and I were driving back home from a weekend trip to the Gorges du Verdon, also known as the French Grand Canyon, when he opened up to me in a way that I had never been able to do with him. He said he had something to tell me. I could see that he was ready to cry.

"What's on your mind?" I asked.

"No, never mind," he said.

"Now you have to tell me," I said.

It was then, with tears in his eyes and a hesitation in his voice, that my son told me that he was gay. I started to say something, but nothing was there. I didn't know what to say. I was actually stunned. Not stunned in a way that I had never suspected it, but more like I couldn't believe this was happening. I glanced at him several times, trying not to crash as I said, "What?" Then I pulled the car over to the side of the road and asked again, "What did you say?"

It's an amazing thing when you realize your child has surpassed you in some way, whether it's in intelligence, maturity, wisdom, common sense, or courage. I looked at my baby and thought he was all of those things, and so brave and honest and much better and stronger than I was. I just wish I could have said it, or something, anything that would have made me sound halfway enlightened.

"Are you shocked?" he asked.

"No, I'm not," I said. "I mean, I don't know what I am. I just wish I was better for you."

"Are you mad?" he asked.

"God no!" I said. "I love you—and I will love you any way you are. I'm so proud of you." (The absolute truth.)

I don't know how he did it, but my kid was already the kind of person I wished that I could have been. With a vision of who he was and who he wanted to be, this was one piece of the puzzle he was addressing so he could get on with the rest of his life. I looked at Duke with envy. At almost fifty, I was still sorting through issues from my childhood. How did he end up this together?

"Did you have any idea?" he asked later.

"No," I said.

That was true at the moment he asked. Later, as I ransacked my memories for clues, I recalled a few times when the thought of him possibly being gay crossed my mind. But it was always one of those things that was easier to ignore—for both of us—until now.

As every parent knows, you spend so many years managing your child's life that it comes as a shock when that relationship changes, when they break the news that certain things about them aren't the way you imagined. This was one of those times. Duke was ready to come out. I wasn't as ready. I know parents react to such news in many different ways. For me, it was more like, wow!

I don't think I was ever less than accepting, but I was still in a fog for three days. I spent part of that time letting the reality soak in and part of that time figuring out how to tell Morgan. My therapist said I should have Duke tell him. However, I knew that was wrong. What if Morgan had a bad reaction? Both of us were very open, accepting, and close to many gay friends. But the issue can play differently when it lands in your living room.

I thought, No, I'll tell Morgan myself.

It's funny. In the time we had known each other, we had talked about every subject imaginable, or so it seemed, except this one, and probably because it was about our little boy, who was not so little but still this human being we had created; it was harder than anything else we had ever discussed.

I needed more than a month to work up the nerve to break the news to Morgan, and as I feared, he struggled with it. From what I read, his was a pretty typical reaction among fathers, who sometimes think their son's homosexuality is a reflection of their own masculinity. We laugh about it now. But Morgan would come up to me and ask, "Are you sure he's gay?" Later, Duke would find me and say, "I can't believe Dad can't accept it."

In the end, Morgan and I both settled down. Not only did we accept Duke's sexuality, we became his biggest supporters—to a point. See, Duke likes to talk and debate. He's a natural politician, a passionate leader with strong views on issues, particularly gay politics. On occasion, we have reached the point where we have said, "All right, we have heard enough! We're all for gay rights. Go tell someone else."

Sometimes he laughs at us. Other times he gets frustrated. And still other times we get into heated debates. He may see us roll our eyes at him, which happens when he goes on one of his diatribes, but he knows we support him 100 percent. He has said and even written that he couldn't ask for any cooler or more accepting parents. We couldn't have hoped for a cooler or better kid.

I've had some pretty big hits in my life—but none bigger than my son. And I know the best is yet to come.

twenty-eight

VOILA

THEN CAME INDIA.

Years earlier, one of my best friends, Rosemarie, had discovered yoga. She had been part of the punk scene in L.A., and I made fun of her for getting into the whole mind-body thing. I jokingly referred to her as Gwyneth. She called me ignorant and close-minded.

She was right. I thought yoga was too trendy and practiced by sweat-soaked fashionistas preening their taut bodies in the latest yoga-wear. No thanks.

Plus I had tried yoga a few times in the past and always ended up injured. In retrospect, I had pushed myself too hard in those classes. Yoga isn't about that at all. But in those early days of my sobriety Rosemarie kept after me to try it.

"Trust me, it will change everything," she said.

As she knew, I needed all the help I could get. I attended daily AA meetings, chanted for hours, and worked out. I focused all my energy on staying sober and being healthy. As long as I was trying to change everything about my lifestyle, I thought, why not try yoga?

I researched classes in the South of France and began attending a branch of the Iyengar Institute in Nice. Iyengar is a form of Hatha yoga that concentrates on body alignment. It focuses on extremely precise poses that put the body into perfect alignment. It's complicated on many levels and frustrating for those same reasons. I started in the beginner's class and gritted my teeth through weeks of criticism and correction from the teacher, a gorgeous woman who came across like a Marine drill sergeant.

She didn't compliment me even when I did the poses correctly. As she later explained, it was to keep the ego from getting in the way. Although I came to understand that approach, it was scary getting yelled at all the time.

I stuck with it, though, and gradually found myself enjoying the discipline—something I obviously needed—and opening up emotionally. I surprised myself when I started to look forward to it, not just the physical and emotional part, but also the mental aspect. I didn't know what it was, but I felt stronger. Something was happening to me. Each week was a different format. One week it was standing, the next forward bends, the fourth third restorative. For me, it was like taking baby steps into a new awareness of myself. I felt like I was breathing differently, sometimes for the first time, and indeed I was.

As I learned, breathing properly opens you up. Each breath carries life and energy, or what the yogis call *prana,* to the rest of your body. Things happened to me in class almost involuntarily. For one, I started to cry in class. I had no idea why—or what triggered it. If I did too many chest or hip openers, I started to break down, felt seized by anger, fear, remorse, and all of a sudden the tears flowed out of me. It happened all the time. Something was shifting around in me.

When I found out the school closed in the summer, I had one of the teachers come to my house for private lessons. I practiced five days a week. My teacher warned me to be careful.

"One day you're going to notice that all your perceptions and your approach to life will have changed," he said. "You can't analyze it. Don't even try. Don't even question it. Just go with it."

And that's what happened. In Los Angeles, instead of hitting my old haunts, I took yoga classes at Golden Bridge, which was designed as more of a community than a school. It was cofounded by Gurmukh Kaur Khalsa, a charismatic, deeply spiritual woman. She was a fun, cool Sikh who could often be spotted dressed in her pristine white robes and turban roller-skating down Santa Monica Boulevard. Her classes in kundalini yoga attracted students from around the world.

I first met her when I was bedridden during my pregnancy with Duke. Someone had suggested I get food delivered from the restaurant that was affiliated with the Golden Bridge. In addition to food, I also got Gurmukh. Well-known in L.A. for her pre- and postnatal yoga and meditation work, she came to my house and gave me private kundalini lessons—as much as I could do in bed—and continued after Duke was born. I didn't care about the yoga, but Gurmukh gave the best foot massage I'd ever had in my life.

I reconnected with her one day in early 2007 when I was waiting for a class at Golden Bridge. She was walking by and stopped to talk.

"What are you doing?" she asked. "You look so happy."

"I'm going to India next month," I said.

"That's great," she said.

I filled her in on some of the details. This was going to be my second trip there. My first time had been with Morgan and my friend Rosemarie in 2000. We had gone on a friend's magnificent yacht. Morgan is like Valentino; he doesn't like anything unpleasant entering his world if possible. So India wasn't for him. I didn't think it was for me either. My friend and I went ashore in Mumbai, where the poverty was more extreme than anyplace I had ever seen. I hadn't led a sheltered life, but I saw people living in conditions that made me grimace and turn away. Yet I couldn't stop looking at the throngs of people and animals. Beggars. Amputees. Small children on their own. Peddlers. Holy men. Everywhere I turned I saw the whole deck of humanity. I kept staring. I was as captivated and curious as I was repulsed.

As I told Gurmukh later, I felt the need to go back. As I got deeper into yoga and related reading, I had the sense that I had missed something in India, something key and important that was there, waiting for me to find it, like a spiritual Where's Waldo.

She smiled.

She mentioned that she was leading a trip there, too.

"Why don't you come with me?" she said.

"Okay."

Saying yes as instantly as I did was one of those turning points in my life, like forming the Go-Go's. I didn't give it any thought. Nor did

I consider any of the arrangements I had to make, the costs, inconveniences, dangers, or hassles. I knew it was something I had to do.

Doors open at different times in your life. Some are presented before you're ready, and others appear at exactly the right time. India was one of those. For years, I had envied people with passions in their life. I had music, but it was my career. It was not until I found yoga, or until yoga found me, that I felt the emptiness in me begin to fill up and my soul burn with a new life force. Having passion in life made me eager to grow and do more. It made me feel alive after so many years of going through the motions of being alive. I know it's what made me eager to plan my trip to India—actually, I planned two: one with friends and then a second one with Gurmukh. But I might not have gone on either one if not for a remarkable woman who passed away in May of that year one month before turning 103.

Lesley Blanch was Morgan's godmother. To say she had a full and rich life is an understatement. She was a writer, artist, editor, adventurer, romantic, dreamer, and lover of life. Her first book, *The Wilder Shores of Love,* had as its theme women escaping the boredom of convention. It was an apt description of Lesley herself. She had studied art as a young woman, designed book jackets for T. S. Eliot, married and divorced French novelist-diplomat Romain Gary, hobnobbed with movie stars and screenwriters, and of course saw the world.

She lived in Paris, Berne, New York, and Los Angeles and traveled the world mostly on her own. As she once said, "I've rather hopped on some trains in my time." In that respect, as well as a few others, we were kindred spirits. I visited with her frequently. I couldn't believe she was 100, then 101, and then 102—with all her teeth, as she liked to joke, and her sense of humor.

She always said, "Belinda, you bring so much light with you. Tell me where you've been lately."

I brought her trinkets from my travels and played her reggae music, which she loved. Her message to me was simple: Live. Don't be afraid. Go for it. I wish I had been able to tell her about India. For my first trip, I went the five-star route. I was there with two girlfriends, and we booked rooms at all the best hotels. I loved seeing the sights, but I was seeing them out the window of a comfortable car. I instinctively knew I wasn't experiencing India the way I wanted or *needed*. I had no stories for Lesley.

Cut to me sitting beside the pool one day at one of India's most luxurious hotels—one of the most luxurious hotels I had ever seen, let alone stayed at. It was an old palace in the mountains. Everything was exquisite: the views, the service, everything. As my friends and I were having our breakfast amid the posh splendor, a dog ran up to our table. She sat down next to me and began licking herself. I looked down at her and saw that her toe was coming off.

"Oh my God," I said. "This is gross."

At the same time, I couldn't stop staring at the dog. She looked back at me, too. After I sensed some kind of contact between us, she got up and left. From then on, I began to see India, really see it as I was meant to. One second it was gorgeous, the next it was gruesome. More often than not, I saw it the other way around: gruesome and then gorgeous.

A few months later, I returned to India as part of Gurmukh's annual Golden Bridge pilgrimage. This time the trappings were extremely different, and so was my experience. I met up with the group in Delhi, took a long bus ride to Amritsar, where we hooked up with Gurmukh and her husband, Gurushabd, and then journeyed to Rishikesh, a holy town in the country's northern highlands.

Rishikesh is best known for two things: it's the place where the Ganges comes down from the Himalayas and it's the yoga center of the world. In the late sixties, the Beatles visited the Maharishi Mahesh Yogi's ashram in Rishikesh and for a moment India was *très* hip.

My arrival drew much less fanfare. It was hard to believe even the Beatles could have caused a stir in the crowded city's hustle and bustle. From my vantage as a new arrival, Rishikesh teemed with the full circus of humanity. I had to take several deep breaths to keep my focus. Even as I was getting my bearings, I knew my pilgrimage to this holy city was going to be either a colossal mistake or an impossibly magical experience. There was no room for anything in between.

Likewise, I was immediately on overload from the city's sights and pungent odors—an acrid foulness mixed with incense and the smell of kerosene. It hung in the air like a thick, exotic perfume. As for the crowds, I didn't know where to look first. There were holy men on the street, people posing as holy men, vendors, peddlers, beggars, blind children, open markets and stands. People wore clothes that were in a whole different color scheme than in the West. And then there was the noise; it was a different soundtrack from that of the life I knew back home. Slowly, I stepped into the churning sea of humanity. I darted between scooters, cows, dogs, and vendors' carts loaded with goods. In the distance was the river with its own craziness along the banks. I lost track of how many times I asked myself, "Where am I?"

It didn't matter.

Within minutes, I knew it was wonderful. I felt strangely comfortable, elated, and at home.

Guided more by curiosity than specific directions, I made it to my destination feeling relief and excitement. I learned quickly that everything in India, no matter where you are, is an adventure. A few days later I set out on what should have been a five-minute walk to see the man who sold shawls. It took me two and a half hours.

Gurmukh and Gurushabd led us to our lodging, Parmarth Niketan, a famous ashram. Although beautiful, the place was surrounded by filth and squalor. Rishikesh was a place where you had to arrive early because the buses and taxis quit driving the mountain roads at dusk, when the elephants began wandering out of the wilds.

After a week, I felt an energy and lightness of being that put me in an altered state of consciousness—but not like a drug high. It was about being open and in touch with myself, unencumbered by the walls that usually kept those feelings at a safe distance, and really just walking around with an appreciation of the miracle of being alive.

Corny? Maybe.

But true.

Early one morning we were on a platform next to the Ganges, participating in a group *sadhana,* which Gurushabd, after I told him about it, described as "dumping your inner garbage can." He was spot-on. After I finished, I felt anxious and irritated. I didn't know why.

Gurmukh then strode into the middle of the platform, looking radiant in white as the morning light wrapped around her. She got everyone's attention and said we were going to be doing rebirthing. People cheered and clapped, as did I, even though I'd never done this exercise.

I had once been in a class she led where I was so relaxed that when she rang a gong to signify the end I literally felt the sound penetrate through the different layers of my consciousness. The sensation of lying on the floor and feeling the kundalini rising within me was something I'll never forget. It was like someone pressing their finger at the base of my spine and moving it up slowly, with a touch that cleansed and awakened as it rose.

The sensation, like a pressure, had stopped between my heart and my throat. It was one of the weirdest and greatest feelings of my life. I'd heard talk of people's kundalini force rising up and coming out of their head. It was the reason some thought the experience, if done incorrectly, could be dangerous.

I had heard about Gurmukh's rebirth class. She did it infrequently, from what I understood, but when she did it was supposed to be one of the most extraordinary experiences. But I'd also heard it could jangle your emotions pretty heavily. Gurmukh told us as much.

"Everyone reacts in a different way," she said as she began taking us through what seemed like a normal kundalini class. A little bit into it, I heard people making strange, almost guttural noises. Then those noises turned into screams and howls. It sounded like people were in pain. There were also sounds of laughter. Giggles. I wondered what was going on.

I wasn't feeling anything different from the class. Then, toward the end, I felt myself get angry. It started in the pit of my stomach and gradually overtook me like a fever. I didn't know where it was coming from or how to manage it. I was like, Screw everyone here. I hate everybody. I got so mad that I couldn't look anyone in the eye, not even those with whom I had shared laughs and hugs a few hours earlier.

At the end of class, we held hands to form a circle and everyone took a turn passing through the symbolic birth canal. People welcomed one another through with an ebullient *satnam*, the traditional Sikh greeting that means "truth," or "truth is my identity." I was cursing those who tried to reach out to me. I still wasn't able to understand this uproar of anger and vitriol. When the last person was through, Gurmukh gathered everyone together. I stood off to the side and said fuck that. Then I started to sob uncontrollably.

I ran to my room and threw myself on the bed. I couldn't stop crying. It went on and on; I had not cried as hard in my entire life. Eventually I got up and paced across my room, trying to figure out why this had happened. As I breathed deeply and looked through my tear-filled eyes, I saw my childhood come into focus, then my parents, and particularly my mother, whom I had always blamed for a lot of the bad things that happened to me as a little girl.

I had forgiven my father—my stepfather, that is—this person who had beaten me and abused me verbally and emotionally. He had turned into an amazing man after he got sober. I understood that he had suffered from a disease. My mom, I had always assumed, should have known better.

But there in India, following this rebirthing class, I had an epiphany. My mom had been eighteen years old when she had me. She hadn't wanted to be pregnant that young or be with my real father. She had been upset about the change in her life. As a fetus in her womb, I had absorbed all of her anger and emotions and now I realized that I had carried those feelings around long enough. I had to let them go. I had to release them like ashes in the Ganges.

All of them.

My mom had done the best she could.

It was time for me to understand, forgive, and let go.

That afternoon I had an appointment. The evening before I had gone into the nearest town to get a few things and the ATM I used to withdraw cash had eaten my card. A nice Indian man who owned a local jewelry store where I shopped saw my frustration at the machine. He said he knew the manager of the bank and would take me to him. He arranged a meeting place and time.

On my way to meet him, I ran into Gurmukh and her husband. She reached out and hugged me.

"What have you done to me?" I said. I started to cry again.

"You're one of the bravest people I saw today," she said, drawing me close again.

"I don't get it," I said. "I don't get any of this. Not what happened. Not why I'm here."

"*Satnam,*" she said, letting me go.

I was sure I looked like a wreck when I arrived at the spot where the jewelry store owner and I had agreed to meet. My eyes were swollen, my face was puffy, and I felt like shit. I had to remind myself this was India, the country where a wise man said, "I once complained about my shoes, until I met a man who had no feet." I looked at the bustling traffic on the street, hoping to see my ride. I had no idea what kind of car he drove.

All of a sudden I heard a loud *put-put-put,* like a souped-up washing machine motor. I turned and suddenly my guy pulled up in front of me on a motorcycle. I stood in place, frozen. A motorcycle? I couldn't believe I had to do this.

"Come, get on," he said.

I didn't want to. But then as clear as I heard everything else around me, I heard the voice of my friend Lesley Blanch say, "Go for it. This is what life is about." I looked up at the clear blue sky, saw a graceful white bird soaring high above, and then without a second thought swung my leg over the motorcycle.

An instant later, we were zipping through traffic, dodging cars and people, turning corners and zigzagging through carts and cows and beggars. It was so unbelievably dangerous and crazy; it was just so unbelievable, period. I was dressed all in white and my red hair was blowing in the wind. As we raced through the city, I felt open and, in a sense, reborn and alive.

They say whatever God is, you can feel it in India. It's there. It's everywhere. It was for me.

Lesley was right, I thought, as I hung on to the back of that motorcycle. This was what life was all about.

Back at the ashram, I felt the invigoration of the bike ride fade and my previous malaise return. I went to my room and found two monkeys going through my suitcase. They had climbed through the open window, as frequently happened there. If it wasn't monkeys, it was rats. After shooing them out, I got back into bed, curled up in the fetal position, and stayed like that for the next three days. I pretended to be asleep as everyone else from my group departed. I couldn't deal.

On the fourth day, I got myself together and moved to a five-star hotel up the hill where I cleaned up—especially my feet, which were black like a hobo's. But no amount of scrubbing got rid of my weird mood. I moved back into bed. Scared, I had the hotel's doctor come check me. Aside from dehydration, he couldn't find anything wrong with me. I was unable to explain my symptoms other than to say I felt like I needed to shed a layer.

And that was exactly it. This emotional thing that I was going through simply had to work its way out of my body. It took a few days, but little by little I felt it pass, and a giddy feeling took its place. I went from one extreme to another. Although I was still totally out of balance, it was better to feel like everything was wonderful than to feel miserable. Before I left, I evened out.

At home, everyone remarked that I looked different. I had been gone only about two weeks, but it felt like two months. I must have looked it, too. Without question, the trip was transformative. Morgan listened attentively to my tales. Although he had no interest in participating in such adventures himself, he saw the benefits manifested in me.

Duke was the one who shook his head. By this time, he had worked as a page in the U.S. House of Representatives, started to write articles for newspapers, and made politically oriented videos, which he posted on YouTube. He was thinking about where he wanted to go to college, and he was looking toward a career in politics. The one blemish on this ambitious landscape was his rock-and-roll mom. He had half-jokingly warned me in the past about staying in the background, and I saw that same look appear on his face as I told my stories from India.

Sure enough, he said, "Mom, as a favor to me, please don't say any of this stuff in the press. It's a little weird."

"So?" I said.

He winced. "You're going to become a political liability."

"A political liability?" I said.

"I'm afraid so," he said. "You're my Lillian Carter."

I laughed to myself and thought, Hey, once a punk rocker, always a punk rocker.

A VISION OF NOWNESS

IN MID-AUGUST 2008, I called home from Los Angeles with bad news. I was on my way to Mexico City for a couple of shows, but I got word that the promoter had run off with the money—or something like that. As a result, the shows were canceled. Now I was stuck on the West Coast just days before my fiftieth birthday.

"I'll meet you," Morgan said.

"Don't spend all that money getting over here," I said. "It will cost a fortune to get a ticket at the last minute."

He wasn't convinced.

"We'll celebrate when I'm back," I said. "I'll be fine. Don't worry."

I was fine with turning fifty. It was easier than forty. I was in a much better place, a really good place in fact. I had worked hard to understand who I was and like myself better. I felt nothing but love and gratitude.

For my actual birthday, I got myself a kick-ass suite at the Helmsley Palace in New York. In the morning, I chanted for a couple hours at the SGI center on Fifteenth Street. I acknowledged gratitude for my first fifty years. One might ask if I really felt gratitude for all the turmoil and problems I had experienced. Yes, I did feel gratitude—gratitude for all I had in spite of that trouble, gratitude for all I had learned, gratitude for all the love that was in my life in spite of me and because of me. It was a sense that transcended the conventional thought of aging as bad and something to be avoided at all costs and by all means; instead it made the years seem fortunate and worthwhile.

At night, I went out for a quiet dinner with some of the guys in my band and my friend Sandra Bernhard and her partner. I had a perfectly nice, laid-back, happy evening. Then I got back to my hotel room and a man from the front desk called. He said there was something for me from Carter.

"Carter?" I said.

"Carter," he repeated.

"Well, send it up, please," I said.

A moment later, a bellman delivered a small box to my room. I saw it and chuckled.

"Oh, Cartier," I said, smiling.

The card was from Morgan and inside the box I found a beautiful pink gold bracelet with a delicate pink sapphire. I held it up and appreciated its simplicity. I was extremely touched and thought of the many ways that bracelet typified our twenty-three-year marriage. We love each other, fight, give each other long leashes, and look forward to being together again. He still makes me laugh like no one else. He's annoying, but funny. I don't want to hear what he has to say about me. A lot of people may not understand what we have, but we do—and it works. To this day, he's my best friend and soul mate.

I put the bracelet on. It was even prettier on my wrist.

I wanted to thank Morgan, but I didn't want to wake him up. I settled for leaving a message on his cell.

Satnam.

In the months that followed, I went back to France and enjoyed being home. I recorded some new music in London and Los Angeles. I appeared on the TV show *Dancing with the Stars,* which was kind of a lark. I had spoken to its producers a year earlier and forgotten about it. Then, the day before I was supposed to make another trip to India, they called and told me to get to Los Angeles immediately to start rehearsing, I was on the show.

So I went and had a good time for the few weeks I was there, but I knew it wasn't for me. I didn't like being judged, and I could tell the pressure I felt wasn't good for my sobriety. I would have liked to have stayed on longer, of course, but I was also very relieved to leave the show. I rejuvenated by making good on my postponed trip to India. I spent the end of 2009 and early 2010 starring in the play *Hairspray* in

London, and afterward I launched an online store offering bags, shawls, jewelry, oils, and other favorite items from my travels around the world, starting with India.

I stayed busy, but not busy without any purpose. I came to an understanding about my past. I let go of the things that had always brought me down, knowing that I had outgrown them. I appreciated the good times and the crazier times for what they were and how they had shaped me. Without them, I wouldn't have ended up in such a better place. I didn't worry about the future either. I thought about a time long ago when I had met Sammy Davis Jr. at a party. He had looked at me and said, "Baby, you are a vision of nowness." As far as I'm concerned, *nowness* is a pretty good place to be.

I am still very much sober and grateful for each day. Once I stopped doing drugs and drinking, the real work began. As you have come to know, my journey to where I am today has been sad, tough, amazing, stupid, silly, and enlightening. I wouldn't have had it any other way.

I'm living proof you can teach old dogs new tricks. With the help of my program and loving, patient, understanding, and remarkable family and friends, I have truly changed. I have done something I never thought possible. I have become the person that I've always wanted to be and knew I could be, if only I could get through the bullshit.

I recently made the trek from my house in the South of France to Austria, one of the world's most beautiful, inspiring drives. The sheer cliffs in the Dolomites always test my courage, but then each time I arrive at the fields and mountains in Austria I feel like I should start singing "The Sound of Music." Anyway, after starting out, I pulled into a gas station in Italy and pinched myself as I got an espresso out of the machine. How amazing was it that I had figured out how to get around—not just these crazy directions from one country to the next, but in my life in general?

I finally appreciate my career. The Go-Go's will always be one of the loves of my life, something that's responsible for so much opportunity and so many memories that I will treasure forever. I'm proud of the music we made and the doors we opened for other girls with dreams of rocking as hard and successfully as the guys. I'm blown away by the many lives we have been able to touch. Music, like all art, is born of a time and spirit, but it lives on if it's any good. I am honored knowing our music continues to be meaningful for so many people.

I wouldn't have wanted to do it with anyone other than Jane, Charlotte, Gina, and Kathy. Although we're grown-ups now, I'll always refer to us as "the girls." Sometimes we're closer than at others, but we have that special bond from having grown up together. Some of my fondest memories, not just of the band but of my life, are when all of us hit the vintage stores together when we were on tour. We got to a town and within minutes were doing what we did almost as well as we played music—shop. I love them like sisters.

Before a show we played in 2009 in Las Vegas, I was walking down the hallway to the elevator, where all of us had agreed to meet. Before heading to the venue, I stopped for some reason and thought about all the years we had played together, all the places we had been, all the memories we had accumulated, and all the people we had entertained, and I really, truly appreciated being a Go-Go.

I have no idea how many more shows we will play or whether we will put out more music. Some days I love being out in front of that band. Other days I ask myself why I'm still doing it. I know I don't want to be doing it when I'm in my mid-fifties. I'd like to end it on a high note, with a little dignity. I hope along the way we have inspired other girls who want to play music. It can be done.

As for the future, I'll likely continue to make albums on my own, at least as long as I find songs that I feel I can sing.

If not, I'm okay with that too. My work does not solely define me, as I had believed for many years. I finally realized that I'm so much more.

I am able to receive love and give love and even love myself. My relationships with my husband and son are better than ever. My one regret is all the hell I put them through. For many years I was too selfish to see that or care. Now that I'm present, all that has changed. I'm blessed to have them in my life.

I'm blessed to have my life—and that's a wonderful way to feel.

I look forward to each day. Sometimes I regret that I didn't get it sooner. I guess I'm just one of those people who had to figure it out the hard way.

But hey, look at me—a Valley girl who ran off to Hollywood, moved to the South of France, and found herself on the Ganges, in India. Who would have thought, back when I was working the photocopy machine with the crappy boss at the Hilton Hotel Corporation, that all this would happen?

Actually, I did.

A girl's gotta dream....

acknowledgments

The following people have each, in some way, made a difference in my life, and I am so thankful.

Morgan, James, Pamela, Portland, Duke, Joanne, Butch, Hope, Mary, Joe, Josh, Sarah, Jane, Charlotte, Kathy, Gina, Ginger, Lorna, Miles Copeland, Pleasant Gehman, Rosemarie Patronette, Jenny Lens, Madness, Richard Gottehrer, the Police, Rodney Bingenheimer, Jack Pinson, Stevie Nicks, Rick Nowels, Irving Azoff, Richard Branson, Diane Keaton, Joe Kelly, Diane Duarte, Jeannine Braden, Michael Lloyd, Mike Curb, John Burnham, George Harrison, Brian Wilson, Danny Goldberg, Ann Sookhoo, Antonia Goodland-Clark, Heidi Cook, Lynne Easton, Jay Boberg, Michael Plen, Deepak Chopra, Jerry and Esther Hicks, Gurmukh Khalsa, Gurushabd, Mitch Clark, Mark Reynolds, Stuart Wilde, Amanda Eliasch, Johann Eliasch, Tony Denton, Bennie Edwards, Janyne Andrews, Dave and Anoushka Stewart, David Russell, Billy Brasfield, Paul Starr, Syd Curry, Connie Clarksville, Soka Gakkai, Joanna Povall, Charles Cartmell, Chirtian Pisano, June Whittaker Pisano, Bks Iyengar, Michelle Nadler, James Nisbet, Gavin De Becker, Rachel Lara, Lesley Blanche, H. H. Swami Chidanand Saraswatiji Maharaj, Simon Watson, Iggy Pop, Dan Rucks, Angie, Mardette Lynch, Lisa and Piero Giramonti, Bradford Cobb, Steve Jensen, Lorenza Marcais, May Fachelan, Tina Constable, Suzanne O'Neill, Penny Simon, Patty Berg, Annsley Rosner, Tricia Wygal, Linnea Knollmueller, Kyle Kolker, Emily Timberlake, Dan Strone, and Todd Gold.

BELINDA CARLISLE is known not only as the lead singer of the Go-Go's, but also as one of the late eighties' most glamorous adult-pop soloists. Since then, Belinda has released five more albums and continues to tour internationally, both with the Go-Go's and as a solo artist. She divides her time between America and the south of France.

Printed in the United States
by Baker & Taylor Publisher Services